Office for Disarmament Affairs
New York, 2010

The United Nations
DISARMAMENT YEARBOOK

Volume 34 (Part I): 2009

*Disarmament Resolutions and Decisions
of the Sixty-fourth Session
of the United Nations General Assembly*

Guide to the user

To facilitate early analysis of the resolutions and decisions on disarmament adopted at the sixty-fourth session of the General Assembly, UNODA offers Part I of the *Yearbook* as a handy, concise reference tool, containing the full texts of all the resolutions and decisions, the date of adoption by the Assembly and the First Committee, the agenda item number, the symbol number of the Report of the Rapporteur, the main sponsors and the voting patterns in the Assembly. For a snapshot of this information in a convenient chart, see "Quick view of votes by cluster". For a list of agenda items and their corresponding reports, see Annex.

Bold type in the list of sponsors indicates the State that introduced the draft resolution or decision. Throughout the book, any deviation in introducing and/or voting on resolutions is asterisked, and explained in a corresponding footnote.

Electronically available in PDF or database format at
www.un.org/disarmament

UNITED NATIONS PUBLICATION
Sales No. E.10.IX.1

ISBN 978-92-1-142273-3

Copyright © United Nations, 2010
All rights reserved
Printed at the United Nations, New York

Contents

	Page
Preface	vii
Quick view of votes by cluster (49 resolutions and 5 decisions)	viii

Resolutions

64/22	Objective information on military matters, including transparency of military expenditures	1
64/23	Implementation of the Declaration of the Indian Ocean as a Zone of Peace	5
64/24	African Nuclear-Weapon-Free Zone Treaty	8
64/25	Developments in the field of information and telecommunications in the context of international security	10
64/26	Establishment of a nuclear-weapon-free zone in the region of the Middle East	14
64/27	Conclusion of effective international arrangements to assure non-nuclear-weapon States against the use or threat of use of nuclear weapons	19
64/28	Prevention of an arms race in outer space	24
64/29	Treaty banning the production of fissile material for nuclear weapons or other nuclear explosive devices	29
64/30	Assistance to States for curbing the illicit traffic in small arms and light weapons and collecting them	31
64/31	Follow-up to nuclear disarmament obligations agreed to at the 1995 and 2000 Review Conferences of the Parties to the Treaty on the Non-Proliferation of Nuclear Weapons	35
64/32	Relationship between disarmament and development	40
64/33	Observance of environmental norms in the drafting and implementation of agreements on disarmament and arms control	43
64/34	Promotion of multilateralism in the area of disarmament and non-proliferation	45
64/35	International Day against Nuclear Tests	50
64/36	Convention on Cluster Munitions	52
64/37	Reducing nuclear danger	53
64/38	Measures to prevent terrorists from acquiring weapons of mass destruction	57

iii

64/39	Treaty on the South-East Asia Nuclear-Weapon-Free Zone (Bangkok Treaty)	60
64/40	National legislation on transfer of arms, military equipment and dual-use goods and technology	64
64/41	Regional disarmament	66
64/42	Conventional arms control at the regional and subregional levels	68
64/43	Confidence-building measures in the regional and subregional context	71
64/44	Nuclear-weapon-free southern hemisphere and adjacent areas	74
64/45	Prohibition of the dumping of radioactive wastes	80
64/46	Implementation of the Convention on the Prohibition of the Development, Production, Stockpiling and Use of Chemical Weapons and on Their Destruction	83
64/47	Renewed determination towards the total elimination of nuclear weapons	86
64/48	The arms trade treaty	92
64/49	Transparency and confidence-building measures in outer space activities	97
64/50	The illicit trade in small arms and light weapons in all its aspects	99
64/51	Problems arising from the accumulation of conventional ammunition stockpiles in surplus	108
64/52	Second Conference of States Parties and Signatories of Treaties that Establish Nuclear-Weapon-Free Zones and Mongolia	111
64/53	Nuclear disarmament	115
64/54	Transparency in armaments	123
64/55	Follow-up to the advisory opinion of the International Court of Justice on the *Legality of the Threat or Use of Nuclear Weapons*	134
64/56	Implementation of the Convention on the Prohibition of the Use, Stockpiling, Production and Transfer of Anti-personnel Mines and on Their Destruction	138
64/57	Towards a nuclear-weapon-free world: accelerating the implementation of nuclear disarmament commitments	142
64/58	United Nations regional centres for peace and disarmament	148

64/59	Convention on the Prohibition of the Use of Nuclear Weapons	150
64/60	United Nations Regional Centre for Peace, Disarmament and Development in Latin America and the Caribbean	153
64/61	Regional confidence-building measures: activities of the United Nations Standing Advisory Committee on Security Questions in Central Africa	156
64/62	United Nations Regional Centre for Peace and Disarmament in Africa	159
64/63	United Nations Regional Centre for Peace and Disarmament in Asia and the Pacific	162
64/64	Report of the Conference on Disarmament	164
64/65	Report of the Disarmament Commission	167
64/66	The risk of nuclear proliferation in the Middle East	170
64/67	Convention on Prohibitions or Restrictions on the Use of Certain Conventional Weapons Which May Be Deemed to Be Excessively Injurious or to Have Indiscriminate Effects	175
64/68	Strengthening of security and cooperation in the Mediterranean region	179
64/69	Comprehensive Nuclear-Test-Ban Treaty	183
64/70	Convention on the Prohibition of the Development, Production and Stockpiling of Bacteriological (Biological) and Toxin Weapons and on Their Destruction	188

Decisions

64/512	Verification in all its aspects, including the role of the United Nations in the field of verification	191
64/513	Review of the implementation of the Declaration on the Strengthening of International Security	192
64/514	Role of science and technology in the context of international security and disarmament	193
64/515	Convening of the fourth special session of the General Assembly devoted to disarmament	194
64/516	Preventing the acquisition by terrorists of radioactive materials and sources	195

Annex

List of reports and notes of the Secretary-General 196

Preface

The *United Nations Disarmament Yearbook* is now in its thirty-fourth year of publication. Part I, which you have in your hands or on screen, presents the official texts on all 49 resolutions and 5 decisions related to disarmament, arms control and international security that were debated in the First Committee and forwarded to the General Assembly for adoption at its sixty-fourth session.

It is issued as a separate publication to provide early access to the resolutions and decisions, each presented with key information: relevant agenda items, main sponsors and co-sponsors, vote counts, including voting patterns in the First Committee and the General Assembly, adoption and meeting number dates and the draft resolution numbers.

A *Quick view by cluster* gives the reader an easy handle (using the First Committee's "cluster" arrangement of agenda items) on resolution numbers, titles and votes in the First Committee and in the Assembly.

The sum of the contents of the resolutions and decisions are the instructions and guideposts for multilateral disarmament and arms control efforts in 2010 and at times beyond. They represent the fullest extent of agreement that could be reached by Member States on the many items before them at that time, from weapons of mass destruction to cluster munitions. Through them, Member States communicated with each other, made recommendations to the Conference on Disarmament, charged the Disarmament Commission with certain tasks, gave instructions to the Secretary-General, provided guidance to intergovernmental bodies and requested the participation of non-governmental organizations and civil society in the work of the United Nations.

As the resolutions and decisions become implemented throughout the year, we hope that Part I furnishes the reader with a handy consolidated multilateral disarmament reference book, in print and electronic form.

Part II of the *Yearbook* will contain main multilateral issues under consideration, including their trends, summaries of First Committee and General Assembly actions taken on resolutions, full texts of principal multilateral agreements reached in 2009, declarations adopted by treaty review conferences and a convenient issue-oriented timeline. This book is forthcoming in early autumn, 2010.

Ed.

Quick view of votes by cluster (49 resolutions and 5 decisions)

No.	Title	First Cttee action (vote, date)	GA action, 2 Dec. (vote)
Cluster 1: Nuclear weapons			
64/24	African Nuclear-Weapon-Free Zone Treaty	w/o vote 27 Oct.	w/o vote
64/26	Establishment of a nuclear-weapon-free zone in the region of the Middle East	w/o vote 166-0-3, o.p. 3 27 Oct.	w/o vote 169-0-3, o.p. 3
64/27	Conclusion of effective international arrangements to assure non-nuclear-weapon States against the use or threat of use of nuclear weapons	119-0-58 27 Oct.	118-0-58
64/29	Treaty banning the production of fissile material for nuclear weapons or other nuclear explosive devices	w/o vote 29 Oct.	w/o vote
64/31	Follow-up to nuclear disarmament obligations agreed to at the 1995 and 2000 Review Conferences of the Parties to the Treaty on the Non-Proliferation of Nuclear Weapons	105-56-12 109-48-10, p.p. 6 27 Oct.	109-56-10 112-50-8, p.p. 6
64/35	International Day against Nuclear Tests	w/o vote 30 Oct.	w/o vote
64/37	Reducing nuclear danger	113-50-15 27 Oct.	115-50-14
64/39	Treaty on the South-East Asia Nuclear-Weapon-Free Zone (Bangkok Treaty)	172-0-5 28 Oct.	174-0-6
64/44	Nuclear-weapon-free southern hemisphere and adjacent areas	168-3-5 165-2-6, o.p. 7 27 Oct.	170-3-6 167-2-7, o.p. 7
64/45	Prohibition of the dumping of radioactive wastes	w/o vote 27 Oct.	w/o vote
64/47	Renewed determination towards the total elimination of nuclear weapons	161-2-8 29 Oct.	171-2-8
64/52	Second Conference of States Parties and Signatories of Treaties that Establish Nuclear-Weapon-Free Zones and Mongolia	159-0-6	166-3-6

No.	Title	First Cttee action (vote, date)	GA action, 2 Dec. (vote)
64/53	Nuclear disarmament	112-43-21 27 Oct.	111-45-19
64/55	Follow-up to the advisory opinion of the International Court of Justice on the *Legality of the Threat or Use of Nuclear Weapons*	126-29-22 30 Oct.	124-31-21
64/57	Towards a nuclear-weapon-free world: accelerating the implementation of nuclear disarmament commitments	165-5-4 159-4-2, o.p. 4 27 Oct.	169-5-5 162-4-2, o.p. 4
64/59	Convention on the Prohibition of the Use of Nuclear Weapons	116-50-11 27 Oct.	116-50-12
64/66	The risk of nuclear proliferation in the Middle East	164-5-6 163-4-6, p.p. 6 27 Oct.	167-6-6 164-5-5, p.p. 6
64/69	Comprehensive Nuclear-Test-Ban Treaty	175-1-3 166-1-5, o.p. 5 30 Oct.	175-1-3 169-1-6, o.p. 5
64/516	Preventing the acquisition by terrorists of radioactive materials and sources (decision)	w/o vote 27 Oct.	w/o vote

Cluster 2: Other weapons of mass destruction

No.	Title	First Cttee action (vote, date)	GA action, 2 Dec. (vote)
64/38	Measures to prevent terrorists from acquiring weapons of mass destruction	w/o vote 28 Oct.	w/o vote
64/46	Implementation of the Convention on the Prohibition of the Development, Production, Stockpiling and Use of Chemical Weapons and on Their Destruction	w/o vote 28 Oct.	w/o vote
64/70	Convention on the Prohibition of the Development, Production and Stockpiling of Bacteriological (Biological) and Toxin Weapons and on Their Destruction	w/o vote 28 Oct.	w/o vote

Cluster 3: Outer space (disarmament aspects)

No.	Title	First Cttee action (vote, date)	GA action, 2 Dec. (vote)
64/28	Prevention of an arms race in outer space	176-0-2 28 Oct.	176-0-2
64/49	Transparency and confidence-building measures in outer space activities	w/o vote 29 Oct.	w/o vote

No.	Title	First Cttee action (vote, date)	GA action, 2 Dec. (vote)
Cluster 4: Conventional weapons			
64/30	Assistance to States for curbing the illicit traffic in small arms and light weapons and collecting them	w/o vote 28 Oct.	w/o vote
64/36	Convention on Cluster Munitions	w/o vote 28 Oct.	w/o vote
64/48	The arms trade treaty	153-1-19 30 Oct.	151-1-20
64/50	The illicit trade in small arms and light weapons in all its aspects	179-0-0 177-0-1, o.p. 4 177-0-1, o.p. 15 29 Oct.	180-0-0 177-0-1, o.p. 4 176-0-1, o.p. 15
64/51	Problems arising from the accumulation of conventional ammunition stockpiles in surplus	w/o vote 28 Oct.	w/o vote
64/56	Implementation of the Convention on the Prohibition of the Use, Stockpiling, Production and Transfer of Anti-personnel Mines and on Their Destruction	158-0-18 29 Oct.	160-0-18
64/67	Convention on Prohibitions or Restrictions on the Use of Certain Conventional Weapons Which May Be Deemed to Be Excessively Injurious or to Have Indiscriminate Effects	w/o vote 29 Oct.	w/o vote
Cluster 5: Regional disarmament and security			
64/23	Implementation of the Declaration of the Indian Ocean as a Zone of Peace	128-3-44 28 Oct.	128-3-45
64/41	Regional disarmament	w/o vote 28 Oct.	w/o vote
64/42	Conventional arms control at the regional and subregional levels	173-1-2 28 Oct.	174-1-2
64/43	Confidence-building measures in the regional and subregional context	w/o vote 28 Oct.	w/o vote
64/61	Regional confidence-building measures: activities of the United Nations Standing Advisory Committee on Security Questions in Central Africa	w/o vote 29 Oct.	w/o vote

No.	Title	First Cttee action (vote, date)	GA action, 2 Dec. (vote)
64/68	Strengthening of security and cooperation in the Mediterranean region	w/o vote 28 Oct.	w/o vote

Cluster 6: Other disarmament measures and international security

No.	Title	First Cttee action (vote, date)	GA action, 2 Dec. (vote)
64/22	Objective information on military matters, including transparency of military expenditures	w/o vote 28 Oct.	w/o vote
64/25	Developments in the field of information and telecommunications in the context of international security	w/o vote 29 Oct.	w/o vote
64/32	Relationship between disarmament and development	w/o vote 28 Oct.	w/o vote
64/33	Observance of environmental norms in the drafting and implementation of agreements on disarmament and arms control	w/o vote 28 Oct.	w/o vote
64/34	Promotion of multilateralism in the area of disarmament and non-proliferation	126-5-49 28 Oct.	122-5-49
64/40	National legislation on transfer of arms, military equipment and dual-use goods and technology	w/o vote 28 Oct.	w/o vote
64/512	Verification in all its aspects, including the role of the United Nations in the field of verification (decision)	w/o vote 28 Oct.	w/o vote
64/513	Review of the implementation of the Declaration on the Strengthening of International Security (decision)	w/o vote 28 Oct.	w/o vote
64/514	Role of science and technology in the context of international security and disarmament (decision)	w/o vote 28 Oct.	w/o vote
64/54	Transparency in armaments	150-0-22 147-0-24, o.p. 3 147-0-24, o.p. 4 149-0-22, o.p. 5 147-0-23, o.p. 6 (d) 148-0-22, o.p. 6 146-0-23, o.p. 8 29 Oct.	153-0-23 149-0-24, o.p. 3 152-0-22, o.p. 4 151-0-22, o.p. 5 151-0-22, o.p. 6 (d) 149-0-24, o.p. 6 152-0-22, o.p. 8

No.	Title	First Cttee action (vote, date)	GA action, 2 Dec. (vote)
Cluster 7: Disarmament machinery			
64/515	Convening of the fourth special session of the General Assembly devoted to disarmament (decision)	w/o vote 28 Oct.	w/o vote
64/58	United Nations regional centres for peace and disarmament	w/o vote 28 Oct.	w/o vote
64/60	United Nations Regional Centre for Peace, Disarmament and Development in Latin America and the Caribbean	w/o vote 28 Oct.	w/o vote
64/62	United Nations Regional Centre for Peace and Disarmament in Africa	w/o vote 30 Oct.	w/o vote
64/63	United Nations Regional Centre for Peace and Disarmament in Asia and the Pacific	w/o vote 28 Oct.	w/o vote
64/64	Report of the Conference on Disarmament	w/o vote 30 Oct.	w/o vote
64/65	Report of the Disarmament Commission	w/o vote 28 Oct.	w/o vote

Resolutions

Agenda item 86 (b)

64/22 Objective information on military matters, including transparency of military expenditures

Text

The General Assembly,

Recalling its resolutions 53/72 of 4 December 1998, 54/43 of 1 December 1999, 56/14 of 29 November 2001, 58/28 of 8 December 2003, 60/44 of 8 December 2005 and 62/13 of 5 December 2007 on objective information on military matters, including transparency of military expenditures,

Recalling also its resolution 35/142 B of 12 December 1980, which introduced the United Nations system for the standardized reporting of military expenditures, its resolutions 48/62 of 16 December 1993, 49/66 of 15 December 1994, 51/38 of 10 December 1996 and 52/32 of 9 December 1997, calling upon all Member States to participate in it, and its resolution 47/54 B of 9 December 1992, endorsing the guidelines and recommendations for objective information on military matters and inviting Member States to provide the Secretary-General with relevant information regarding their implementation,

Noting that since then, national reports on military expenditures and on the guidelines and recommendations for objective information on military matters have been submitted by a number of Member States belonging to different geographical regions,

Convinced that the improvement of international relations forms a sound basis for promoting further openness and transparency in all military matters,

Convinced also that transparency in military matters is an essential element for building a climate of trust and confidence between States worldwide and that a better flow of objective information on military matters can help to relieve international tension and is therefore an important contribution to conflict prevention,

Noting the role of the standardized reporting system, as instituted through its resolution 35/142 B, as an important instrument to enhance transparency in military matters,

Conscious that the value of the standardized reporting system would be enhanced by a broader participation of Member States,

Noting that the continuing operation of the standardized reporting system should be reviewed with a view to improving its further development and to broadening participation in it,

Welcoming, therefore, the report of the Secretary-General[1] on ways and means to implement the guidelines and recommendations for objective information on military matters, including, in particular, how to strengthen and broaden participation in the standardized reporting system,

Recalling that the guidelines and recommendations for objective information on military matters recommended certain areas for further consideration, such as the improvement of the standardized reporting system,

Noting the efforts of several regional organizations to promote transparency of military expenditures, including standardized annual exchanges of relevant information among their member States,

Recalling the establishment of a group of governmental experts, on the basis of equitable geographical representation, to review the operation and further development of the Standardized Instrument for Reporting Military Expenditures, commencing in 2010, taking into account the views expressed by Member States on the subject and the reports of the Secretary-General on objective information on military matters, including transparency of military expenditures,[2]

Emphasizing the continuing importance of the Standardized Instrument under the current political and economic circumstances,

1. *Calls upon* Member States to report annually to the Secretary-General, by 30 April, their military expenditures for the latest fiscal year for which data are available, using, preferably and to the extent possible, the reporting instrument[3] as recommended in its resolution 35/142 B or, as appropriate, any other format developed in conjunction with similar reporting on military expenditures to other international or regional organizations, and, in the same context, encourages Member States to submit nil returns, if appropriate;

2. *Recommends* the guidelines and recommendations for objective information on military matters to all Member States for implementation, fully taking into account specific political, military and other conditions prevailing in a region, on the basis of initiatives and with the agreement of the States of the region concerned;

3. *Encourages* relevant international bodies and regional organizations to promote transparency of military expenditures and to enhance complementarities among reporting systems, taking into account the particular

---

[1] A/54/298.
[2] See resolution 62/13, para. 5.
[3] Available from www.un.org/disarmament/convarms/Milex/html/MilexIndex.shtml.

characteristics of each region, and to consider the possibility of an exchange of information with the United Nations;

4. *Takes note* of the reports of the Secretary-General;[4]

5. *Requests* the Secretary-General, within available resources:

(*a*) To continue the practice of sending an annual note verbale to Member States requesting the submission of data to the United Nations system for the standardized reporting of military expenditures, together with the reporting format and related instructions, and to publish in a timely fashion in appropriate United Nations media the due date for transmitting data on military expenditures;

(*b*) To circulate annually the reports on military expenditures as received from Member States, taking into account in his 2010 report the information received from Member States in accordance with paragraph 6 (*b*) below;

(*c*) To transmit the report of the group of governmental experts to the General Assembly for consideration at its sixty-sixth session;

(*d*) To continue consultations with relevant international bodies, with a view to ascertaining requirements for adjusting the present instrument, with a view to encouraging wider participation, and to make recommendations, based on the outcome of those consultations and taking into account the views of Member States, on necessary changes to the content and structure of the standardized reporting system;

(*e*) To encourage relevant international bodies and organizations to promote transparency of military expenditures and to consult with those bodies and organizations with emphasis on examining possibilities for enhancing complementarities among international and regional reporting systems and for exchanging related information between those bodies and the United Nations;

(*f*) To encourage the United Nations regional centres for peace and disarmament in Africa, in Asia and the Pacific, and in Latin America and the Caribbean to assist Member States in their regions in enhancing their knowledge of the standardized reporting system;

(*g*) To promote international and regional/subregional symposiums and training seminars to explain the purpose of the standardized reporting system and to give relevant technical instructions;

(*h*) To report on experiences gained during such symposiums and training seminars;

6. *Encourages* Member States:

---

[4] A/58/202 and Add.1–3, A/59/192 and Add.1, A/60/159 and Add.1–3, A/61/133 and Add.1–3, A/62/158 and Add.1 and 2, A/63/97 and Add.1 and 2 and A/64/113 and Add.1.

(*a*) To inform the Secretary-General about possible problems with the standardized reporting system and their reasons for not submitting the requested data;

(*b*) To continue to provide the Secretary-General with their views and suggestions on ways and means to improve the future functioning of and broaden participation in the standardized reporting system, including necessary changes to its content and structure, which could be taken into account by the group of governmental experts during its mandated activity;

7. *Decides* to include in the provisional agenda of its sixty-sixth session the item entitled "Objective information on military matters, including transparency of military expenditures".

Action by the General Assembly

Date: 2 December 2009　　Meeting: 55th plenary meeting
Vote: Adopted without a vote　Report: A/64/381

Sponsors

Albania, Argentina, Armenia, Australia, Austria, Belgium, Brazil, Bulgaria, Canada, Chile, Costa Rica, Croatia, Cyprus, Czech Republic, Denmark, Dominican Republic, Ecuador, Estonia, Finland, France, Georgia, **Germany**, Ghana, Greece, Grenada, Guatemala, Hungary, Iceland, Ireland, Italy, Japan, Latvia, Lesotho, Liberia, Liechtenstein, Lithuania, Luxembourg, Madagascar, Mali, Montenegro, Netherlands, New Zealand, Norway, Peru, Poland, Portugal, Republic of Korea, Republic of Moldova, Romania, Russian Federation, Senegal, Serbia, Slovakia, Slovenia, Spain, Sweden, Switzerland, the former Yugoslav Republic of Macedonia, Trinidad and Tobago, Turkey, Ukraine, United Kingdom, Uruguay, Zambia

Co-sponsors

Andorra, Bolivia (Plurinational State of), Comoros, India, Kazakhstan, Malta, Mauritius, Monaco, San Marino, Thailand, Timor-Leste

Action by the First Committee

Date: 28 October 2009　　Meeting: 20th meeting
Vote: Adopted without a vote　Draft resolution: A/C.1/64/L.43

Agenda item 87

64/23 Implementation of the Declaration of the Indian Ocean as a Zone of Peace

Text

The General Assembly,

Recalling the Declaration of the Indian Ocean as a Zone of Peace, contained in its resolution 2832 (XXVI) of 16 December 1971, and recalling also its resolutions 54/47 of 1 December 1999, 56/16 of 29 November 2001, 58/29 of 8 December 2003, 60/48 of 8 December 2005 and 62/14 of 5 December 2007 and other relevant resolutions,

Recalling also the report of the Meeting of the Littoral and Hinterland States of the Indian Ocean held in July 1979,[1]

Recalling further paragraph 102 of the Final Document of the Thirteenth Conference of Heads of State or Government of Non-Aligned Countries, held at Kuala Lumpur on 24 and 25 February 2003,[2] in which it was noted, inter alia, that the Chairperson of the Ad Hoc Committee on the Indian Ocean would continue his informal consultations on the future work of the Committee,

Emphasizing the need to foster consensual approaches that are conducive to the pursuit of such endeavours,

Noting the initiatives taken by countries of the region to promote cooperation, in particular economic cooperation, in the Indian Ocean area and the possible contribution of such initiatives to overall objectives of a zone of peace,

Convinced that the participation of all permanent members of the Security Council and the major maritime users of the Indian Ocean in the work of the Ad Hoc Committee is important and would assist the progress of a mutually beneficial dialogue to develop conditions of peace, security and stability in the Indian Ocean region,

Considering that greater efforts and more time are required to develop a focused discussion on practical measures to ensure conditions of peace, security and stability in the Indian Ocean region,

Having considered the report of the Ad Hoc Committee on the Indian Ocean,[3]

---

[1] *Official Records of the General Assembly, Thirty-fourth Session, Supplement No. 45* and corrigendum (A/34/45 and Corr.1).
[2] See A/57/759-S/2003/332, annex I.
[3] *Official Records of the General Assembly, Sixty-fourth Session, Supplement No. 29* (A/64/29).

1. *Takes note* of the report of the Ad Hoc Committee on the Indian Ocean;[3]

2. *Reiterates its conviction* that the participation of all permanent members of the Security Council and the major maritime users of the Indian Ocean in the work of the Ad Hoc Committee is important and would greatly facilitate the development of a mutually beneficial dialogue to advance peace, security and stability in the Indian Ocean region;

3. *Requests* the Chairman of the Ad Hoc Committee to continue his informal consultations with the members of the Committee and to report through the Committee to the General Assembly at its sixty-sixth session;

4. *Requests* the Secretary-General to continue to render, within existing resources, all necessary assistance to the Ad Hoc Committee, including the provision of summary records;

5. *Decides* to include in the provisional agenda of its sixty-sixth session the item entitled "Implementation of the Declaration of the Indian Ocean as a Zone of Peace".

Action by the General Assembly

Date: 2 December 2009 Meeting: 55th plenary meeting
Vote: 128-3-45 Report: A/64/382

Sponsors

Indonesia, on behalf of the States Members of the United Nations that are members of the Non-Aligned Movement

*Recorded vote**

In favour:

Afghanistan, Algeria, Angola, Antigua and Barbuda, Argentina, Armenia, Australia, Azerbaijan, Bahamas, Bahrain, Barbados, Belarus, Belize, Benin, Bhutan, Bolivia (Plurinational State of), Bosnia and Herzegovina, Botswana, Brazil, Brunei Darussalam, Burundi, Cambodia, Cameroon, Cape Verde, Chile, China, Colombia, Comoros, Congo, Costa Rica, Côte d'Ivoire, Cuba, Democratic People's Republic of Korea, Democratic Republic of the Congo, Djibouti, Dominica, Dominican Republic, Ecuador, Egypt, El Salvador, Eritrea, Fiji, Gambia, Ghana, Grenada, Guatemala, Guinea, Guinea-Bissau, Guyana, Haiti, Honduras, India, Indonesia, Iran (Islamic Republic of), Iraq, Jamaica, Japan, Jordan, Kazakhstan, Kenya, Kuwait, Kyrgyzstan, Lao People's Democratic Republic, Lebanon, Lesotho, Liberia, Libyan Arab Jamahiriya,

---

* Subsequently, the delegations of Bangladesh, Burkina Faso, Ethiopia, Swaziland and Tajikistan advised the Secretariat that they had intended to vote in favour. The voting tally above does not reflect this information.

Madagascar, Malawi, Malaysia, Maldives, Mali, Mauritania, Mauritius, Mexico, Mongolia, Morocco, Mozambique, Myanmar, Namibia, Nepal, New Zealand, Nicaragua, Niger, Nigeria, Oman, Pakistan, Panama, Papua New Guinea, Paraguay, Peru, Philippines, Qatar, Republic of Korea, Russian Federation, Rwanda, Saint Kitts and Nevis, Saint Lucia, Saint Vincent and the Grenadines, Samoa, Saudi Arabia, Senegal, Serbia, Sierra Leone, Singapore, Solomon Islands, Somalia, South Africa, Sri Lanka, Sudan, Suriname, Syrian Arab Republic, Thailand, Togo, Tonga, Trinidad and Tobago, Tunisia, Turkmenistan, Uganda, United Arab Emirates, United Republic of Tanzania, Uruguay, Uzbekistan, Venezuela (Bolivarian Republic of), Viet Nam, Yemen, Zambia, Zimbabwe

Against:
France, United Kingdom, United States

Abstaining:
Albania, Andorra, Austria, Belgium, Bulgaria, Canada, Croatia, Cyprus, Czech Republic, Denmark, Estonia, Finland, Georgia, Germany, Greece, Hungary, Iceland, Ireland, Israel, Italy, Latvia, Liechtenstein, Lithuania, Luxembourg, Malta, Marshall Islands, Micronesia (Federated States of), Monaco, Montenegro, Netherlands, Norway, Palau, Poland, Portugal, Republic of Moldova, Romania, San Marino, Slovakia, Slovenia, Spain, Sweden, Switzerland, the former Yugoslav Republic of Macedonia, Turkey, Ukraine

Action by the First Committee

Date: 28 October 2009　　　Meeting: 20th meeting
Vote: 128-3-44　　　Draft resolution: A/C.1/64/L.8

Agenda item 88

64/24 African Nuclear-Weapon-Free Zone Treaty

Text

The General Assembly,

Recalling its resolutions 51/53 of 10 December 1996 and 56/17 of 29 November 2001 and all its other relevant resolutions, as well as those of the Organization of African Unity,

Recalling also the signing of the African Nuclear-Weapon-Free Zone Treaty (Treaty of Pelindaba)[1] at Cairo on 11 April 1996,

Recalling further the Cairo Declaration adopted on that occasion,[2] which emphasized that nuclear-weapon-free zones, especially in regions of tension, such as the Middle East, enhance global and regional peace and security,

Taking note of the statement made by the President of the Security Council on behalf of the members of the Council on 12 April 1996,[3] affirming that the signature of the African Nuclear-Weapon-Free Zone Treaty constituted an important contribution by the African countries to the maintenance of international peace and security,

Considering that the establishment of nuclear-weapon-free zones, especially in the Middle East, would enhance the security of Africa and the viability of the African nuclear-weapon-free zone,

1. *Notes with satisfaction* the entry into force of the African Nuclear-Weapon-Free-Zone Treaty (Treaty of Pelindaba)[1] on 15 July 2009;

2. *Calls upon* African States that have not yet done so to sign and ratify the Treaty as soon as possible;

3. *Expresses its appreciation* to the nuclear-weapon States that have signed the Protocols to the Treaty[1] that concern them, and calls upon those that have not yet ratified the Protocols concerning them to do so as soon as possible;

4. *Calls upon* the States contemplated in Protocol III to the Treaty that have not yet done so to take all necessary measures to ensure the speedy application of the Treaty to territories for which they are, de jure or de facto, internationally responsible and that lie within the limits of the geographical zone established in the Treaty;

---

[1] See A/50/426, annex.
[2] A/51/113-S/1996/276, annex.
[3] S/PRST/1996/17; see *Resolutions and Decisions of the Security Council*, 1996.

5. *Calls upon* the African States parties to the Treaty on the Non-Proliferation of Nuclear Weapons[4] that have not yet done so to conclude comprehensive safeguards agreements with the International Atomic Energy Agency pursuant to the Treaty, thereby satisfying the requirements of article 9 (*b*) of and annex II to the Treaty of Pelindaba, and to conclude additional protocols to their safeguards agreements on the basis of the Model Protocol approved by the Board of Governors of the Agency on 15 May 1997;[5]

6. *Expresses its gratitude* to the Secretary-General, the Chairperson of the African Union Commission and the Director General of the International Atomic Energy Agency for the diligence with which they have rendered effective assistance to the signatories to the Treaty;

7. *Decides* to include in the provisional agenda of its sixty-fifth session the item entitled "African Nuclear-Weapon-Free Zone Treaty".

Action by the General Assembly

Date: 2 December 2009　　Meeting: 55th plenary meeting
Vote: Adopted without a vote　　Report: A/64/383

Sponsors

Nigeria, on behalf of the States Members of the United Nations that are Members of the Group of African States

Action by the First Committee

Date: 27 October 2009　　Meeting: 19th meeting
Vote: Adopted without a vote　　Draft resolution: A/C.1/64/L.33

---

[4] United Nations, *Treaty Series*, vol. 729, No. 10485.
[5] Model Protocol Additional to the Agreement(s) between State(s) and the International Atomic Energy Agency for the Application of Safeguards (International Atomic Energy Agency, INFCIRC/540 (Corrected)).

Agenda item 91

64/25 Developments in the field of information and telecommunications in the context of international security

Text

The General Assembly,

Recalling its resolutions 53/70 of 4 December 1998, 54/49 of 1 December 1999, 55/28 of 20 November 2000, 56/19 of 29 November 2001, 57/53 of 22 November 2002, 58/32 of 8 December 2003, 59/61 of 3 December 2004, 60/45 of 8 December 2005, 61/54 of 6 December 2006, 62/17 of 5 December 2007 and 63/37 of 2 December 2008,

Recalling also its resolutions on the role of science and technology in the context of international security, in which, inter alia, it recognized that scientific and technological developments could have both civilian and military applications and that progress in science and technology for civilian applications needed to be maintained and encouraged,

Noting that considerable progress has been achieved in developing and applying the latest information technologies and means of telecommunication,

Affirming that it sees in this process the broadest positive opportunities for the further development of civilization, the expansion of opportunities for cooperation for the common good of all States, the enhancement of the creative potential of humankind and additional improvements in the circulation of information in the global community,

Recalling, in this connection, the approaches and principles outlined at the Information Society and Development Conference, held in Midrand, South Africa, from 13 to 15 May 1996,

Bearing in mind the results of the Ministerial Conference on Terrorism, held in Paris on 30 July 1996, and the recommendations that it made,[1]

Bearing in mind also the results of the World Summit on the Information Society, held in Geneva from 10 to 12 December 2003 (first phase) and in Tunis from 16 to 18 November 2005 (second phase),[2]

Noting that the dissemination and use of information technologies and means affect the interests of the entire international community and that optimum effectiveness is enhanced by broad international cooperation,

Expressing its concern that these technologies and means can potentially be used for purposes that are inconsistent with the objectives of maintaining

---

[1] See A/51/261, annex.
[2] See A/C.2/59/3 and A/60/687.

international stability and security and may adversely affect the integrity of the infrastructure of States to the detriment of their security in both civil and military fields,

Considering that it is necessary to prevent the use of information resources or technologies for criminal or terrorist purposes,

Noting the contribution of those Member States that have submitted their assessments on issues of information security to the Secretary-General pursuant to paragraphs 1 to 3 of resolutions 53/70, 54/49, 55/28, 56/19, 57/53, 58/32, 59/61, 60/45, 61/54, 62/17 and 63/37,

Taking note of the reports of the Secretary-General containing those assessments,[3]

Welcoming the initiative taken by the Secretariat and the United Nations Institute for Disarmament Research in convening international meetings of experts in Geneva in August 1999 and April 2008 on developments in the field of information and telecommunications in the context of international security, as well as the results of those meetings,

Considering that the assessments of the Member States contained in the reports of the Secretary-General and the international meetings of experts have contributed to a better understanding of the substance of issues of international information security and related notions,

Bearing in mind that the Secretary-General, in fulfilment of resolution 58/32, established in 2004 a group of governmental experts, which, in accordance with its mandate, considered existing and potential threats in the sphere of information security and possible cooperative measures to address them and conducted a study on relevant international concepts aimed at strengthening the security of global information and telecommunications systems,

Taking note of the report of the Secretary-General on the Group of Governmental Experts on Developments in the Field of Information and Telecommunications in the Context of International Security, prepared on the basis of the results of the Group's work,[4]

1. *Calls upon* Member States to promote further at multilateral levels the consideration of existing and potential threats in the field of information security, as well as possible measures to limit the threats emerging in this field, consistent with the need to preserve the free flow of information;

---

[3] A/54/213, A/55/140 and Corr.1 and Add.1, A/56/164 and Add.1, A/57/166 and Add.1, A/58/373, A/59/116 and Add.1, A/60/95 and Add.1, A/61/161 and Add.1, A/62/98 and Add.1 and A/64/129 and Add.1.
[4] A/60/202.

2. *Considers* that the purpose of such measures could be served through the examination of relevant international concepts aimed at strengthening the security of global information and telecommunications systems;

3. *Invites* all Member States to continue to inform the Secretary-General of their views and assessments on the following questions:

(*a*) General appreciation of the issues of information security;

(*b*) Efforts taken at the national level to strengthen information security and promote international cooperation in this field;

(*c*) The content of the concepts mentioned in paragraph 2 above;

(*d*) Possible measures that could be taken by the international community to strengthen information security at the global level;

4. *Requests* the Secretary-General, with the assistance of the group of governmental experts, established in 2009 on the basis of equitable geographical distribution pursuant to General Assembly resolution 63/37, to continue to study existing and potential threats in the sphere of information security and possible cooperative measures to address them, as well as the concepts referred to in paragraph 2 above, and to submit a report on the results of this study to the Assembly at its sixty-fifth session;

5. *Notes with satisfaction* the holding, in Geneva in November 2009, of the first session of the group of governmental experts established by the Secretary-General and the intention of the group to convene three more sessions in 2010 in order to fulfil its mandate as specified in resolution 63/37;

6. *Decides* to include in the provisional agenda of its sixty-fifth session the item entitled "Developments in the field of information and telecommunications in the context of international security".

Action by the General Assembly

Date: 2 December 2009 Meeting: 55th plenary meeting
Vote: Adopted without a vote Report: A/64/386

Sponsors

Armenia, Azerbaijan, Belarus, Brazil, Chile, China, Cuba, Ethiopia, Haiti, India, Kazakhstan, Kyrgyzstan, Madagascar, Mali, Myanmar, Nicaragua, **Russian Federation**, Serbia, Sudan, Turkmenistan, Uzbekistan, Viet Nam, Zimbabwe

Co-sponsors

Bolivia (Plurinational State of), Japan, Rwanda, Saint Lucia, Syrian Arab Republic, Tajikistan

Action by the First Committee

Date: 29 October 2009 　　Meeting: 　　21st meeting
Vote: Adopted without a vote 　Draft resolution: A/C.1/64/L.39

Agenda item 92

64/26   Establishment of a nuclear-weapon-free zone in the region of the Middle East

Text

The General Assembly,

Recalling its resolutions 3263 (XXIX) of 9 December 1974, 3474 (XXX) of 11 December 1975, 31/71 of 10 December 1976, 32/82 of 12 December 1977, 33/64 of 14 December 1978, 34/77 of 11 December 1979, 35/147 of 12 December 1980, 36/87 A and B of 9 December 1981, 37/75 of 9 December 1982, 38/64 of 15 December 1983, 39/54 of 12 December 1984, 40/82 of 12 December 1985, 41/48 of 3 December 1986, 42/28 of 30 November 1987, 43/65 of 7 December 1988, 44/108 of 15 December 1989, 45/52 of 4 December 1990, 46/30 of 6 December 1991, 47/48 of 9 December 1992, 48/71 of 16 December 1993, 49/71 of 15 December 1994, 50/66 of 12 December 1995, 51/41 of 10 December 1996, 52/34 of 9 December 1997, 53/74 of 4 December 1998, 54/51 of 1 December 1999, 55/30 of 20 November 2000, 56/21 of 29 November 2001, 57/55 of 22 November 2002, 58/34 of 8 December 2003, 59/63 of 3 December 2004, 60/52 of 8 December 2005, 61/56 of 6 December 2006, 62/18 of 5 December 2007 and 63/38 of 2 December 2008 on the establishment of a nuclear-weapon-free zone in the region of the Middle East,

Recalling also the recommendations for the establishment of a nuclear-weapon-free zone in the region of the Middle East consistent with paragraphs 60 to 63, and in particular paragraph 63 (*d*), of the Final Document of the Tenth Special Session of the General Assembly,[1]

Emphasizing the basic provisions of the above-mentioned resolutions, which call upon all parties directly concerned to consider taking the practical and urgent steps required for the implementation of the proposal to establish a nuclear-weapon-free zone in the region of the Middle East and, pending and during the establishment of such a zone, to declare solemnly that they will refrain, on a reciprocal basis, from producing, acquiring or in any other way possessing nuclear weapons and nuclear explosive devices and from permitting the stationing of nuclear weapons on their territory by any third party, to agree to place their nuclear facilities under International Atomic Energy Agency safeguards and to declare their support for the establishment of the zone and to deposit such declarations with the Security Council for consideration, as appropriate,

Reaffirming the inalienable right of all States to acquire and develop nuclear energy for peaceful purposes,

---

[1] Resolution S-10/2.

Emphasizing the need for appropriate measures on the question of the prohibition of military attacks on nuclear facilities,

Bearing in mind the consensus reached by the General Assembly since its thirty-fifth session that the establishment of a nuclear-weapon-free zone in the region of the Middle East would greatly enhance international peace and security,

Desirous of building on that consensus so that substantial progress can be made towards establishing a nuclear-weapon-free zone in the region of the Middle East,

Welcoming all initiatives leading to general and complete disarmament, including in the region of the Middle East, and in particular on the establishment therein of a zone free of weapons of mass destruction, including nuclear weapons,

Noting the peace negotiations in the Middle East, which should be of a comprehensive nature and represent an appropriate framework for the peaceful settlement of contentious issues in the region,

Recognizing the importance of credible regional security, including the establishment of a mutually verifiable nuclear-weapon-free zone,

Emphasizing the essential role of the United Nations in the establishment of a mutually verifiable nuclear-weapon-free zone,

Having examined the report of the Secretary-General on the implementation of resolution 63/38,[2]

1. *Urges* all parties directly concerned seriously to consider taking the practical and urgent steps required for the implementation of the proposal to establish a nuclear-weapon-free zone in the region of the Middle East in accordance with the relevant resolutions of the General Assembly, and, as a means of promoting this objective, invites the countries concerned to adhere to the Treaty on the Non-Proliferation of Nuclear Weapons;[3]

2. *Calls upon* all countries of the region that have not yet done so, pending the establishment of the zone, to agree to place all their nuclear activities under International Atomic Energy Agency safeguards;

3. *Takes note* of resolution GC(53)/RES/16, adopted on 17 September 2009 by the General Conference of the International Atomic Energy Agency at its fifty-third regular session, concerning the application of Agency safeguards in the Middle East;[4]

---

[2] A/64/124 (Part I) and Add.1.
[3] United Nations, *Treaty Series*, vol. 729, No. 10485.
[4] See International Atomic Energy Agency, *Resolutions and Other Decisions of the General Conference*, Fifty-third Regular Session, 14–18 September 2009 (GC(53)/RES/DEC(2009)).

4. *Notes* the importance of the ongoing bilateral Middle East peace negotiations and the activities of the multilateral Working Group on Arms Control and Regional Security in promoting mutual confidence and security in the Middle East, including the establishment of a nuclear-weapon-free zone;

5. *Invites* all countries of the region, pending the establishment of a nuclear-weapon-free zone in the region of the Middle East, to declare their support for establishing such a zone, consistent with paragraph 63 (*d*) of the Final Document of the Tenth Special Session of the General Assembly,[1] and to deposit those declarations with the Security Council;

6. *Also invites* those countries, pending the establishment of the zone, not to develop, produce, test or otherwise acquire nuclear weapons or permit the stationing on their territories, or territories under their control, of nuclear weapons or nuclear explosive devices;

7. *Invites* the nuclear-weapon States and all other States to render their assistance in the establishment of the zone and at the same time to refrain from any action that runs counter to both the letter and the spirit of the present resolution;

8. *Takes note* of the report of the Secretary-General;[2]

9. *Invites* all parties to consider the appropriate means that may contribute towards the goal of general and complete disarmament and the establishment of a zone free of weapons of mass destruction in the region of the Middle East;

10. *Requests* the Secretary-General to continue to pursue consultations with the States of the region and other concerned States, in accordance with paragraph 7 of resolution 46/30 and taking into account the evolving situation in the region, and to seek from those States their views on the measures outlined in chapters III and IV of the study annexed to the report of the Secretary-General of 10 October 1990[5] or other relevant measures, in order to move towards the establishment of a nuclear-weapon-free zone in the region of the Middle East;

11. *Also requests* the Secretary-General to submit to the General Assembly at its sixty-fifth session a report on the implementation of the present resolution;

12. *Decides* to include in the provisional agenda of its sixty-fifth session the item entitled "Establishment of a nuclear-weapon-free zone in the region of the Middle East".

---

[5] A/45/435.

Action by the General Assembly

Date: 2 December 2009 Meeting: 55th plenary meeting
Vote: Adopted without a vote, Report: A/64/387
as a whole
169-0-3, o.p. 3

Sponsors

Egypt

Recorded vote

As a whole

Adopted without a vote

Operative paragraph 3*

In favour:

Afghanistan, Albania, Algeria, Andorra, Angola, Antigua and Barbuda, Argentina, Armenia, Australia, Austria, Azerbaijan, Bahamas, Bahrain, Barbados, Belarus, Belgium, Belize, Benin, Bhutan, Bolivia (Plurinational State of), Bosnia and Herzegovina, Botswana, Brazil, Brunei Darussalam, Bulgaria, Burundi, Cambodia, Cameroon, Canada, Cape Verde, Chile, China, Colombia, Comoros, Congo, Costa Rica, Côte d'Ivoire, Croatia, Cuba, Cyprus, Czech Republic, Democratic Republic of the Congo, Denmark, Djibouti, Dominica, Dominican Republic, Ecuador, Egypt, El Salvador, Equatorial Guinea, Eritrea, Estonia, Finland, France, Gambia, Georgia, Germany, Ghana, Greece, Grenada, Guatemala, Guinea, Guinea-Bissau, Guyana, Haiti, Honduras, Hungary, Iceland, Indonesia, Iran (Islamic Republic of), Iraq, Ireland, Italy, Jamaica, Japan, Jordan, Kazakhstan, Kenya, Kuwait, Kyrgyzstan, Lao People's Democratic Republic, Latvia, Lebanon, Lesotho, Liberia, Libyan Arab Jamahiriya, Liechtenstein, Lithuania, Luxembourg, Madagascar, Malawi, Malaysia, Maldives, Mali, Malta, Mauritania, Mauritius, Mexico, Monaco, Mongolia, Montenegro, Morocco, Mozambique, Myanmar, Namibia, Nepal, Netherlands, New Zealand, Nicaragua, Niger, Nigeria, Norway, Oman, Pakistan, Panama, Papua New Guinea, Paraguay, Peru, Philippines, Poland, Portugal, Qatar, Republic of Korea, Republic of Moldova, Romania, Russian Federation, Rwanda, Saint Kitts and Nevis, Saint Lucia, Saint Vincent and the Grenadines, Samoa, San Marino, Saudi Arabia, Senegal, Serbia, Sierra Leone, Singapore, Slovakia, Slovenia, Solomon Islands, Somalia, South Africa, Spain, Sri Lanka, Sudan, Suriname, Sweden, Switzerland, Syrian Arab Republic,

---

* Subsequently, the delegations of Bangladesh, Burkina Faso, Ethiopia and Tajikistan advised the Secretariat that they had intended to vote in favour. The voting tally above does not reflect this information.

Thailand, the former Yugoslav Republic of Macedonia, Togo, Trinidad and Tobago, Tunisia, Turkey, Turkmenistan, Uganda, Ukraine, United Arab Emirates, United Kingdom, United Republic of Tanzania, United States, Uruguay, Uzbekistan, Venezuela (Bolivarian Republic of), Viet Nam, Yemen, Zambia, Zimbabwe

Against:
   None

Abstaining:
   India, Israel, Marshall Islands

Action by the First Committee

Date: 27 October 2009   Meeting: 19th meeting
Vote: Adopted without a vote   Draft resolution: A/C.1/64/L.3
      166-0-3, o.p. 3

Agenda item 93

64/27 Conclusion of effective international arrangements to assure non-nuclear-weapon States against the use or threat of use of nuclear weapons

Text

The General Assembly,

Bearing in mind the need to allay the legitimate concern of the States of the world with regard to ensuring lasting security for their peoples,

Convinced that nuclear weapons pose the greatest threat to mankind and to the survival of civilization,

Noting that the renewed interest in nuclear disarmament should be translated into concrete actions for the achievement of general and complete disarmament under effective international control,

Convinced that nuclear disarmament and the complete elimination of nuclear weapons are essential to remove the danger of nuclear war,

Determined to abide strictly by the relevant provisions of the Charter of the United Nations on the non-use of force or threat of force,

Recognizing that the independence, territorial integrity and sovereignty of non-nuclear-weapon States need to be safeguarded against the use or threat of use of force, including the use or threat of use of nuclear weapons,

Considering that, until nuclear disarmament is achieved on a universal basis, it is imperative for the international community to develop effective measures and arrangements to ensure the security of non-nuclear-weapon States against the use or threat of use of nuclear weapons from any quarter,

Recognizing that effective measures and arrangements to assure non-nuclear-weapon States against the use or threat of use of nuclear weapons can contribute positively to the prevention of the spread of nuclear weapons,

Bearing in mind paragraph 59 of the Final Document of the Tenth Special Session of the General Assembly, the first special session devoted to disarmament,[1] in which it urged the nuclear-weapon States to pursue efforts to conclude, as appropriate, effective arrangements to assure non-nuclear-weapon States against the use or threat of use of nuclear weapons, and desirous of promoting the implementation of the relevant provisions of the Final Document,

---

[1] Resolution S-10/2.

Recalling the relevant parts of the special report of the Committee on Disarmament[2] submitted to the General Assembly at its twelfth special session, the second special session devoted to disarmament,[3] and of the special report of the Conference on Disarmament submitted to the Assembly at its fifteenth special session, the third special session devoted to disarmament,[4] as well as the report of the Conference on its 1992 session,[5]

Recalling also paragraph 12 of the Declaration of the 1980s as the Second Disarmament Decade, contained in the annex to its resolution 35/46 of 3 December 1980, which states, inter alia, that all efforts should be exerted by the Committee on Disarmament urgently to negotiate with a view to reaching agreement on effective international arrangements to assure non-nuclear-weapon States against the use or threat of use of nuclear weapons,

Noting the in-depth negotiations undertaken in the Conference on Disarmament and its Ad Hoc Committee on Effective International Arrangements to Assure Non-Nuclear-Weapon States against the Use or Threat of Use of Nuclear Weapons,[6] with a view to reaching agreement on this question,

Taking note of the proposals submitted under the item in the Conference on Disarmament, including the drafts of an international convention,

Taking note also of the relevant decision of the Thirteenth Conference of Heads of State or Government of Non-Aligned Countries, held at Kuala Lumpur on 24 and 25 February 2003,[7] which was reiterated at the Fourteenth and Fifteenth Conferences of Heads of State or Government of Non-Aligned Countries, held at Havana and Sharm el-Sheik, Egypt, on 15 and 16 September 2006,[8] and 15 and 16 July 2009,[9] respectively, as well as the relevant recommendations of the Organization of the Islamic Conference,

Taking note further of the unilateral declarations made by all the nuclear-weapon States on their policies of non-use or non-threat of use of nuclear weapons against the non-nuclear-weapon States,

Noting the support expressed in the Conference on Disarmament and in the General Assembly for the elaboration of an international convention to assure non-nuclear-weapon States against the use or threat of use of nuclear

---

[2] The Committee on Disarmament was redesignated the Conference on Disarmament as from 7 February 1984.
[3] *Official Records of the General Assembly, Twelfth Special Session, Supplement No. 2* (A/S-12/2), sect. III.C.
[4] Ibid., *Fifteenth Special Session, Supplement No. 2* (A/S-15/2), sect. III.F.
[5] Ibid., *Forty-seventh Session, Supplement No. 27* (A/47/27), sect. III.F.
[6] Ibid., *Forty-eighth Session, Supplement No. 27* (A/48/27), para. 39.
[7] See A/57/759-S/2003/332, annex I.
[8] See A/61/472-S/2006/780, annex I.
[9] See S/2009/459, annex, para. 118.

weapons, as well as the difficulties pointed out in evolving a common approach acceptable to all,

Taking note of Security Council resolution 984 (1995) of 11 April 1995 and the views expressed on it,

Recalling its relevant resolutions adopted in previous years, in particular resolutions 45/54 of 4 December 1990, 46/32 of 6 December 1991, 47/50 of 9 December 1992, 48/73 of 16 December 1993, 49/73 of 15 December 1994, 50/68 of 12 December 1995, 51/43 of 10 December 1996, 52/36 of 9 December 1997, 53/75 of 4 December 1998, 54/52 of 1 December 1999, 55/31 of 20 November 2000, 56/22 of 29 November 2001, 57/56 of 22 November 2002, 58/35 of 8 December 2003, 59/64 of 3 December 2004, 60/53 of 8 December 2005, 61/57 of 6 December 2006, 62/19 of 5 December 2007 and 63/39 of 2 December 2008,

1. *Reaffirms* the urgent need to reach an early agreement on effective international arrangements to assure non-nuclear-weapon States against the use or threat of use of nuclear weapons;

2. *Notes with satisfaction* that in the Conference on Disarmament there is no objection, in principle, to the idea of an international convention to assure non-nuclear-weapon States against the use or threat of use of nuclear weapons, although the difficulties with regard to evolving a common approach acceptable to all have also been pointed out;

3. *Appeals* to all States, especially the nuclear-weapon States, to work actively towards an early agreement on a common approach and, in particular, on a common formula that could be included in an international instrument of a legally binding character;

4. *Recommends* that further intensive efforts be devoted to the search for such a common approach or common formula and that the various alternative approaches, including, in particular, those considered in the Conference on Disarmament, be explored further in order to overcome the difficulties;

5. *Also recommends* that the Conference on Disarmament actively continue intensive negotiations with a view to reaching early agreement and concluding effective international agreements to assure the non-nuclear-weapon States against the use or threat of use of nuclear weapons, taking into account the widespread support for the conclusion of an international convention and giving consideration to any other proposals designed to secure the same objective;

6. *Decides* to include in the provisional agenda of its sixty-fifth session the item entitled "Conclusion of effective international arrangements to assure non-nuclear-weapon States against the use or threat of use of nuclear weapons".

Action by the General Assembly

Date: 2 December 2009   Meeting: 55th plenary meeting
Vote: 118-0-58   Report: A/64/388

Sponsors

Bangladesh, Benin, Brunei Darussalam, Cuba, Egypt, El Salvador, Ghana, Haiti, Honduras, Indonesia, Iran (Islamic Republic of), Iraq, Kuwait, Libyan Arab Jamahiriya, Malawi, Malaysia, Myanmar, **Pakistan**, Peru, Philippines, Qatar, Saudi Arabia, Sri Lanka, Syrian Arab Republic, Uzbekistan, Viet Nam

Co-sponsors

Cambodia, Colombia, Fiji

Recorded vote*

In favour:

Afghanistan, Algeria, Angola, Antigua and Barbuda, Azerbaijan, Bahamas, Bahrain, Barbados, Belarus, Belize, Benin, Bhutan, Bolivia (Plurinational State of), Botswana, Brazil, Brunei Darussalam, Burundi, Cambodia, Cameroon, Cape Verde, Chile, China, Colombia, Comoros, Congo, Costa Rica, Côte d'Ivoire, Cuba, Democratic People's Republic of Korea, Djibouti, Dominica, Dominican Republic, Ecuador, Egypt, El Salvador, Equatorial Guinea, Eritrea, Fiji, Gambia, Ghana, Grenada, Guatemala, Guinea, Guinea-Bissau, Guyana, Haiti, Honduras, India, Indonesia, Iran (Islamic Republic of), Iraq, Jamaica, Japan, Jordan, Kazakhstan, Kenya, Kuwait, Kyrgyzstan, Lao People's Democratic Republic, Lebanon, Lesotho, Liberia, Libyan Arab Jamahiriya, Madagascar, Malawi, Malaysia, Maldives, Mali, Mauritania, Mauritius, Mexico, Mongolia, Morocco, Mozambique, Myanmar, Namibia, Nepal, Nicaragua, Niger, Nigeria, Oman, Pakistan, Panama, Papua New Guinea, Paraguay, Peru, Philippines, Qatar, Rwanda, Saint Kitts and Nevis, Saint Lucia, Saint Vincent and the Grenadines, Samoa, Saudi Arabia, Senegal, Singapore, Solomon Islands, Somalia, Sri Lanka, Sudan, Suriname, Syrian Arab Republic, Thailand, Togo, Tonga, Trinidad and Tobago, Tunisia, Turkmenistan, Uganda, United Arab Emirates, United Republic of Tanzania, Uruguay, Uzbekistan, Venezuela (Bolivarian Republic of), Viet Nam, Yemen, Zambia, Zimbabwe

Against:
None

---

* Subsequently, the delegations of Bangladesh, Burkina Faso, Ethiopia and Swaziland advised the Secretariat that they had intended to vote in favour, and the delegation of Tajikistan advised that it had intended to abstain. The voting tally above does not reflect this information.

Abstaining:
Albania, Andorra, Argentina, Armenia, Australia, Austria, Belgium, Bosnia and Herzegovina, Bulgaria, Canada, Croatia, Cyprus, Czech Republic, Democratic Republic of the Congo, Denmark, Estonia, Finland, France, Georgia, Germany, Greece, Hungary, Iceland, Ireland, Israel, Italy, Latvia, Liechtenstein, Lithuania, Luxembourg, Malta, Marshall Islands, Micronesia (Federated States of), Monaco, Montenegro, Netherlands, New Zealand, Norway, Palau, Poland, Portugal, Republic of Korea, Republic of Moldova, Romania, Russian Federation, San Marino, Serbia, Slovakia, Slovenia, South Africa, Spain, Sweden, Switzerland, the former Yugoslav Republic of Macedonia, Turkey, Ukraine, United Kingdom, United States

Action by the First Committee

Date: 27 October 2009　　　Meeting:　　　19th meeting
Vote: 119-0-58　　　　　　　Draft resolution: A/C.1/64/L.24

Agenda item 94

64/28   Prevention of an arms race in outer space

Text

The General Assembly,

Recognizing the common interest of all mankind in the exploration and use of outer space for peaceful purposes,

Reaffirming the will of all States that the exploration and use of outer space, including the Moon and other celestial bodies, shall be for peaceful purposes and shall be carried out for the benefit and in the interest of all countries, irrespective of their degree of economic or scientific development,

Reaffirming also the provisions of articles III and IV of the Treaty on Principles Governing the Activities of States in the Exploration and Use of Outer Space, including the Moon and Other Celestial Bodies,[1]

Recalling the obligation of all States to observe the provisions of the Charter of the United Nations regarding the use or threat of use of force in their international relations, including in their space activities,

Reaffirming paragraph 80 of the Final Document of the Tenth Special Session of the General Assembly,[2] in which it is stated that in order to prevent an arms race in outer space, further measures should be taken and appropriate international negotiations held in accordance with the spirit of the Treaty,

Recalling its previous resolutions on this issue, and taking note of the proposals submitted to the General Assembly at its tenth special session and at its regular sessions, and of the recommendations made to the competent organs of the United Nations and to the Conference on Disarmament,

Recognizing that prevention of an arms race in outer space would avert a grave danger for international peace and security,

Emphasizing the paramount importance of strict compliance with existing arms limitation and disarmament agreements relevant to outer space, including bilateral agreements, and with the existing legal regime concerning the use of outer space,

Considering that wide participation in the legal regime applicable to outer space could contribute to enhancing its effectiveness,

Noting that the Ad Hoc Committee on the Prevention of an Arms Race in Outer Space, taking into account its previous efforts since its establishment in 1985 and seeking to enhance its functioning in qualitative terms, continued the examination and identification of various issues, existing agreements and

---

[1] United Nations, *Treaty Series*, vol. 610, No. 8843.
[2] Resolution S-10/2.

existing proposals, as well as future initiatives relevant to the prevention of an arms race in outer space,[3] and that this contributed to a better understanding of a number of problems and to a clearer perception of the various positions,

Noting also that there were no objections in principle in the Conference on Disarmament to the re-establishment of the Ad Hoc Committee, subject to re-examination of the mandate contained in the decision of the Conference on Disarmament of 13 February 1992,[4]

Emphasizing the mutually complementary nature of bilateral and multilateral efforts for the prevention of an arms race in outer space, and hoping that concrete results will emerge from those efforts as soon as possible,

Convinced that further measures should be examined in the search for effective and verifiable bilateral and multilateral agreements in order to prevent an arms race in outer space, including the weaponization of outer space,

Stressing that the growing use of outer space increases the need for greater transparency and better information on the part of the international community,

Recalling, in this context, its previous resolutions, in particular resolutions 45/55 B of 4 December 1990, 47/51 of 9 December 1992 and 48/74 A of 16 December 1993, in which, inter alia, it reaffirmed the importance of confidence-building measures as a means conducive to ensuring the attainment of the objective of the prevention of an arms race in outer space,

Conscious of the benefits of confidence- and security-building measures in the military field,

Recognizing that negotiations for the conclusion of an international agreement or agreements to prevent an arms race in outer space remain a priority task of the Conference on Disarmament and that the concrete proposals on confidence-building measures could form an integral part of such agreements,

Noting with satisfaction the constructive, structured and focused debate on the prevention of an arms race in outer space at the Conference on Disarmament in 2009,

Taking note of the introduction by China and the Russian Federation at the Conference on Disarmament of the draft treaty on the prevention of the placement of weapons in outer space and of the threat or use of force against outer space objects,[5]

---

[3] *Official Records of the General Assembly, Forty-ninth Session, Supplement No. 27* (A/49/27), sect. III.D (para. 5 of the quoted text).
[4] CD/1125.
[5] See CD/1839.

Taking note also of the decision of the Conference on Disarmament to establish for its 2009 session a working group to discuss, substantially, without limitation, all issues related to the prevention of an arms race in outer space,

1. *Reaffirms* the importance and urgency of preventing an arms race in outer space and the readiness of all States to contribute to that common objective, in conformity with the provisions of the Treaty on Principles Governing the Activities of States in the Exploration and Use of Outer Space, including the Moon and Other Celestial Bodies;[1]

2. *Reaffirms its recognition*, as stated in the report of the Ad Hoc Committee on the Prevention of an Arms Race in Outer Space, that the legal regime applicable to outer space does not in and of itself guarantee the prevention of an arms race in outer space, that the regime plays a significant role in the prevention of an arms race in that environment, that there is a need to consolidate and reinforce that regime and enhance its effectiveness and that it is important to comply strictly with existing agreements, both bilateral and multilateral;

3. *Emphasizes* the necessity of further measures with appropriate and effective provisions for verification to prevent an arms race in outer space;

4. *Calls upon* all States, in particular those with major space capabilities, to contribute actively to the objective of the peaceful use of outer space and of the prevention of an arms race in outer space and to refrain from actions contrary to that objective and to the relevant existing treaties in the interest of maintaining international peace and security and promoting international cooperation;

5. *Reiterates* that the Conference on Disarmament, as the sole multilateral disarmament negotiating forum, has the primary role in the negotiation of a multilateral agreement or agreements, as appropriate, on the prevention of an arms race in outer space in all its aspects;

6. *Invites* the Conference on Disarmament to establish a working group under its agenda item entitled "Prevention of an arms race in outer space" as early as possible during its 2010 session;

7. *Recognizes*, in this respect, the growing convergence of views on the elaboration of measures designed to strengthen transparency, confidence and security in the peaceful uses of outer space;

8. *Urges* States conducting activities in outer space, as well as States interested in conducting such activities, to keep the Conference on Disarmament informed of the progress of bilateral and multilateral negotiations on the matter, if any, so as to facilitate its work;

9. *Decides* to include in the provisional agenda of its sixty-fifth session the item entitled "Prevention of an arms race in outer space".

Action by the General Assembly

Date: 2 December 2009   Meeting: 55th plenary meeting
Vote: 176-0-2   Report: A/64/389

Sponsors

Algeria, Armenia, Belarus, Bhutan, Burkina Faso, China, Cuba, Egypt, Guatemala, India, Jordan, Libyan Arab Jamahiriya, Mongolia, Myanmar, Nepal, Nigeria, Pakistan, Russian Federation, **Sri Lanka**, Syrian Arab Republic, Uganda, Venezuela (Bolivarian Republic of)

Co-sponsors

Antigua and Barbuda, Bolivia (Plurinational State of), Brazil, Comoros, Democratic People's Republic of Korea, Dominican Republic, Fiji, Honduras, Kazakhstan, Madagascar, Malaysia, Philippines, Tajikistan, Trinidad and Tobago, Uruguay, Uzbekistan

*Recorded vote**

In favour:

Afghanistan, Albania, Algeria, Andorra, Angola, Antigua and Barbuda, Argentina, Armenia, Australia, Austria, Azerbaijan, Bahamas, Bahrain, Barbados, Belarus, Belgium, Belize, Benin, Bhutan, Bolivia (Plurinational State of), Bosnia and Herzegovina, Botswana, Brazil, Brunei Darussalam, Bulgaria, Burundi, Cambodia, Cameroon, Canada, Cape Verde, Chile, China, Colombia, Comoros, Congo, Costa Rica, Côte d'Ivoire, Croatia, Cuba, Cyprus, Czech Republic, Democratic People's Republic of Korea, Democratic Republic of the Congo, Denmark, Djibouti, Dominica, Dominican Republic, Ecuador, Egypt, El Salvador, Equatorial Guinea, Eritrea, Estonia, Fiji, Finland, France, Gambia, Georgia, Germany, Ghana, Greece, Grenada, Guatemala, Guinea, Guinea-Bissau, Guyana, Haiti, Honduras, Hungary, Iceland, India, Indonesia, Iran (Islamic Republic of), Iraq, Ireland, Italy, Jamaica, Japan, Jordan, Kazakhstan, Kenya, Kuwait, Kyrgyzstan, Lao People's Democratic Republic, Latvia, Lebanon, Lesotho, Liberia, Libyan Arab Jamahiriya, Liechtenstein, Lithuania, Luxembourg, Madagascar, Malawi, Malaysia, Maldives, Mali, Malta, Marshall Islands, Mauritania, Mauritius, Mexico, Micronesia (Federated States of), Monaco, Mongolia, Montenegro, Morocco, Mozambique, Myanmar, Namibia,

---

* Subsequently, the delegations of Bangladesh, Burkina Faso, Ethiopia, Swaziland and Tajikistan advised the Secretariat that they had intended to vote in favour. The voting tally above does not reflect this information.

Nepal, Netherlands, New Zealand, Nicaragua, Niger, Nigeria, Norway, Oman, Pakistan, Palau, Panama, Papua New Guinea, Paraguay, Peru, Philippines, Poland, Portugal, Qatar, Republic of Korea, Republic of Moldova, Romania, Russian Federation, Rwanda, Saint Kitts and Nevis, Saint Lucia, Saint Vincent and the Grenadines, Samoa, San Marino, Saudi Arabia, Senegal, Serbia, Seychelles, Sierra Leone, Singapore, Slovakia, Slovenia, Solomon Islands, Somalia, South Africa, Spain, Sri Lanka, Sudan, Suriname, Sweden, Switzerland, Syrian Arab Republic, Thailand, the former Yugoslav Republic of Macedonia, Togo, Tonga, Trinidad and Tobago, Tunisia, Turkey, Turkmenistan, Uganda, Ukraine, United Arab Emirates, United Kingdom, United Republic of Tanzania, Uruguay, Uzbekistan, Venezuela (Bolivarian Republic of), Viet Nam, Yemen, Zambia, Zimbabwe

Against:
None

Abstaining:
Israel, United States

Action by the First Committee

Date: 28 October 2009　　Meeting:　　20th meeting
Vote: 176-0-2　　　　　　Draft resolution: A/C.1/64/L.25

Agenda item 96

64/29 Treaty banning the production of fissile material for nuclear weapons or other nuclear explosive devices

Text

The General Assembly,

Recalling its resolutions 48/75 L of 16 December 1993, 53/77 I of 4 December 1998, 55/33 Y of 20 November 2000, 56/24 J of 29 November 2001, 57/80 of 22 November 2002, 58/57 of 8 December 2003 and 59/81 of 3 December 2004 on the subject of banning the production of fissile material for nuclear weapons or other nuclear explosive devices, and noting in this regard the support for the Conference on Disarmament expressed by the Security Council summit on nuclear disarmament and nuclear non-proliferation, held on 24 September 2009,

Convinced that a non-discriminatory, multilateral and internationally and effectively verifiable treaty banning the production of fissile material for nuclear weapons or other nuclear explosive devices would be a significant contribution to nuclear disarmament and non-proliferation,

Welcoming, after years of stalemate, the consensus adoption by the Conference on Disarmament of its decision (CD/1864) of 29 May 2009 on the establishment of a programme of work for its 2009 session, by which the Conference, inter alia, and without prejudice to any past, present or future position, established a Working Group to negotiate a treaty banning the production of fissile material for nuclear weapons or other nuclear explosive devices on the basis of document CD/1299 of 24 March 1995 and the mandate contained therein,

1. *Urges* the Conference on Disarmament to agree early in 2010 on a programme of work that includes the immediate commencement of negotiations on a treaty banning the production of fissile material for nuclear weapons or other nuclear explosive devices;

2. *Decides* to include in the provisional agenda of its sixty-fifth session an item entitled "Treaty banning the production of fissile material for nuclear weapons or other nuclear explosive devices".

Action by the General Assembly

Date: 2 December 2009 Meeting: 55th plenary meeting
Vote: Adopted without a vote Report: A/64/391

Sponsors
> **Canada**

Action by the First Committee
> Date: 29 October 2009 Meeting: 21st meeting
> Vote: Adopted without a vote Draft resolution: A/C.1/64/L.1/Rev.1

Agenda item 96 (u)

64/30　Assistance to States for curbing the illicit traffic in small arms and light weapons and collecting them

Text

The General Assembly,

Recalling its resolution 63/66 of 2 December 2008 on assistance to States for curbing the illicit traffic in small arms and light weapons and collecting them,

Deeply concerned by the magnitude of human casualty and suffering, especially among children, caused by the illicit proliferation and use of small arms and light weapons,

Concerned by the negative impact that the illicit proliferation and use of those weapons continue to have on the efforts of States in the Sahelo-Saharan subregion in the areas of poverty eradication, sustainable development and the maintenance of peace, security and stability,

Bearing in mind the Bamako Declaration on an African Common Position on the Illicit Proliferation, Circulation and Trafficking of Small Arms and Light Weapons, adopted at Bamako on 1 December 2000,[1]

Recalling the report of the Secretary-General entitled "In larger freedom: towards development, security and human rights for all",[2] in which he emphasized that States must strive just as hard to eliminate the threat of illicit small arms and light weapons as they do to eliminate the threat of weapons of mass destruction,

Recalling also the International Instrument to Enable States to Identify and Trace, in a Timely and Reliable Manner, Illicit Small Arms and Light Weapons, adopted on 8 December 2005,[3]

Welcoming the expression of support in the 2005 World Summit Outcome for the implementation of the Programme of Action to Prevent, Combat and Eradicate the Illicit Trade in Small Arms and Light Weapons in All Its Aspects,[4]

Welcoming also the adoption, at the thirtieth ordinary summit of the Economic Community of West African States, held in Abuja in June 2006, of the Convention on Small Arms and Light Weapons, Their Ammunition and

---

[1] A/CONF.192/PC/23, annex.
[2] A/59/2005.
[3] A/60/88 and Corr.2, annex; see also decision 60/519.
[4] See resolution 60/1, para. 94.

Other Related Materials, in replacement of the moratorium on the importation, exportation and manufacture of small arms and light weapons in West Africa,

Welcoming further the decision taken by the Economic Community to establish a Small Arms Unit responsible for advocating appropriate policies and developing and implementing programmes, as well as the establishment of the Economic Community's Small Arms Control Programme, launched on 6 June 2006 in Bamako, in replacement of the Programme for Coordination and Assistance for Security and Development,

Taking note of the latest report of the Secretary-General on assistance to States for curbing the illicit traffic in small arms and light weapons and collecting them and the illicit trade in small arms and light weapons in all its aspects,[5]

Welcoming, in that regard, the decision of the European Union to significantly support the Economic Community in its efforts to combat the illicit proliferation of small arms and light weapons,

Recognizing the important role that civil society organizations play, by raising public awareness, in efforts to curb the illicit traffic in small arms and light weapons,

Taking note of the report of the United Nations Conference to Review Progress Made in the Implementation of the Programme of Action to Prevent, Combat and Eradicate the Illicit Trade in Small Arms and Light Weapons in All Its Aspects, held in New York from 26 June to 7 July 2006,[6]

1. *Commends* the United Nations and international, regional and other organizations for their assistance to States for curbing the illicit traffic in small arms and light weapons and collecting them;

2. *Encourages* the Secretary-General to pursue his efforts in the context of the implementation of General Assembly resolution 49/75 G of 15 December 1994 and the recommendations of the United Nations advisory missions aimed at curbing the illicit circulation of small arms and light weapons and collecting them in the affected States that so request, with the support of the United Nations Regional Centre for Peace and Disarmament in Africa and in close cooperation with the African Union;

3. *Encourages* the international community to support the implementation of the Economic Community of West African States Convention on Small Arms and Light Weapons, Their Ammunition and Other Related Materials;

4. *Encourages* the countries of the Sahelo-Saharan subregion to facilitate the effective functioning of national commissions to combat the

---

[5] A/64/173.
[6] A/CONF.192/2006/RC/9.

illicit proliferation of small arms and light weapons, and, in that regard, invites the international community to lend its support wherever possible;

5. *Encourages* the collaboration of civil society organizations and associations in the efforts of the national commissions to combat the illicit traffic in small arms and light weapons and in the implementation of the Programme of Action to Prevent, Combat and Eradicate the Illicit Trade in Small Arms and Light Weapons in All Its Aspects;[7]

6. *Also encourages* cooperation among State organs, international organizations and civil society in support of programmes and projects aimed at combating the illicit traffic in small arms and light weapons and collecting them;

7. *Calls upon* the international community to provide technical and financial support to strengthen the capacity of civil society organizations to take action to help to combat the illicit trade in small arms and light weapons;

8. *Invites* the Secretary-General and those States and organizations that are in a position to do so to continue to provide assistance to States for curbing the illicit traffic in small arms and light weapons and collecting them;

9. *Requests* the Secretary-General to continue to consider the matter and to report to the General Assembly at its sixty-fifth session on the implementation of the present resolution;

10. *Decides* to include in the provisional agenda of its sixty-fifth session the item entitled "Assistance to States for curbing the illicit traffic in small arms and light weapons and collecting them".

Action by the General Assembly

Date: 2 December 2009   Meeting: 55th plenary meeting
Vote: Adopted without a vote   Report: A/64/391

Sponsors

Mali, on behalf of the States Members of the United Nations which are members of the Economic Community of West African States

Co-sponsors

Albania, Algeria, Andorra, Angola, Antigua and Barbuda, Austria, Belgium, Belize, Bosnia and Herzegovina, Bulgaria, Burundi, Cameroon, Canada, Central African Republic, Chile, Colombia, Comoros, Congo, Croatia, Cyprus, Czech Republic, Democratic Republic of the Congo, Denmark, Djibouti, Dominica, Dominican Republic, Eritrea, Estonia,

---

[7] See *Report of the United Nations Conference on the Illicit Trade in Small Arms and Light Weapons in All Its Aspects, New York, 9–20 July 2001* (A/CONF.192/15), chap. IV, para. 24.

Ethiopia, Fiji, Finland, France, Gabon, Germany, Greece, Grenada, Guatemala, Guyana, Haiti, Honduras, Hungary, Iceland, Ireland, Italy, Jamaica, Kenya, Latvia, Lesotho, Liechtenstein, Lithuania, Luxembourg, Madagascar, Malawi, Malta, Mauritania, Montenegro, Morocco, Mozambique, Netherlands, Norway, Papua New Guinea, Poland, Portugal, Republic of Moldova, Romania, Saint Kitts and Nevis, Saint Lucia, Saint Vincent and the Grenadines, San Marino, Serbia, Slovakia, Slovenia, South Africa, Spain, Sudan, Sweden, Switzerland, the former Yugoslav Republic of Macedonia, Trinidad and Tobago, Turkey, Uganda, United Kingdom, United Republic of Tanzania, Zambia, Zimbabwe

Action by the First Committee

Date: 28 October 2009	Meeting: 20th meeting
Vote: Adopted without a vote	Draft resolution: A/C.1/64/L.5

Agenda item 96 (b)

64/31 Follow-up to nuclear disarmament obligations agreed to at the 1995 and 2000 Review Conferences of the Parties to the Treaty on the Non-Proliferation of Nuclear Weapons

Text

The General Assembly,

Recalling its various resolutions in the field of nuclear disarmament, including its most recent, resolutions 62/24 of 5 December 2007, and 63/46, 63/49 and 63/75 of 2 December 2008,

Bearing in mind its resolution 2373 (XXII) of 12 June 1968, the annex to which contains the Treaty on the Non-Proliferation of Nuclear Weapons,[1]

Noting the provisions of article VIII, paragraph 3, of the Treaty regarding the convening of review conferences at five-year intervals,

Recalling its resolution 50/70 Q of 12 December 1995, in which the General Assembly noted that the States parties to the Treaty affirmed the need to continue to move with determination towards the full realization and effective implementation of the provisions of the Treaty, and accordingly adopted a set of principles and objectives,

Recalling also that, on 11 May 1995, the 1995 Review and Extension Conference of the Parties to the Treaty on the Non-Proliferation of Nuclear Weapons adopted three decisions on strengthening the review process for the Treaty, principles and objectives for nuclear non-proliferation and disarmament, and extension of the Treaty,[2]

Reaffirming the resolution on the Middle East adopted on 11 May 1995 by the 1995 Review and Extension Conference of the Parties to the Treaty,[2] in which the Conference reaffirmed the importance of the early realization of universal adherence to the Treaty and placement of nuclear facilities under full-scope International Atomic Energy Agency safeguards,

Reaffirming also its resolution 55/33 D of 20 November 2000, in which the General Assembly welcomed the adoption by consensus on 19 May 2000 of the Final Document of the 2000 Review Conference of the Parties to the Treaty on the Non-Proliferation of Nuclear Weapons,[3] including, in particular,

---

[1] See also United Nations, *Treaty Series*, vol. 729, No. 10485.
[2] See *1995 Review and Extension Conference of the Parties to the Treaty on the Non-Proliferation of Nuclear Weapons, Final Document, Part I* (NPT/CONF.1995/32 (Part I) and Corr.2), annex.
[3] *2000 Review Conference of the Parties to the Treaty on the Non-Proliferation of Nuclear Weapons, Final Document*, vols. I–III (NPT/CONF.2000/28 (Parts I-IV)).

the documents entitled "Review of the operation of the Treaty, taking into account the decisions and the resolution adopted by the 1995 Review and Extension Conference" and "Improving the effectiveness of the strengthened review process for the Treaty",[4]

Taking into consideration the unequivocal undertaking by the nuclear-weapon States, in the Final Document of the 2000 Review Conference of the Parties to the Treaty, to accomplish the total elimination of their nuclear arsenals leading to nuclear disarmament, to which all States parties to the Treaty are committed under article VI of the Treaty,

Gravely concerned over the failure of the 2005 Review Conference of the Parties to the Treaty to reach any substantive agreement on the follow-up to the nuclear disarmament obligations,

Noting with satisfaction that the Preparatory Committee for the 2010 Review Conference of the Parties to the Treaty finalized the procedural arrangements for the Review Conference,

1. *Determines* to pursue practical steps for systematic and progressive efforts to implement article VI of the Treaty on the Non-Proliferation of Nuclear Weapons[1] and paragraphs 3 and 4 (*c*) of the decision on principles and objectives for nuclear non-proliferation and disarmament of the 1995 Review and Extension Conference of the Parties to the Treaty on the Non-Proliferation of Nuclear Weapons;[2]

2. *Calls for* practical steps, as agreed to at the 2000 Review Conference of the Parties to the Treaty on the Non-Proliferation of Nuclear Weapons, to be taken by all nuclear-weapon States, which would lead to nuclear disarmament in a way that promotes international stability and, based on the principle of undiminished security for all:

(*a*) Further efforts to be made by the nuclear-weapon States to reduce their nuclear arsenals unilaterally;

(*b*) Increased transparency by the nuclear-weapon States with regard to nuclear weapons capabilities and the implementation of agreements pursuant to article VI of the Treaty and as a voluntary confidence-building measure to support further progress in nuclear disarmament;

(*c*) The further reduction of non-strategic nuclear weapons, based on unilateral initiatives and as an integral part of the nuclear arms reduction and disarmament process;

(*d*) Concrete agreed measures to reduce further the operational status of nuclear weapons systems;

---

[4] Ibid., vol. I (NPT/CONF.2000/28 (Parts I and II)), part I.

(e) A diminishing role for nuclear weapons in security policies so as to minimize the risk that these weapons will ever be used and to facilitate the process of their total elimination;

(f) The engagement, as soon as appropriate, of all the nuclear-weapon States in the process leading to the total elimination of their nuclear weapons;

3. *Notes* that the 2000 Review Conference of the Parties to the Treaty agreed that legally binding security assurances by the five nuclear-weapon States to the non-nuclear-weapon States parties to the Treaty strengthen the nuclear non-proliferation regime;

4. *Urges* the States parties to the Treaty to follow up on the implementation of the nuclear disarmament obligations under the Treaty agreed to at the 1995 and 2000 Review Conferences of the Parties to the Treaty within the framework of Review Conferences of the Parties to the Treaty and their Preparatory Committees;

5. *Decides* to include in the provisional agenda of its sixty-sixth session the item entitled "Follow-up to nuclear disarmament obligations agreed to at the 1995 and 2000 Review Conferences of the Parties to the Treaty on the Non-Proliferation of Nuclear Weapons".

Action by the General Assembly

Date: 2 December 2009
Vote: 109-56-10, as a whole
112-50-8, p.p. 6

Meeting: 55th plenary meeting
Report: A/64/391

Sponsors

Iran (Islamic Republic of)

Recorded vote

As a whole*

In favour:
Algeria, Angola, Antigua and Barbuda, Argentina, Bahamas, Bahrain, Barbados, Belarus, Belize, Benin, Bhutan, Bolivia (Plurinational State of), Botswana, Brazil, Brunei Darussalam, Burundi, Cambodia, Cameroon, Cape Verde, Chile, Congo, Côte d'Ivoire, Cuba, Democratic People's Republic of Korea, Democratic Republic of the Congo, Djibouti, Dominica, Dominican Republic, Ecuador, Egypt, El Salvador, Equatorial Guinea, Eritrea, Fiji, Gambia, Ghana, Grenada, Guatemala, Guinea, Guinea-Bissau, Guyana, Haiti, Honduras, Indonesia, Iran

---

* Subsequently, the delegations of Bangladesh, Burkina Faso, Ethiopia and Swaziland advised the Secretariat that they had intended to vote in favour; the delegation of Turkey advised that it had intended to vote against. The voting tally above does not reflect this information.

(Islamic Republic of), Iraq, Jamaica, Jordan, Kazakhstan, Kenya, Kuwait, Kyrgyzstan, Lao People's Democratic Republic, Lebanon, Lesotho, Liberia, Libyan Arab Jamahiriya, Madagascar, Malawi, Malaysia, Maldives, Mali, Mauritania, Mauritius, Mexico, Mongolia, Morocco, Mozambique, Myanmar, Namibia, Nepal, Nicaragua, Niger, Nigeria, Oman, Papua New Guinea, Paraguay, Philippines, Qatar, Rwanda, Saint Kitts and Nevis, Saint Lucia, Saint Vincent and the Grenadines, Saudi Arabia, Senegal, Singapore, Solomon Islands, Somalia, South Africa, Sri Lanka, Sudan, Suriname, Syrian Arab Republic, Tajikistan, Thailand, Togo, Trinidad and Tobago, Tunisia, Turkmenistan, Uganda, United Arab Emirates, United Republic of Tanzania, Uruguay, Uzbekistan, Venezuela (Bolivarian Republic of), Viet Nam, Yemen, Zambia, Zimbabwe

Against:
Albania, Andorra, Australia, Austria, Belgium, Bosnia and Herzegovina, Bulgaria, Canada, Comoros, Croatia, Cyprus, Czech Republic, Denmark, Estonia, Finland, France, Georgia, Germany, Greece, Hungary, Iceland, Ireland, Israel, Italy, Japan, Latvia, Liechtenstein, Lithuania, Luxembourg, Malta, Marshall Islands, Micronesia (Federated States of), Monaco, Montenegro, Netherlands, New Zealand, Norway, Palau, Panama, Poland, Portugal, Republic of Korea, Republic of Moldova, Romania, Russian Federation, San Marino, Serbia, Slovakia, Slovenia, Spain, Sweden, Switzerland, the former Yugoslav Republic of Macedonia, Ukraine, United Kingdom, United States

Abstaining:
Armenia, Azerbaijan, China, Colombia, Costa Rica, India, Pakistan, Peru, Samoa, Tonga

Sixth preambular paragaph*

In favour:
Afghanistan, Algeria, Angola, Antigua and Barbuda, Argentina, Bahamas, Bahrain, Barbados, Belarus, Belize, Benin, Bhutan, Bolivia (Plurinational State of), Botswana, Brazil, Brunei Darussalam, Burundi, Cambodia, Cameroon, Cape Verde, Chile, Colombia, Comoros, Congo, Costa Rica, Côte d'Ivoire, Cuba, Democratic Republic of the Congo, Djibouti, Dominica, Dominican Republic, Ecuador, Egypt, El Salvador, Equatorial Guinea, Eritrea, Fiji, Gambia, Ghana, Grenada, Guatemala, Guinea, Guinea-Bissau, Guyana, Haiti, Honduras, Indonesia, Iran (Islamic Republic of), Iraq, Jamaica, Jordan, Kazakhstan, Kenya, Kuwait, Kyrgyzstan, Lao People's Democratic Republic, Lebanon, Liberia, Libyan Arab Jamahiriya, Liechtenstein, Madagascar, Malawi, Malaysia,

---

* Subsequently the delegations of Bangladesh, Burkina Faso, Ethiopia, Lesotho and Tajikistan advised the Secretariat that they had intended to vote in favour. The voting tally above does not reflect this information.

Maldives, Mali, Mauritania, Mexico, Mongolia, Morocco, Mozambique, Myanmar, Namibia, Nepal, New Zealand, Nicaragua, Niger, Nigeria, Oman, Papua New Guinea, Paraguay, Philippines, Qatar, Rwanda, Saint Kitts and Nevis, Saint Lucia, Saint Vincent and the Grenadines, Saudi Arabia, Senegal, Singapore, Solomon Islands, Somalia, South Africa, Sri Lanka, Sudan, Suriname, Switzerland, Syrian Arab Republic, Thailand, Togo, Trinidad and Tobago, Tunisia, Turkmenistan, Uganda, United Arab Emirates, United Republic of Tanzania, Uruguay, Uzbekistan, Venezuela (Bolivarian Republic of), Viet Nam, Yemen, Zambia, Zimbabwe

Against:

Albania, Andorra, Australia, Austria, Belgium, Bosnia and Herzegovina, Bulgaria, Canada, Croatia, Cyprus, Czech Republic, Denmark, Estonia, Finland, France, Georgia, Germany, Greece, Hungary, Iceland, Ireland, Israel, Italy, Japan, Latvia, Lithuania, Luxembourg, Malta, Marshall Islands, Micronesia (Federated States of), Monaco, Montenegro, Netherlands, Norway, Panama, Poland, Portugal, Republic of Korea, Republic of Moldova, Romania, San Marino, Slovakia, Slovenia, Spain, Sweden, the former Yugoslav Republic of Macedonia, Turkey, Ukraine, United Kingdom, United States

Abstaining:

Armenia, Azerbaijan, India, Pakistan, Peru, Russian Federation, Samoa, Serbia

Action by the First Committee

Date: 27 October 2009　　Meeting:　　19th meeting
Vote: 105-56-12, as a whole　　Draft resolution: A/C.1/64/L.6
　　　109-48-10, p.p. 6

Agenda item 96 (o)

64/32   Relationship between disarmament and development

Text

The General Assembly,

Recalling that the Charter of the United Nations envisages the establishment and maintenance of international peace and security with the least diversion for armaments of the world's human and economic resources,

Recalling also the provisions of the Final Document of the Tenth Special Session of the General Assembly concerning the relationship between disarmament and development,[1] as well as the adoption on 11 September 1987 of the Final Document of the International Conference on the Relationship between Disarmament and Development,[2]

Recalling further its resolutions 49/75 J of 15 December 1994, 50/70 G of 12 December 1995, 51/45 D of 10 December 1996, 52/38 D of 9 December 1997, 53/77 K of 4 December 1998, 54/54 T of 1 December 1999, 55/33 L of 20 November 2000, 56/24 E of 29 November 2001, 57/65 of 22 November 2002, 59/78 of 3 December 2004, 60/61 of 8 December 2005, 61/64 of 6 December 2006, 62/48 of 5 December 2007 and 63/52 of 2 December 2008, and its decision 58/520 of 8 December 2003,

Bearing in mind the Final Document of the Twelfth Conference of Heads of State or Government of Non-Aligned Countries, held in Durban, South Africa, from 29 August to 3 September 1998,[3] and the Final Document of the Thirteenth Ministerial Conference of the Movement of Non-Aligned Countries, held in Cartagena, Colombia, on 8 and 9 April 2000,[4]

Mindful of the changes in international relations that have taken place since the adoption on 11 September 1987 of the Final Document of the International Conference on the Relationship between Disarmament and Development, including the development agenda that has emerged over the past decade,

Bearing in mind the new challenges for the international community in the field of development, poverty eradication and the elimination of the diseases that afflict humanity,

Stressing the importance of the symbiotic relationship between disarmament and development and the important role of security in this

---

[1] See resolution S-10/2.
[2] United Nations publication, Sales No. E.87.IX.8.
[3] A/53/667-S/1998/1071, annex I.
[4] A/54/917-S/2000/580, annex.

connection, and concerned at increasing global military expenditure, which could otherwise be spent on development needs,

Recalling the report of the Group of Governmental Experts on the relationship between disarmament and development[5] and its reappraisal of this significant issue in the current international context,

Bearing in mind the importance of following up on the implementation of the action programme adopted at the 1987 International Conference on the Relationship between Disarmament and Development,[2]

1. *Stresses* the central role of the United Nations in the disarmament-development relationship, and requests the Secretary-General to strengthen further the role of the Organization in this field, in particular the high-level Steering Group on Disarmament and Development, in order to ensure continued and effective coordination and close cooperation between the relevant United Nations departments, agencies and sub-agencies;

2. *Requests* the Secretary-General to continue to take action, through appropriate organs and within available resources, for the implementation of the action programme adopted at the 1987 International Conference on the Relationship between Disarmament and Development;[2]

3. *Urges* the international community to devote part of the resources made available by the implementation of disarmament and arms limitation agreements to economic and social development, with a view to reducing the ever-widening gap between developed and developing countries;

4. *Encourages* the international community to achieve the Millennium Development Goals and to make reference to the contribution that disarmament could provide in meeting them when it reviews its progress towards this purpose in 2010, as well as to make greater efforts to integrate disarmament, humanitarian and development activities;

5. *Encourages* the relevant regional and subregional organizations and institutions, non-governmental organizations and research institutes to incorporate issues related to the relationship between disarmament and development in their agendas and, in this regard, to take into account the report of the Group of Governmental Experts on the relationship between disarmament and development;[5]

6. *Reiterates its invitation* to Member States to provide the Secretary-General with information regarding measures and efforts to devote part of the resources made available by the implementation of disarmament and arms limitation agreements to economic and social development, with a view to reducing the ever-widening gap between developed and developing countries;

---

[5] See A/59/119.

7. *Requests* the Secretary-General to report to the General Assembly at its sixty-fifth session on the implementation of the present resolution, including the information provided by Member States pursuant to paragraph 6 above;

8. *Decides* to include in the provisional agenda of its sixty-fifth session the item entitled "Relationship between disarmament and development".

Action by the General Assembly

Date: 2 December 2009　　　Meeting: 55th plenary meeting
Vote: Adopted without a vote　　Report: A/64/391

Sponsors

Indonesia, on behalf of the States Members of the United Nations that are members of the Movement of Non-Aligned Countries

Co-sponsors

Fiji, Uruguay

Action by the First Committee

Date: 28 October 2009　　　Meeting: 20th meeting
Vote: Adopted without a vote　　Draft resolution: A/C.1/64/L.10

Agenda item 96 (n)

64/33 Observance of environmental norms in the drafting and implementation of agreements on disarmament and arms control

Text

The General Assembly,

Recalling its resolutions 50/70 M of 12 December 1995, 51/45 E of 10 December 1996, 52/38 E of 9 December 1997, 53/77 J of 4 December 1998, 54/54 S of 1 December 1999, 55/33 K of 20 November 2000, 56/24 F of 29 November 2001, 57/64 of 22 November 2002, 58/45 of 8 December 2003, 59/68 of 3 December 2004, 60/60 of 8 December 2005, 61/63 of 6 December 2006, 62/28 of 5 December 2007 and 63/51 of 2 December 2008,

Emphasizing the importance of the observance of environmental norms in the preparation and implementation of disarmament and arms limitation agreements,

Recognizing that it is necessary to take duly into account the agreements adopted at the United Nations Conference on Environment and Development, as well as prior relevant agreements, in the drafting and implementation of agreements on disarmament and arms limitation,

Taking note of the report of the Secretary-General submitted pursuant to resolution 63/51,[1]

Noting that the Fifteenth Summit Conference of Heads of State and Government of the Movement of Non-Aligned Countries, held in Sharm el-Sheikh, Egypt, from 11 to 16 July 2009, welcomed the adoption of resolution 63/51, the first resolution adopted without a vote by the General Assembly on the observance of environmental norms in the drafting and implementation of agreements on disarmament and arms control,

Mindful of the detrimental environmental effects of the use of nuclear weapons,

1. *Reaffirms* that international disarmament forums should take fully into account the relevant environmental norms in negotiating treaties and agreements on disarmament and arms limitation and that all States, through their actions, should contribute fully to ensuring compliance with the aforementioned norms in the implementation of treaties and conventions to which they are parties;

2. *Calls upon* States to adopt unilateral, bilateral, regional and multilateral measures so as to contribute to ensuring the application of scientific

---

[1] A/64/118 and Add.1.

and technological progress within the framework of international security, disarmament and other related spheres, without detriment to the environment or to its effective contribution to attaining sustainable development;

3. *Welcomes* the information provided by Member States on the implementation of the measures they have adopted to promote the objectives envisaged in the present resolution;[1]

4. *Invites* all Member States to communicate to the Secretary-General information on the measures they have adopted to promote the objectives envisaged in the present resolution, and requests the Secretary-General to submit a report containing that information to the General Assembly at its sixty-fifth session;

5. *Decides* to include in the provisional agenda of its sixty-fifth session the item entitled "Observance of environmental norms in the drafting and implementation of agreements on disarmament and arms control".

Action by the General Assembly

Date: 2 December 2009 Meeting: 55th plenary meeting
Vote: Adopted without a vote Report: A/64/391

Sponsors

Indonesia, on behalf of the States Members of the United Nations that are members of the Movement of Non-Aligned Countries

Co-sponsors

Fiji

Action by the First Committee

Date: 28 October 2009 Meeting: 20th meeting
Vote: Adopted without a vote Draft resolution: A/C.1/64/L.12

Agenda item 96 (m)

64/34   Promotion of multilateralism in the area of disarmament and non-proliferation

Text

The General Assembly,

Determined to foster strict respect for the purposes and principles enshrined in the Charter of the United Nations,

Recalling its resolution 56/24 T of 29 November 2001 on multilateral cooperation in the area of disarmament and non-proliferation and global efforts against terrorism and other relevant resolutions, as well as its resolutions 57/63 of 22 November 2002, 58/44 of 8 December 2003, 59/69 of 3 December 2004, 60/59 of 8 December 2005, 61/62 of 6 December 2006, 62/27 of 5 December 2007 and 63/50 of 2 December 2008 on the promotion of multilateralism in the area of disarmament and non-proliferation,

Recalling also the purpose of the United Nations to maintain international peace and security and, to that end, to take effective collective measures for the prevention and removal of threats to the peace and for the suppression of acts of aggression or other breaches of the peace, and to bring about by peaceful means, and in conformity with the principles of justice and international law, adjustment or settlement of international disputes or situations which might lead to a breach of the peace, as enshrined in the Charter,

Recalling further the United Nations Millennium Declaration,[1] which states, inter alia, that the responsibility for managing worldwide economic and social development, as well as threats to international peace and security, must be shared among the nations of the world and should be exercised multilaterally and that, as the most universal and most representative organization in the world, the United Nations must play the central role,

Convinced that, in the globalization era and with the information revolution, arms regulation, non-proliferation and disarmament problems are more than ever the concern of all countries in the world, which are affected in one way or another by these problems and, therefore, should have the possibility to participate in the negotiations that arise to tackle them,

Bearing in mind the existence of a broad structure of disarmament and arms regulation agreements resulting from non-discriminatory and transparent multilateral negotiations with the participation of a large number of countries, regardless of their size and power,

Aware of the need to advance further in the field of arms regulation, non-proliferation and disarmament on the basis of universal, multilateral,

---

[1] See resolution 55/2.

non-discriminatory and transparent negotiations with the goal of reaching general and complete disarmament under strict international control,

Recognizing the complementarity of bilateral, plurilateral and multilateral negotiations on disarmament,

Recognizing also that the proliferation and development of weapons of mass destruction, including nuclear weapons, are among the most immediate threats to international peace and security which need to be dealt with, with the highest priority,

Considering that the multilateral disarmament agreements provide the mechanism for States parties to consult one another and to cooperate in solving any problems which may arise in relation to the objective of, or in the application of, the provisions of the agreements and that such consultations and cooperation may also be undertaken through appropriate international procedures within the framework of the United Nations and in accordance with the Charter,

Stressing that international cooperation, the peaceful settlement of disputes, dialogue and confidence-building measures would contribute essentially to the creation of multilateral and bilateral friendly relations among peoples and nations,

Being concerned at the continuous erosion of multilateralism in the field of arms regulation, non-proliferation and disarmament, and recognizing that a resort to unilateral actions by Member States in resolving their security concerns would jeopardize international peace and security and undermine confidence in the international security system as well as the foundations of the United Nations itself,

Noting that the Fifteenth Summit Conference of Heads of State and Government of the Movement of Non-Aligned Countries, held in Sharm el-Sheikh, Egypt, from 11 to 16 July 2009, welcomed the adoption of resolution 63/50 on the promotion of multilateralism in the area of disarmament and non-proliferation, and underlined the fact that multilateralism and multilaterally agreed solutions, in accordance with the Charter, provide the only sustainable method of addressing disarmament and international security issues,

Reaffirming the absolute validity of multilateral diplomacy in the field of disarmament and non-proliferation, and determined to promote multilateralism as an essential way to develop arms regulation and disarmament negotiations,

1. *Reaffirms* multilateralism as the core principle in negotiations in the area of disarmament and non-proliferation with a view to maintaining and strengthening universal norms and enlarging their scope;

2. *Also reaffirms* multilateralism as the core principle in resolving disarmament and non-proliferation concerns;

3. *Urges* the participation of all interested States in multilateral negotiations on arms regulation, non-proliferation and disarmament in a non-discriminatory and transparent manner;

4. *Underlines* the importance of preserving the existing agreements on arms regulation and disarmament, which constitute an expression of the results of international cooperation and multilateral negotiations in response to the challenges facing mankind;

5. *Calls once again upon* all Member States to renew and fulfil their individual and collective commitments to multilateral cooperation as an important means of pursuing and achieving their common objectives in the area of disarmament and non-proliferation;

6. *Requests* the States parties to the relevant instruments on weapons of mass destruction to consult and cooperate among themselves in resolving their concerns with regard to cases of non-compliance as well as on implementation, in accordance with the procedures defined in those instruments, and to refrain from resorting or threatening to resort to unilateral actions or directing unverified non-compliance accusations against one another to resolve their concerns;

7. *Takes note* of the report of the Secretary-General containing the replies of Member States on the promotion of multilateralism in the area of disarmament and non-proliferation, submitted pursuant to resolution 63/50;[2]

8. *Requests* the Secretary-General to seek the views of Member States on the issue of the promotion of multilateralism in the area of disarmament and non-proliferation and to submit a report thereon to the General Assembly at its sixty-fifth session;

9. *Decides* to include in the provisional agenda of its sixty-fifth session the item entitled "Promotion of multilateralism in the area of disarmament and non-proliferation".

Action by the General Assembly

Date: 2 December 2009　　Meeting: 55th plenary meeting
Vote: 122-5-49　　Report: A/64/391

Sponsors

Indonesia, on behalf of the States Members of the United Nations that are members of the Movement of Non-Aligned Countries

---

[2] A/64/117 and Add.1.

Co-sponsors

Fiji, Uruguay

*Recorded vote**

In favour:
Afghanistan, Algeria, Angola, Antigua and Barbuda, Argentina, Azerbaijan, Bahamas, Bahrain, Barbados, Belarus, Belize, Benin, Bhutan, Bolivia (Plurinational State of), Botswana, Brazil, Brunei Darussalam, Burundi, Cambodia, Cameroon, Cape Verde, Chile, China, Colombia, Comoros, Congo, Costa Rica, Côte d'Ivoire, Cuba, Democratic People's Republic of Korea, Democratic Republic of the Congo, Djibouti, Dominica, Dominican Republic, Ecuador, Egypt, El Salvador, Equatorial Guinea, Eritrea, Fiji, Gambia, Ghana, Grenada, Guatemala, Guinea, Guinea-Bissau, Guyana, Haiti, Honduras, India, Indonesia, Iran (Islamic Republic of), Iraq, Jamaica, Jordan, Kazakhstan, Kenya, Kuwait, Kyrgyzstan, Lao People's Democratic Republic, Lebanon, Lesotho, Liberia, Libyan Arab Jamahiriya, Madagascar, Malawi, Malaysia, Maldives, Mali, Marshall Islands, Mauritania, Mauritius, Mexico, Mongolia, Morocco, Mozambique, Myanmar, Namibia, Nepal, Nicaragua, Niger, Nigeria, Oman, Pakistan, Panama, Papua New Guinea, Paraguay, Peru, Philippines, Qatar, Russian Federation, Saint Kitts and Nevis, Saint Lucia, Saint Vincent and the Grenadines, Saudi Arabia, Senegal, Serbia, Singapore, Solomon Islands, Somalia, South Africa, Sri Lanka, Sudan, Suriname, Syrian Arab Republic, Tajikistan, Thailand, Togo, Tonga, Trinidad and Tobago, Tunisia, Turkmenistan, Uganda, United Arab Emirates, United Republic of Tanzania, Uruguay, Uzbekistan, Venezuela (Bolivarian Republic of), Viet Nam, Yemen, Zambia, Zimbabwe

Against:
Israel, Micronesia (Federated States of), Palau, United Kingdom, United States

Abstaining:
Albania, Andorra, Armenia, Australia, Austria, Belgium, Bosnia and Herzegovina, Bulgaria, Canada, Croatia, Cyprus, Czech Republic, Denmark, Estonia, Finland, France, Georgia, Germany, Greece, Hungary, Iceland, Ireland, Italy, Japan, Latvia, Liechtenstein, Lithuania, Luxembourg, Malta, Monaco, Montenegro, Netherlands, New Zealand, Norway, Poland, Portugal, Republic of Korea, Republic of Moldova, Romania, Samoa, San Marino, Slovakia, Slovenia, Spain, Sweden,

---

* Subsequently, the delegations of Bangladesh, Burkina Faso and Ethiopia advised the Secretariat that they had intended to vote in favour. The voting tally above does not reflect this information.

Switzerland, the former Yugoslav Republic of Macedonia, Turkey, Ukraine

Action by the First Committee

Date: 28 October 2009 Meeting: 20th meeting
Vote: 126-5-49 Draft resolution: A/C.1/64/L.13

Agenda item 96

64/35 International Day against Nuclear Tests

Text

The General Assembly,

Recalling that the promotion of peace and security is among the main purposes and principles of the United Nations embodied in the Charter,

Convinced that every effort should be made to end nuclear tests in order to avert devastating and harmful effects on the lives and health of people and the environment,

Convinced also that the end of nuclear tests is one of the key means of achieving the goal of a nuclear-weapon-free world,

Welcoming the recent positive momentum in the international community to work towards this goal,

Emphasizing in this context the essential role of Governments, intergovernmental organizations, civil society, academia and mass media,

Acknowledging the related importance of education as a tool for peace, security, disarmament and non-proliferation,

1. *Declares* 29 August as the International Day against Nuclear Tests, devoted to enhancing public awareness and education about the effects of nuclear weapon test explosions or any other nuclear explosions and the need for their cessation as one of the means of achieving the goal of a nuclear-weapon-free world;

2. *Invites* Member States, the United Nations system, civil society, academia, the mass media and individuals to commemorate the International Day against Nuclear Tests in an appropriate manner, including through all means of educational and public awareness-raising activities.

Action by the General Assembly

Date: 2 December 2009　　Meeting: 55th plenary meeting
Vote: Adopted without a vote　　Report: A/64/391

Sponsors

Belarus, Belize, Brazil, Chile, Comoros, Congo, Dominican Republic, El Salvador, **Kazakhstan**, Kyrgyzstan, Nepal, Niger, Qatar, Philippines, Tajikistan, Turkmenistan

Co-sponsors

Armenia, Burkina Faso, Gambia, Guyana, Jamaica, Japan, Kenya, Mongolia, Papua New Guinea, Saudi Arabia

Action by the First Committee

Date: 30 October 2009　　　Meeting:　　22nd meeting
Vote: Adopted without a vote　　Draft resolution: A/C.1/64/L.14/Rev.1

Agenda item 96

64/36   Convention on Cluster Munitions

Text

The General Assembly,

Recalling its resolution 63/71 of 2 December 2008,

Recalling also the conclusion of negotiations on the Convention on Cluster Munitions[1] in Dublin on 30 May 2008 and the opening for signature of the Convention in Oslo on 3 December 2008, and thereafter at United Nations Headquarters pending its entry into force,

Noting the signature of the Convention on behalf of many States and the growing number of ratifications by signatories, which now approaches that required for entry into force of the Convention in accordance with its terms,

1.   *Welcomes* the offer of the Government of the Lao People's Democratic Republic to host the First Meeting of States Parties to the Convention on Cluster Munitions[1] following its entry into force;

2.   *Requests* the Secretary-General, in accordance with article 11, paragraph 2, of the Convention, to undertake the preparations necessary to convene the First Meeting of States Parties to the Convention following its entry into force.

Action by the General Assembly

Date: 2 December 2009   Meeting: 55th plenary meeting
Vote: Adopted without a vote   Report: A/64/391

Sponsors

Ireland, Lao People's Democratic Republic

Action by the First Committee

Date: 28 October 2009   Meeting: 20th meeting
Vote: Adopted without a vote   Draft resolution: A/C.1/64/L.16

---

[1] A/C.1/63/5, enclosure, part II.

Agenda item 96 (j)

64/37 Reducing nuclear danger

Text

The General Assembly,

Bearing in mind that the use of nuclear weapons poses the most serious threat to mankind and to the survival of civilization,

Reaffirming that any use or threat of use of nuclear weapons would constitute a violation of the Charter of the United Nations,

Convinced that the proliferation of nuclear weapons in all its aspects would seriously enhance the danger of nuclear war,

Convinced also that nuclear disarmament and the complete elimination of nuclear weapons are essential to remove the danger of nuclear war,

Considering that, until nuclear weapons cease to exist, it is imperative on the part of the nuclear-weapon States to adopt measures that assure non-nuclear-weapon States against the use or threat of use of nuclear weapons,

Considering also that the hair-trigger alert of nuclear weapons carries unacceptable risks of unintentional or accidental use of nuclear weapons, which would have catastrophic consequences for all mankind,

Emphasizing the need to adopt measures to avoid accidental, unauthorized or unexplained incidents arising from computer anomaly or other technical malfunctions,

Conscious that limited steps relating to de-alerting and de-targeting have been taken by the nuclear-weapon States and that further practical, realistic and mutually reinforcing steps are necessary to contribute to the improvement in the international climate for negotiations leading to the elimination of nuclear weapons,

Mindful that a diminishing role for nuclear weapons in the security policies of nuclear-weapon States would positively impact on international peace and security and improve the conditions for the further reduction and the elimination of nuclear weapons,

Reiterating the highest priority accorded to nuclear disarmament in the Final Document of the Tenth Special Session of the General Assembly[1] and by the international community,

---

[1] Resolution S-10/2.

Recalling the advisory opinion of the International Court of Justice on the *Legality of the Threat or Use of Nuclear Weapons*[2] that there exists an obligation for all States to pursue in good faith and bring to a conclusion negotiations leading to nuclear disarmament in all its aspects under strict and effective international control,

Recalling also the call in the United Nations Millennium Declaration[3] to seek to eliminate the dangers posed by weapons of mass destruction and the resolve to strive for the elimination of weapons of mass destruction, particularly nuclear weapons, including the possibility of convening an international conference to identify ways of eliminating nuclear dangers,

1. *Calls for* a review of nuclear doctrines and, in this context, immediate and urgent steps to reduce the risks of unintentional and accidental use of nuclear weapons, including through the de-alerting and de-targeting of nuclear weapons;

2. *Requests* the five nuclear-weapon States to take measures towards the implementation of paragraph 1 above;

3. *Calls upon* Member States to take the necessary measures to prevent the proliferation of nuclear weapons in all its aspects and to promote nuclear disarmament, with the objective of eliminating nuclear weapons;

4. *Takes note* of the report of the Secretary-General submitted pursuant to paragraph 5 of resolution 63/47 of 2 December 2008;[4]

5. *Requests* the Secretary-General to intensify efforts and support initiatives that would contribute towards the full implementation of the seven recommendations identified in the report of the Advisory Board on Disarmament Matters that would significantly reduce the risk of nuclear war,[5] and also to continue to encourage Member States to consider the convening of an international conference, as proposed in the United Nations Millennium Declaration,[3] to identify ways of eliminating nuclear dangers, and to report thereon to the General Assembly at its sixty-fifth session;

6. *Decides* to include in the provisional agenda of its sixty-fifth session the item entitled "Reducing nuclear danger".

Action by the General Assembly

Date: 2 December 2009 Meeting: 55th plenary meeting
Vote: 115-50-14 Report: A/64/391

---

[2] A/51/218, annex; see also *Legality of the Threat or Use of Nuclear Weapons, Advisory Opinion, I.C.J. Reports 1996*, p. 226.
[3] See resolution 55/2.
[4] A/64/139.
[5] See A/56/400, para. 3.

Sponsors

Afghanistan, Bangladesh, Bhutan, Cambodia, Chile, Cuba, Democratic Republic of the Congo, El Salvador, Fiji, Haiti, **India**, Jamaica, Jordan, Libyan Arab Jamahiriya, Madagascar, Malaysia, Mauritius, Myanmar, Nepal, Nicaragua, Sudan, Viet Nam, Zambia

Co-sponsors

Bolivia (Plurinational State of), Comoros, Gabon

*Recorded vote**

In favour:

Afghanistan, Algeria, Angola, Antigua and Barbuda, Bahamas, Bahrain, Bangladesh, Barbados, Belize, Benin, Bhutan, Bolivia (Plurinational State of), Botswana, Brazil, Brunei Darussalam, Burkina Faso, Burundi, Cambodia, Cameroon, Cape Verde, Chile, Colombia, Comoros, Congo, Costa Rica, Côte d'Ivoire, Cuba, Democratic People's Republic of Korea, Democratic Republic of the Congo, Djibouti, Dominica, Dominican Republic, Ecuador, Egypt, El Salvador, Equatorial Guinea, Eritrea, Fiji, Gambia, Ghana, Grenada, Guatemala, Guinea, Guinea-Bissau, Guyana, Haiti, Honduras, India, Indonesia, Iran (Islamic Republic of), Iraq, Jamaica, Jordan, Kenya, Kuwait, Lao People's Democratic Republic, Lebanon, Lesotho, Liberia, Libyan Arab Jamahiriya, Madagascar, Malawi, Malaysia, Maldives, Mali, Mauritania, Mauritius, Mexico, Mongolia, Morocco, Mozambique, Myanmar, Namibia, Nepal, Nicaragua, Niger, Nigeria, Oman, Pakistan, Panama, Papua New Guinea, Paraguay, Peru, Philippines, Qatar, Saint Kitts and Nevis, Saint Lucia, Saint Vincent and the Grenadines, Samoa, Saudi Arabia, Senegal, Singapore, Solomon Islands, Somalia, South Africa, Sri Lanka, Sudan, Suriname, Swaziland, Syrian Arab Republic, Thailand, Togo, Tonga, Trinidad and Tobago, Tunisia, Turkmenistan, Uganda, United Arab Emirates, United Republic of Tanzania, Uruguay, Venezuela (Bolivarian Republic of), Viet Nam, Yemen, Zambia, Zimbabwe

Against:

Albania, Andorra, Australia, Austria, Belgium, Bosnia and Herzegovina, Bulgaria, Canada, Croatia, Cyprus, Czech Republic, Denmark, Estonia, Finland, France, Georgia, Germany, Greece, Hungary, Iceland, Ireland, Israel, Italy, Latvia, Liechtenstein, Lithuania, Luxembourg, Malta, Micronesia (Federated States of), Monaco, Montenegro, Netherlands, New Zealand, Norway, Palau, Poland, Portugal, Republic of Moldova, Romania, San Marino, Slovakia, Slovenia, Spain, Sweden, Switzerland,

---

* Subsequently, the delegation of Ethiopia advised the Secretariat that it had intended to vote in favour. The voting tally above does not reflect this information.

the former Yugoslav Republic of Macedonia, Turkey, Ukraine, United Kingdom, United States

Abstaining:
Argentina, Armenia, Azerbaijan, Belarus, China, Japan, Kazakhstan, Kyrgyzstan, Marshall Islands, Republic of Korea, Russian Federation, Serbia, Tajikistan, Uzbekistan

Action by the First Committee

Date: 27 October 2009 Meeting: 19th meeting
Vote: 113-50-15 Draft resolution: A/C.1/64/L.18

Agenda item 96 (q)

64/38   Measures to prevent terrorists from acquiring weapons of mass destruction

Text

The General Assembly,

Recalling its resolution 63/60 of 2 December 2008,

Recognizing the determination of the international community to combat terrorism, as evidenced in relevant General Assembly and Security Council resolutions,

Deeply concerned by the growing risk of linkages between terrorism and weapons of mass destruction, and in particular by the fact that terrorists may seek to acquire weapons of mass destruction,

Cognizant of the steps taken by States to implement Security Council resolution 1540 (2004) on the non-proliferation of weapons of mass destruction, adopted on 28 April 2004,

Welcoming the entry into force on 7 July 2007 of the International Convention for the Suppression of Acts of Nuclear Terrorism,[1]

Welcoming also the adoption, by consensus, of amendments to strengthen the Convention on the Physical Protection of Nuclear Material[2] by the International Atomic Energy Agency on 8 July 2005,

Noting the support expressed in the Final Document of the Fifteenth Summit Conference of Heads of State and Government of the Movement of Non-Aligned Countries, which was held in Sharm-el Sheikh, Egypt, from 11 to 16 July 2009,[3] for measures to prevent terrorists from acquiring weapons of mass destruction,

Noting also that the Group of Eight, the European Union, the Regional Forum of the Association of Southeast Asian Nations and others have taken into account in their deliberations the dangers posed by the likely acquisition by terrorists of weapons of mass destruction, and the need for international cooperation in combating it,

Noting further the Global Initiative to Combat Nuclear Terrorism, launched jointly by the Russian Federation and the United States of America, and the proposed Global Summit on Nuclear Security to be hosted by the United States of America in 2010,

---

[1] Resolution 59/290, annex.
[2] United Nations, *Treaty Series*, vol. 1456, No. 24631.
[3] See A/63/965-S/2009/514, annex.

Acknowledging the consideration of issues relating to terrorism and weapons of mass destruction by the Advisory Board on Disarmament Matters,[4]

Taking note of the relevant resolutions adopted by the General Conference of the International Atomic Energy Agency at its fifty-third regular session,[5]

Taking note also of the 2005 World Summit Outcome adopted at the High-level Plenary Meeting of the General Assembly in September 2005[6] and adoption of the United Nations Global Counter-Terrorism Strategy on 8 September 2006,[7]

Taking note further of the report of the Secretary-General, submitted pursuant to paragraph 5 of resolution 63/60,[8]

Mindful of the urgent need for addressing, within the United Nations framework and through international cooperation, this threat to humanity,

Emphasizing that progress is urgently needed in the area of disarmament and non-proliferation in order to maintain international peace and security and to contribute to global efforts against terrorism,

1. *Calls upon* all Member States to support international efforts to prevent terrorists from acquiring weapons of mass destruction and their means of delivery;

2. *Appeals* to all Member States to consider early accession to and ratification of the International Convention for the Suppression of Acts of Nuclear Terrorism;[1]

3. *Urges* all Member States to take and strengthen national measures, as appropriate, to prevent terrorists from acquiring weapons of mass destruction, their means of delivery and materials and technologies related to their manufacture;

4. *Encourages* cooperation among and between Member States and relevant regional and international organizations for strengthening national capacities in this regard;

5. *Requests* the Secretary-General to compile a report on measures already taken by international organizations on issues relating to the linkage between the fight against terrorism and the proliferation of weapons of mass destruction and to seek the views of Member States on additional relevant measures, including national measures, for tackling the global threat posed by

---

[4] See A/59/361.
[5] See International Atomic Energy Agency, *Resolutions and Other Decisions of the General Conference, Fifty-third Regular Session, 14–18 September 2009* (GC(53)/RES/DEC(2009)).
[6] See resolution 60/1.
[7] Resolution 60/288.
[8] See A/64/140 and Add.1.

the acquisition by terrorists of weapons of mass destruction and to report to the General Assembly at its sixty-fifth session;

6. *Decides* to include in the provisional agenda of its sixty-fifth session the item entitled "Measures to prevent terrorists from acquiring weapons of mass destruction".

Action by the General Assembly

Date: 2 December 2009　　Meeting: 55th plenary meeting
Vote: Adopted without a vote　　Report: A/64/391

Sponsors

Afghanistan, Argentina, Armenia, Australia, Austria, Bangladesh, Belgium, Bhutan, Bulgaria, Cambodia, Chile, Croatia, Cyprus, Czech Republic, Democratic Republic of the Congo, Denmark, Finland, France, Germany, Greece, Guatemala, Haiti, Honduras, Hungary, Iceland, **India**, Ireland, Kuwait, Lithuania, Luxembourg, Malta, Mauritius, Monaco, Myanmar, Nepal, Norway, Philippines, Poland, Romania, Russian Federation, Serbia, Singapore, Slovakia, Slovenia, Spain, Sri Lanka, Thailand, Turkey, United Kingdom, Zambia

Co-sponsors

Albania, Antigua and Barbuda, Azerbaijan, Belize, Central African Republic, Dominica, El Salvador, Estonia, Fiji, Grenada, Guyana, Italy, Jamaica, Kyrgyzstan, Latvia, Montenegro, Netherlands, Portugal, Sweden, the former Yugoslav Republic of Macedonia, Trinidad and Tobago, United States

Action by the First Committee

Date: 28 October 2009　　Meeting: 20th meeting
Vote: Adopted without a vote　　Draft resolution: A/C.1/64/L.19

Agenda item 96 (c)

64/39 Treaty on the South-East Asia Nuclear-Weapon-Free Zone (Bangkok Treaty)

Text

The General Assembly,

Recalling its resolution 62/31 of 5 December 2007, entitled "Treaty on the South-East Asia Nuclear-Weapon-Free-Zone (Bangkok Treaty)",

Welcoming the desire of the South-East Asian States to maintain peace and stability in the region in the spirit of peaceful coexistence and mutual understanding and cooperation,

Noting the entry into force of the Charter of the Association of Southeast Asian Nations on 15 December 2008, which states, inter alia, that one of the purposes of the Association is to preserve South-East Asia as a nuclear-weapon-free zone, free of all other weapons of mass destruction,

Noting also the convening of the second Conference of States Parties and Signatories of Treaties that Establish Nuclear-Weapon-Free Zones and Mongolia,

Reaffirming its conviction of the important role of nuclear-weapon-free zones in strengthening the nuclear non-proliferation regime and in extending the areas of the world that are nuclear-weapon-free, and, with particular reference to the responsibilities of the nuclear-weapon States, calling upon all States to support the process of nuclear disarmament and to work for the total elimination of all nuclear weapons,

Convinced that the establishment of a South-East Asia Nuclear-Weapon-Free Zone, as an essential component of the Declaration on the Zone of Peace, Freedom and Neutrality, signed in Kuala Lumpur on 27 November 1971, will contribute towards strengthening the security of States within the Zone and towards enhancing international peace and security as a whole,

Noting the entry into force of the Treaty on the South-East Asia Nuclear-Weapon-Free Zone on 27 March 1997[1] and the tenth anniversary of its entry into force in 2007,

Welcoming the reaffirmation of South-East Asian States that the South-East Asia Nuclear-Weapon-Free Zone shall continue to play a pivotal role in the area of confidence-building measures, preventive diplomacy and the approaches to conflict resolution as enshrined in the Declaration of the Association of Southeast Asian Nations Concord II (Bali Concord II),[2]

---

[1] United Nations, *Treaty Series*, vol. 1981, No. 33873.
[2] A/58/548, annex I.

Reaffirming the inalienable right of all the parties to the Treaty on the South-East Asia Nuclear-Weapon-Free Zone to develop research, production and use of nuclear energy for peaceful purposes without discrimination and in conformity with the Treaty on the Non-Proliferation of Nuclear Weapons,[3]

Recognizing that by signing and ratifying the relevant protocols to the treaties establishing nuclear-weapon-free zones, nuclear-weapon States undertake legally binding commitments to respect the status of such zones and not to use or threaten to use nuclear weapons against States parties to such treaties,

Recalling the applicable principles and rules of international law relating to the freedom of the high seas and the rights of innocent passage, archipelagic sea lanes passage or transit passage of ships and aircraft, particularly those of the United Nations Convention on the Law of the Sea,[4]

1. *Welcomes* the commitment and efforts of the Commission for the Treaty on the South-East Asia Nuclear-Weapon-Free Zone to further enhance and strengthen the implementation of the Bangkok Treaty[1] by implementing the Plan of Action for the period 2007–2012, adopted in Manila on 29 July 2007, and the recent decision of the Association of Southeast Asian Nations Political-Security Community Council, established under the Charter of the Association, to give priority to the implementation of the Plan of Action;

2. *Encourages* States parties to the Treaty to resume direct consultations with the five nuclear-weapon States to resolve comprehensively, in accordance with the objectives and principles of the Treaty, existing outstanding issues on a number of provisions of the Treaty and the Protocol thereto;

3. *Encourages* nuclear-weapon States and States parties to the Treaty to work constructively with a view to ensuring the early accession of the nuclear-weapon States to the Protocol to the Treaty;

4. *Underlines* the value of enhancing and implementing further ways and means of cooperation among nuclear-weapon-free zones;

5. *Decides* to include in the provisional agenda of its sixty-sixth session the item entitled "Treaty on the South-East Asia Nuclear-Weapon-Free Zone (Bangkok Treaty)".

Action by the General Assembly

Date: 2 December 2009　　　Meeting: 55th plenary meeting
Vote: 174-0-6　　　　　　　　Report: A/64/391

---

[3] United Nations, *Treaty Series*, vol. 729, No. 10485.
[4] Ibid., vol. 1833, No. 31363.

Sponsors

Thailand, on behalf of the States Members of the United Nations that are members of the Association of Southeast Asian Nations and the States parties to the Treaty on the South-East Asia Nuclear-Weapon-Free Zone (Bangkok Treaty)

Co-sponsors

Australia, Brazil, Burkina Faso, Chile, Colombia, Comoros, Democratic People's Republic of Korea, Egypt, Grenada, Jamaica, Mexico, Mongolia, Nepal, New Zealand, Saint Lucia, Saint Vincent and the Grenadines, Timor-Leste, Turkmenistan, Uzbekistan, Zambia

Recorded vote*

In favour:

Afghanistan, Albania, Algeria, Andorra, Angola, Antigua and Barbuda, Argentina, Armenia, Australia, Austria, Azerbaijan, Bahamas, Bahrain, Bangladesh, Barbados, Belarus, Belgium, Belize, Benin, Bhutan, Bolivia (Plurinational State of), Bosnia and Herzegovina, Botswana, Brazil, Brunei Darussalam, Bulgaria, Burkina Faso, Burundi, Cambodia, Cameroon, Canada, Cape Verde, Chile, China, Colombia, Comoros, Congo, Costa Rica, Côte d'Ivoire, Croatia, Cuba, Cyprus, Czech Republic, Democratic People's Republic of Korea, Democratic Republic of the Congo, Denmark, Djibouti, Dominica, Dominican Republic, Ecuador, Egypt, El Salvador, Equatorial Guinea, Eritrea, Estonia, Fiji, Finland, Gambia, Georgia, Germany, Ghana, Greece, Grenada, Guatemala, Guinea, Guinea-Bissau, Guyana, Haiti, Honduras, Hungary, Iceland, India, Indonesia, Iran (Islamic Republic of), Iraq, Ireland, Italy, Jamaica, Japan, Jordan, Kazakhstan, Kenya, Kuwait, Kyrgyzstan, Lao People's Democratic Republic, Latvia, Lebanon, Lesotho, Liberia, Libyan Arab Jamahiriya, Liechtenstein, Lithuania, Luxembourg, Madagascar, Malawi, Malaysia, Maldives, Mali, Malta, Mauritania, Mauritius, Mexico, Monaco, Mongolia, Montenegro, Morocco, Mozambique, Myanmar, Namibia, Nepal, Netherlands, New Zealand, Nicaragua, Niger, Nigeria, Norway, Oman, Pakistan, Panama, Papua New Guinea, Paraguay, Peru, Philippines, Poland, Portugal, Qatar, Republic of Korea, Republic of Moldova, Romania, Russian Federation, Saint Kitts and Nevis, Saint Lucia, Saint Vincent and the Grenadines, Samoa, San Marino, Saudi Arabia, Senegal, Serbia, Seychelles, Singapore, Slovakia, Slovenia, Solomon Islands, Somalia, South Africa, Spain, Sri Lanka, Sudan, Suriname, Swaziland, Sweden, Switzerland, Syrian Arab Republic, Tajikistan, Thailand, the former Yugoslav Republic of Macedonia, Togo,

---

* Subsequently, the delegation of Ethiopia advised the Secretariat that it had intended to vote in favour. The voting tally above does not reflect this information.

Tonga, Trinidad and Tobago, Tunisia, Turkey, Turkmenistan, Uganda, Ukraine, United Arab Emirates, United Kingdom, United Republic of Tanzania, Uruguay, Uzbekistan, Venezuela (Bolivarian Republic of), Viet Nam, Yemen, Zambia, Zimbabwe

Against:
None

Abstaining:
France, Israel, Marshall Islands, Micronesia (Federated States of), Palau, United States

Action by the First Committee

Date: 27 October 2009   Meeting: 19th meeting
Vote: 172-0-5   Draft resolution: A/C.1/64/L.23

Agenda item 96

64/40   National legislation on transfer of arms, military equipment and dual-use goods and technology

Text

The General Assembly,

Recognizing that disarmament, arms control and non-proliferation are essential for the maintenance of international peace and security,

Recalling that effective national control of the transfer of arms, military equipment and dual-use goods and technology, including those transfers that could contribute to proliferation activities, is an important tool for achieving those objectives,

Recalling also that the States parties to the international disarmament and non-proliferation treaties have undertaken to facilitate the fullest possible exchange of materials, equipment and technological information for peaceful purposes, in accordance with the provisions of those treaties,

Considering that the exchange of national legislation, regulations and procedures on the transfer of arms, military equipment and dual-use goods and technology contributes to mutual understanding and confidence among Member States,

Convinced that such an exchange would be beneficial to Member States that are in the process of developing such legislation,

Welcoming the electronic database established by the Office for Disarmament Affairs,[1] in which all information exchanged pursuant to General Assembly resolutions 57/66 of 22 November 2002, 58/42 of 8 December 2003, 59/66 of 3 December 2004, 60/69 of 8 December 2005 and 62/26 of 5 December 2007, entitled "National legislation on transfer of arms, military equipment and dual-use goods and technology", can be consulted,

Reaffirming the inherent right of individual or collective self-defence in accordance with Article 51 of the Charter of the United Nations,

1. *Invites* Member States that are in a position to do so, without prejudice to the provisions contained in Security Council resolution 1540 (2004) of 28 April 2004 and subsequent relevant Council resolutions, to enact or improve national legislation, regulations and procedures to exercise effective control over the transfer of arms, military equipment and dual-use goods and technology, while ensuring that such legislation, regulations and procedures are consistent with the obligations of States parties under international treaties;

---

[1] Available at www.un.org/disarmament/convarms/NLDU/html/NLDU.shtml.

2. *Encourages* Member States to provide, on a voluntary basis, information to the Secretary-General on their national legislation, regulations and procedures on the transfer of arms, military equipment and dual-use goods and technology, as well as the changes therein, and requests the Secretary-General to make that information accessible to Member States;

3. *Decides* to remain attentive to the matter.

Action by the General Assembly

Date: 2 December 2009 Meeting: 55th plenary meeting
Vote: Adopted without a vote Report: A/64/391

Sponsors

Netherlands

Action by the First Committee

Date: 28 October 2009 Meeting: 20th meeting
Vote: Adopted without a vote Draft resolution: A/C.1/64/L.26

Agenda item 96 (f)

64/41   Regional disarmament

Text

The General Assembly,

Recalling its resolutions 45/58 P of 4 December 1990, 46/36 I of 6 December 1991, 47/52 J of 9 December 1992, 48/75 I of 16 December 1993, 49/75 N of 15 December 1994, 50/70 K of 12 December 1995, 51/45 K of 10 December 1996, 52/38 P of 9 December 1997, 53/77 O of 4 December 1998, 54/54 N of 1 December 1999, 55/33 O of 20 November 2000, 56/24 H of 29 November 2001, 57/76 of 22 November 2002, 58/38 of 8 December 2003, 59/89 of 3 December 2004, 60/63 of 8 December 2005, 61/80 of 6 December 2006, 62/38 of 5 December 2007 and 63/43 of 2 December 2008 on regional disarmament,

Believing that the efforts of the international community to move towards the ideal of general and complete disarmament are guided by the inherent human desire for genuine peace and security, the elimination of the danger of war and the release of economic, intellectual and other resources for peaceful pursuits,

Affirming the abiding commitment of all States to the purposes and principles enshrined in the Charter of the United Nations in the conduct of their international relations,

Noting that essential guidelines for progress towards general and complete disarmament were adopted at the tenth special session of the General Assembly,[1]

Taking note of the guidelines and recommendations for regional approaches to disarmament within the context of global security adopted by the Disarmament Commission at its 1993 substantive session,[2]

Welcoming the prospects of genuine progress in the field of disarmament engendered in recent years as a result of negotiations between the two super-Powers,

Taking note of the recent proposals for disarmament at the regional and subregional levels,

Recognizing the importance of confidence-building measures for regional and international peace and security,

---

[1] See resolution S-10/2.
[2] *Official Records of the General Assembly, Forty-eighth Session, Supplement No. 42* (A/48/42), annex II.

Convinced that endeavours by countries to promote regional disarmament, taking into account the specific characteristics of each region and in accordance with the principle of undiminished security at the lowest level of armaments, would enhance the security of all States and would thus contribute to international peace and security by reducing the risk of regional conflicts,

1. *Stresses* that sustained efforts are needed, within the framework of the Conference on Disarmament and under the umbrella of the United Nations, to make progress on the entire range of disarmament issues;

2. *Affirms* that global and regional approaches to disarmament complement each other and should therefore be pursued simultaneously to promote regional and international peace and security;

3. *Calls upon* States to conclude agreements, wherever possible, for nuclear non-proliferation, disarmament and confidence-building measures at the regional and subregional levels;

4. *Welcomes* the initiatives towards disarmament, nuclear non-proliferation and security undertaken by some countries at the regional and subregional levels;

5. *Supports and encourages* efforts aimed at promoting confidence-building measures at the regional and subregional levels to ease regional tensions and to further disarmament and nuclear non-proliferation measures at the regional and subregional levels;

6. *Decides* to include in the provisional agenda of its sixty-fifth session the item entitled "Regional disarmament".

Action by the General Assembly

Date: 2 December 2009   Meeting: 55th plenary meeting
Vote: Adopted without a vote   Report: A/64/391

Sponsors

Ecuador, Egypt, Indonesia, Jordan, Kuwait, Nepal, **Pakistan**, Peru, Saudi Arabia, Sri Lanka, Turkey

Co-sponsors

Comoros, Fiji

Action by the First Committee

Date: 28 October 2009   Meeting: 20th meeting
Vote: Adopted without a vote   Draft resolution: A/C.1/64/L.28

Agenda item 96 (g)

64/42 Conventional arms control at the regional and subregional levels

Text

The General Assembly,

Recalling its resolutions 48/75 J of 16 December 1993, 49/75 O of 15 December 1994, 50/70 L of 12 December 1995, 51/45 Q of 10 December 1996, 52/38 Q of 9 December 1997, 53/77 P of 4 December 1998, 54/54 M of 1 December 1999, 55/33 P of 20 November 2000, 56/24 I of 29 November 2001, 57/77 of 22 November 2002, 58/39 of 8 December 2003, 59/88 of 3 December 2004, 60/75 of 8 December 2005, 61/82 of 6 December 2006, 62/44 of 5 December 2007 and 63/44 of 2 December 2008,

Recognizing the crucial role of conventional arms control in promoting regional and international peace and security,

Convinced that conventional arms control needs to be pursued primarily in the regional and subregional contexts since most threats to peace and security in the post-cold-war era arise mainly among States located in the same region or subregion,

Aware that the preservation of a balance in the defence capabilities of States at the lowest level of armaments would contribute to peace and stability and should be a prime objective of conventional arms control,

Desirous of promoting agreements to strengthen regional peace and security at the lowest possible level of armaments and military forces,

Noting with particular interest the initiatives taken in this regard in different regions of the world, in particular the commencement of consultations among a number of Latin American countries and the proposals for conventional arms control made in the context of South Asia, and recognizing, in the context of this subject, the relevance and value of the Treaty on Conventional Armed Forces in Europe,[1] which is a cornerstone of European security,

Believing that militarily significant States and States with larger military capabilities have a special responsibility in promoting such agreements for regional security,

Believing also that an important objective of conventional arms control in regions of tension should be to prevent the possibility of military attack launched by surprise and to avoid aggression,

---

[1] CD/1064.

1. *Decides* to give urgent consideration to the issues involved in conventional arms control at the regional and subregional levels;

2. *Requests* the Conference on Disarmament to consider the formulation of principles that can serve as a framework for regional agreements on conventional arms control, and looks forward to a report of the Conference on this subject;

3. *Requests* the Secretary-General, in the meantime, to seek the views of Member States on the subject and to submit a report to the General Assembly at its sixty-fifth session;

4. *Decides* to include in the provisional agenda of its sixty-fifth session the item entitled "Conventional arms control at the regional and subregional levels".

Action by the General Assembly

Date: 2 December 2009   Meeting: 55th plenary meeting
Vote: 174-1-2   Report: A/64/391

Sponsors

Belarus, Egypt, Nepal, **Pakistan**, Peru, Syrian Arab Republic, Ukraine

Co-sponsors

Comoros, Dominican Republic, Fiji, Italy

Recorded vote*

In favour:
Afghanistan, Albania, Algeria, Andorra, Angola, Antigua and Barbuda, Argentina, Armenia, Australia, Austria, Azerbaijan, Bahamas, Bahrain, Bangladesh, Barbados, Belarus, Belgium, Belize, Benin, Bolivia (Plurinational State of), Bosnia and Herzegovina, Botswana, Brazil, Brunei Darussalam, Bulgaria, Burkina Faso, Burundi, Cambodia, Cameroon, Canada, Cape Verde, Chile, China, Colombia, Comoros, Congo, Costa Rica, Côte d'Ivoire, Croatia, Cyprus, Czech Republic, Democratic People's Republic of Korea, Democratic Republic of the Congo, Denmark, Djibouti, Dominica, Dominican Republic, Ecuador, Egypt, El Salvador, Equatorial Guinea, Eritrea, Estonia, Fiji, Finland, France, Gambia, Georgia, Germany, Ghana, Greece, Grenada, Guatemala, Guinea, Guinea-Bissau, Guyana, Haiti, Honduras, Hungary, Iceland, Indonesia, Iran (Islamic Republic of), Iraq, Ireland, Israel, Italy, Jamaica, Japan, Jordan, Kazakhstan, Kenya, Kuwait, Kyrgyzstan, Latvia, Lebanon, Lesotho, Liberia, Libyan Arab Jamahiriya, Liechtenstein, Lithuania,

---

* Subsequently, the delegation of Ethiopia advised the Secretariat that it had intended to vote in favour. The voting tally above does not reflect this information.

Luxembourg, Madagascar, Malawi, Malaysia, Maldives, Mali, Malta, Marshall Islands, Mauritania, Mauritius, Mexico, Micronesia (Federated States of), Monaco, Mongolia, Montenegro, Morocco, Mozambique, Myanmar, Namibia, Nepal, Netherlands, New Zealand, Nicaragua, Niger, Nigeria, Norway, Oman, Pakistan, Palau, Panama, Papua New Guinea, Paraguay, Peru, Philippines, Poland, Portugal, Qatar, Republic of Korea, Republic of Moldova, Romania, Saint Kitts and Nevis, Saint Lucia, Saint Vincent and the Grenadines, Samoa, San Marino, Saudi Arabia, Senegal, Serbia, Seychelles, Sierra Leone, Singapore, Slovakia, Slovenia, Solomon Islands, Somalia, South Africa, Spain, Sri Lanka, Sudan, Suriname, Swaziland, Sweden, Switzerland, Syrian Arab Republic, Tajikistan, Thailand, the former Yugoslav Republic of Macedonia, Togo, Tonga, Trinidad and Tobago, Tunisia, Turkey, Turkmenistan, Ukraine, United Arab Emirates, United Kingdom, United Republic of Tanzania, United States, Uruguay, Uzbekistan, Venezuela (Bolivarian Republic of), Yemen, Zambia, Zimbabwe

Against:
India

Abstaining:
Bhutan, Russian Federation

Action by the First Committee

Date: 28 October 2009   Meeting: 20th meeting
Vote: 173-1-2   Draft resolution: A/C.1/64/L.29

Agenda item 96 (h)

64/43 Confidence-building measures in the regional and subregional context

Text

The General Assembly,

Guided by the purposes and principles enshrined in the Charter of the United Nations,

Recalling its resolutions 58/43 of 8 December 2003, 59/87 of 3 December 2004, 60/64 of 8 December 2005, 61/81 of 6 December 2006, 62/45 of 5 December 2007 and 63/45 of 2 December 2008,

Recalling also its resolution 57/337 of 3 July 2003 entitled "Prevention of armed conflict", in which it calls upon Member States to settle their disputes by peaceful means, as set out in Chapter VI of the Charter, inter alia, by any procedures adopted by the parties,

Recalling further the resolutions and guidelines adopted by consensus by the General Assembly and the Disarmament Commission relating to confidence-building measures and their implementation at the global, regional and subregional levels,

Considering the importance and effectiveness of confidence-building measures taken at the initiative and with the agreement of all States concerned and taking into account the specific characteristics of each region, since such measures can contribute to regional stability,

Convinced that resources released by disarmament, including regional disarmament, can be devoted to economic and social development and to the protection of the environment for the benefit of all peoples, in particular those of the developing countries,

Recognizing the need for meaningful dialogue among States concerned to avert conflict,

Welcoming the peace processes already initiated by States concerned to resolve their disputes through peaceful means bilaterally or through mediation, inter alia, by third parties, regional organizations or the United Nations,

Recognizing that States in some regions have already taken steps towards confidence-building measures at the bilateral, subregional and regional levels in the political and military fields, including arms control and disarmament, and noting that such confidence-building measures have improved peace and security in those regions and contributed to progress in the socio-economic conditions of their people,

Concerned that the continuation of disputes among States, particularly in the absence of an effective mechanism to resolve them through peaceful means, may contribute to the arms race and endanger the maintenance of international peace and security and the efforts of the international community to promote arms control and disarmament,

1. *Calls upon* Member States to refrain from the use or threat of use of force in accordance with the purposes and principles of the Charter of the United Nations;

2. *Reaffirms its commitment* to the peaceful settlement of disputes under Chapter VI of the Charter, in particular Article 33, which provides for a solution by negotiation, enquiry, mediation, conciliation, arbitration, judicial settlement, resort to regional agencies or arrangements or other peaceful means chosen by the parties;

3. *Reaffirms* the ways and means regarding confidence- and security-building measures set out in the report of the Disarmament Commission on its 1993 session;[1]

4. *Calls upon* Member States to pursue these ways and means through sustained consultations and dialogue, while at the same time avoiding actions that may hinder or impair such a dialogue;

5. *Urges* States to comply strictly with all bilateral, regional and international agreements, including arms control and disarmament agreements, to which they are party;

6. *Emphasizes* that the objective of confidence-building measures should be to help to strengthen international peace and security and to be consistent with the principle of undiminished security at the lowest level of armaments;

7. *Encourages* the promotion of bilateral and regional confidence-building measures, with the consent and participation of the parties concerned, to avoid conflict and prevent the unintended and accidental outbreak of hostilities;

8. *Requests* the Secretary-General to submit a report to the General Assembly at its sixty-fifth session containing the views of Member States on confidence-building measures in the regional and subregional context;

9. *Decides* to include in the provisional agenda of its sixty-fifth session the item entitled "Confidence-building measures in the regional and subregional context".

---

[1] *Official Records of the General Assembly, Forty-eighth Session, Supplement No. 42* (A/48/42), annex II, sect. III.A.

Action by the General Assembly

    Date: 2 December 2009   Meeting: 55th plenary meeting
    Vote: Adopted without a vote   Report: A/64/391

Sponsors

    Kazakhstan, Kuwait, **Pakistan**, Syrian Arab Republic, Ukraine

Co-sponsors

    Comoros, Dominica, Fiji, Philippines, Uruguay

Action by the First Committee

    Date: 28 October 2009   Meeting: 20th meeting
    Vote: Adopted without a vote   Draft resolution: A/C.1/64/L.30

Agenda item 96 (t)

64/44   Nuclear-weapon-free southern hemisphere and adjacent areas

Text

The General Assembly,

Recalling its resolutions 51/45 B of 10 December 1996, 52/38 N of 9 December 1997, 53/77 Q of 4 December 1998, 54/54 L of 1 December 1999, 55/33 I of 20 November 2000, 56/24 G of 29 November 2001, 57/73 of 22 November 2002, 58/49 of 8 December 2003, 59/85 of 3 December 2004, 60/58 of 8 December 2005, 61/69 of 6 December 2006, 62/35 of 5 December 2007 and 63/65 of 2 December 2008,

Recalling also the adoption by the Disarmament Commission at its 1999 substantive session of a text entitled "Establishment of nuclear-weapon-free zones on the basis of arrangements freely arrived at among the States of the region concerned",[1]

Determined to pursue the total elimination of nuclear weapons,

Determined also to continue to contribute to the prevention of the proliferation of nuclear weapons in all its aspects and to the process of general and complete disarmament under strict and effective international control, in particular in the field of nuclear weapons and other weapons of mass destruction, with a view to strengthening international peace and security, in accordance with the purposes and principles of the Charter of the United Nations,

Recalling the provisions on nuclear-weapon-free zones of the Final Document of the Tenth Special Session of the General Assembly, the first special session devoted to disarmament,[2]

Stressing the importance of the treaties of Tlatelolco,[3] Rarotonga,[4] Bangkok[5] and Pelindaba[6] establishing nuclear-weapon-free zones, as well as the Antarctic Treaty,[7] to, inter alia, achieve a world entirely free of nuclear weapons,

---

[1] *Official Records of the General Assembly, Fifty-fourth Session, Supplement No. 42* (A/54/42), annex I.
[2] Resolution S-10/2.
[3] United Nations, *Treaty Series*, vol. 634, No. 9068.
[4] See *The United Nations Disarmament Yearbook*, vol. 10: 1985 (United Nations publication, Sales No. E.86.IX.7), appendix VII.
[5] United Nations, *Treaty Series*, vol. 1981, No. 33873.
[6] A/50/426, annex.
[7] United Nations, *Treaty Series*, vol. 402, No. 5778.

Noting the adoption of the Declaration of the first Conference of States Parties and Signatories to Treaties that Establish Nuclear-Weapon-Free-Zones, held in Tlatelolco, Mexico, from 26 to 28 April 2005,[8] where nuclear-weapon-free-zone States met for the purpose of strengthening the nuclear-weapon-free zone regime and contributing to the disarmament and the non-proliferation processes, and in particular to analyse ways of cooperating that could contribute to achieving the universal goal of a nuclear-weapon-free world,

Underlining the value of enhancing cooperation among the nuclear-weapon-free-zone treaty members by means of mechanisms such as joint meetings of States parties, signatories and observers to those treaties, and in that regard, notes with satisfaction the meeting of focal points of nuclear-weapon-free zones and Mongolia, held in Ulaanbaatar on 27 and 28 April 2009,

Reaffirming the applicable principles and rules of international law relating to the freedom of the high seas and the rights of passage through maritime space, including those of the United Nations Convention on the Law of the Sea,[9]

1. *Welcomes* the continued contribution that the Antarctic Treaty[7] and the treaties of Tlatelolco,[3] Rarotonga,[4] Bangkok[5] and Pelindaba[6] are making towards freeing the southern hemisphere and adjacent areas covered by those treaties from nuclear weapons;

2. *Notes with satisfaction* that all nuclear-weapon-free zones in the southern hemisphere and adjacent areas are now in force;

3. *Welcomes* the ratification by all original parties of the Treaty of Rarotonga, and calls upon eligible States to adhere to the Treaty and the protocols thereto;

4. *Also welcomes* the entry into force, on 15 July 2009, of the Treaty of Pelindaba, which establishes a nuclear-weapon-free zone in Africa;

5. *Calls upon* all concerned States to continue to work together in order to facilitate adherence to the protocols to nuclear-weapon-free zone treaties by all relevant States that have not yet adhered to them;

6. *Urges* all relevant States to cooperate in resolving outstanding issues with a view to the full implementation of the Treaty on a Nuclear-Weapon-Free Zone in Central Asia, which entered into force on 21 March 2009;

7. *Welcomes* the steps taken to conclude further nuclear-weapon-free-zone treaties on the basis of arrangements freely arrived at among the States of the region concerned, and calls upon all States to consider all relevant

---

[8] A/60/121, annex III.
[9] United Nations, *Treaty Series*, vol. 1833, No. 31363.

proposals, including those reflected in its resolutions on the establishment of nuclear-weapon-free zones in the Middle East and South Asia;

8. *Affirms its conviction* of the important role of nuclear-weapon-free zones in strengthening the nuclear non-proliferation regime and in extending the areas of the world that are nuclear-weapon-free, and, with particular reference to the responsibilities of the nuclear-weapon States, calls upon all States to support the process of nuclear disarmament and to work for the total elimination of all nuclear weapons;

9. *Welcomes* the progress made on increased collaboration within and between zones at the first Conference of States Parties and Signatories to Treaties that Establish Nuclear-Weapon-Free-Zones, held in Tlatelolco, Mexico, from 26 to 28 April 2005, at which States reaffirmed their need to cooperate in order to achieve their common objectives, and looks forward to the second Conference planned for 2010, which aims to further develop this collaboration;

10. *Congratulates* the States parties and signatories to the treaties of Tlatelolco, Rarotonga, Bangkok and Pelindaba, as well as Mongolia, for their efforts to pursue the common goals envisaged in those treaties and to promote the nuclear-weapon-free status of the southern hemisphere and adjacent areas, and calls upon them to explore and implement further ways and means of cooperation among themselves and their treaty agencies;

11. *Encourages* the competent authorities of the nuclear-weapon-free-zone treaties to provide assistance to the States parties and signatories to those treaties so as to facilitate the accomplishment of the goals;

12. *Decides* to include in the provisional agenda of its sixty-fifth session the item entitled "Nuclear-weapon-free southern hemisphere and adjacent areas".

Action by the General Assembly

Date: 2 December 2009
Vote: 170-3-6, as a whole
167-2-7, o.p. 7

Meeting: 55th plenary meeting
Report: A/64/391

Sponsors

Brazil, **New Zealand**

Co-sponsors

Antigua and Barbuda, Argentina, Australia, Bangladesh, Belize, Brunei Darussalam, Cambodia, Chile, Costa Rica, Cuba, Dominican Republic, Fiji, Grenada, Guatemala, Guyana, Haiti, Honduras, Indonesia, Jamaica, Kenya, Mexico, Mongolia, Nigeria, Panama, Papua New Guinea, Peru, Philippines, Saint Vincent and the Grenadines, Samoa, Singapore, South Africa, Thailand, Timor-Leste, Tonga, Trinidad and Tobago, Uruguay, Venezuela (Bolivarian Republic of), Zambia

Recorded vote

As a whole*

In favour:

Afghanistan, Albania, Algeria, Andorra, Angola, Antigua and Barbuda, Argentina, Armenia, Australia, Austria, Azerbaijan, Bahamas, Bahrain, Bangladesh, Barbados, Belarus, Belgium, Belize, Benin, Bhutan, Bolivia (Plurinational State of), Bosnia and Herzegovina, Botswana, Brazil, Brunei Darussalam, Bulgaria, Burkina Faso, Burundi, Cambodia, Cameroon, Canada, Cape Verde, Chile, China, Colombia, Comoros, Congo, Costa Rica, Côte d'Ivoire, Croatia, Cuba, Cyprus, Czech Republic, Democratic People's Republic of Korea, Democratic Republic of the Congo, Denmark, Djibouti, Dominica, Dominican Republic, Ecuador, Egypt, El Salvador, Equatorial Guinea, Eritrea, Estonia, Fiji, Finland, Gambia, Georgia, Germany, Ghana, Greece, Grenada, Guatemala, Guinea, Guinea-Bissau, Guyana, Haiti, Honduras, Hungary, Iceland, Indonesia, Iran (Islamic Republic of), Iraq, Ireland, Italy, Jamaica, Japan, Jordan, Kazakhstan, Kenya, Kuwait, Kyrgyzstan, Lao People's Democratic Republic, Latvia, Lebanon, Lesotho, Liberia, Libyan Arab Jamahiriya, Liechtenstein, Lithuania, Luxembourg, Madagascar, Malawi, Malaysia, Maldives, Mali, Malta, Mauritania, Mauritius, Mexico, Mongolia, Montenegro, Morocco, Mozambique, Myanmar, Namibia, Nepal, Netherlands, New Zealand, Nicaragua, Niger, Nigeria, Norway, Oman, Panama, Papua New Guinea, Paraguay, Peru, Philippines, Poland, Portugal, Qatar, Republic of Korea, Republic of Moldova, Romania, Russian Federation, Saint Kitts and Nevis, Saint Lucia, Saint Vincent and the Grenadines, Samoa, San Marino, Saudi Arabia, Senegal, Serbia, Seychelles, Sierra Leone, Singapore, Slovakia, Slovenia, Solomon Islands, Somalia, South Africa, Spain, Sri Lanka, Sudan, Suriname, Swaziland, Sweden, Switzerland, Syrian Arab Republic, Tajikistan, Thailand, the former Yugoslav Republic of Macedonia, Togo, Tonga, Trinidad and Tobago, Tunisia, Turkmenistan, Uganda, Ukraine, United Arab Emirates, United Republic of Tanzania,

---

* Subsequently, the delegations of Ethiopia and Turkey advised the Secretariat that they had intended to vote in favour. The voting tally above does not reflect this information.

Uruguay, Uzbekistan, Venezuela (Bolivarian Republic of), Viet Nam, Yemen, Zambia, Zimbabwe

Against:
France, United Kingdom, United States

Abstaining:
India, Israel, Marshall Islands, Micronesia (Federated States of), Pakistan, Palau

Operative paragraph 7*

In favour:
Afghanistan, Albania, Algeria, Andorra, Angola, Antigua and Barbuda, Argentina, Armenia, Australia, Austria, Azerbaijan, Bahamas, Bahrain, Bangladesh, Barbados, Belarus, Belgium, Belize, Benin, Bolivia (Plurinational State of), Bosnia and Herzegovina, Botswana, Brazil, Brunei Darussalam, Bulgaria, Burkina Faso, Burundi, Cambodia, Cameroon, Canada, Cape Verde, Chile, China, Colombia, Comoros, Congo, Costa Rica, Côte d'Ivoire, Croatia, Cuba, Cyprus, Czech Republic, Democratic People's Republic of Korea, Democratic Republic of the Congo, Denmark, Djibouti, Dominica, Dominican Republic, Ecuador, Egypt, El Salvador, Equatorial Guinea, Eritrea, Estonia, Fiji, Finland, Gambia, Georgia, Germany, Ghana, Greece, Grenada, Guatemala, Guinea, Guinea-Bissau, Guyana, Haiti, Honduras, Hungary, Iceland, Indonesia, Iran (Islamic Republic of), Iraq, Ireland, Italy, Jamaica, Japan, Jordan, Kazakhstan, Kenya, Kuwait, Kyrgyzstan, Latvia, Lebanon, Lesotho, Liberia, Libyan Arab Jamahiriya, Liechtenstein, Lithuania, Luxembourg, Madagascar, Malawi, Malaysia, Maldives, Mali, Malta, Mauritania, Mauritius, Mexico, Mongolia, Montenegro, Morocco, Mozambique, Myanmar, Namibia, Nepal, Netherlands, New Zealand, Nicaragua, Niger, Nigeria, Norway, Oman, Panama, Papua New Guinea, Paraguay, Peru, Philippines, Poland, Portugal, Qatar, Republic of Korea, Republic of Moldova, Romania, Russian Federation, Saint Kitts and Nevis, Saint Lucia, Saint Vincent and the Grenadines, Samoa, San Marino, Saudi Arabia, Senegal, Serbia, Singapore, Slovakia, Slovenia, Solomon Islands, Somalia, South Africa, Spain, Sri Lanka, Sudan, Suriname, Swaziland, Sweden, Switzerland, Syrian Arab Republic, Tajikistan, Thailand, the former Yugoslav Republic of Macedonia, Togo, Tonga, Trinidad and Tobago, Tunisia, Turkey, Turkmenistan, Uganda, Ukraine, United Arab Emirates, United Republic of Tanzania, Uruguay, Uzbekistan, Venezuela (Bolivarian Republic of), Viet Nam, Yemen, Zambia, Zimbabwe

---

* Subsequently, the delegation of Ethiopia advised the Secretariat that it had intended to vote in favour. The voting tally above does not reflect this information.

Against:
India, Pakistan

Abstaining:
Bhutan, France, Israel, Marshall Islands, Palau, United Kingdom, United States

Action by the First Committee

Date: 27 October 2009 Meeting: 19th meeting
Vote: 168-3-5, as a whole Draft resolution: A/C.1/64/L.31
165-2-6, o.p. 7

Agenda item 96 (d)

64/45   Prohibition of the dumping of radioactive wastes

Text

The General Assembly,

Bearing in mind resolutions CM/Res.1153 (XLVIII) of 1988[1] and CM/Res.1225 (L) of 1989,[2] adopted by the Council of Ministers of the Organization of African Unity, concerning the dumping of nuclear and industrial wastes in Africa,

Welcoming resolution GC(XXXIV)/RES/530 establishing a Code of Practice on the International Transboundary Movement of Radioactive Waste, adopted on 21 September 1990 by the General Conference of the International Atomic Energy Agency at its thirty-fourth regular session,[3]

Taking note of the commitment by the participants in the Summit on Nuclear Safety and Security, held in Moscow on 19 and 20 April 1996, to ban the dumping at sea of radioactive wastes,[4]

Considering its resolution 2602 C (XXIV) of 16 December 1969, in which it requested the Conference of the Committee on Disarmament,[5] inter alia, to consider effective methods of control against the use of radiological methods of warfare,

Aware of the potential hazards underlying any use of radioactive wastes that would constitute radiological warfare and its implications for regional and international security, in particular for the security of developing countries,

Recalling all its resolutions on the matter since its forty-third session in 1988, including its resolution 51/45 J of 10 December 1996,

Recalling also resolution GC(45)/RES/10 adopted by consensus on 21 September 2001 by the General Conference of the International Atomic Energy Agency at its forty-fifth regular session,[6] in which States shipping radioactive materials are invited to provide, as appropriate, assurances

---

[1] See A/43/398, annex I.
[2] See A/44/603, annex I.
[3] See International Atomic Energy Agency, *Resolutions and Other Decisions of the General Conference, Thirty-fourth Regular Session, 17–21 September 1990* (GC(XXXIV)/RESOLUTIONS (1990)).
[4] A/51/131, annex I, para. 20.
[5] The Conference of the Committee on Disarmament became the Committee on Disarmament as from the tenth special session of the General Assembly. The Committee on Disarmament was redesignated the Conference on Disarmament as from 7 February 1984.
[6] See International Atomic Energy Agency, *Resolutions and Other Decisions of the General Conference, Forty-fifth Regular Session, 17–21 September 2001* (GC(45)/RES/DEC(2001)).

to concerned States, upon their request, that the national regulations of the shipping State take into account the Agency's transport regulations and to provide them with relevant information relating to the shipment of such materials; the information provided should in no case be contradictory to the measures of physical security and safety,

Welcoming the adoption at Vienna, on 5 September 1997, of the Joint Convention on the Safety of Spent Fuel Management and on the Safety of Radioactive Waste Management,[7] as recommended by the participants in the Summit on Nuclear Safety and Security,

Noting with satisfaction that the Joint Convention entered into force on 18 June 2001,

Noting that the first Review Meeting of the Contracting Parties to the Joint Convention on the Safety of Spent Fuel Management and on the Safety of Radioactive Waste Management was convened in Vienna from 3 to 14 November 2003,

Desirous of promoting the implementation of paragraph 76 of the Final Document of the Tenth Special Session of the General Assembly, the first special session devoted to disarmament,[8]

1. *Takes note* of the part of the report of the Conference on Disarmament relating to radiological weapons;[9]

2. *Expresses grave concern* regarding any use of nuclear wastes that would constitute radiological warfare and have grave implications for the national security of all States;

3. *Calls upon* all States to take appropriate measures with a view to preventing any dumping of nuclear or radioactive wastes that would infringe upon the sovereignty of States;

4. *Requests* the Conference on Disarmament to take into account, in the negotiations for a convention on the prohibition of radiological weapons, radioactive wastes as part of the scope of such a convention;

5. *Also requests* the Conference on Disarmament to intensify efforts towards an early conclusion of such a convention and to include in its report to the General Assembly at its sixty-sixth session the progress recorded in the negotiations on this subject;

6. *Takes note* of resolution CM/Res.1356 (LIV) of 1991, adopted by the Council of Ministers of the Organization of African Unity,[10] on the Bamako

---

[7] United Nations, *Treaty Series*, vol. 2153, No. 37605.
[8] Resolution S-10/2.
[9] See *Official Records of the General Assembly, Sixty-fourth Session, Supplement No. 27* (A/64/27), chap. III, sect. E.
[10] See A/46/390, annex I.

Convention on the Ban on the Import of Hazardous Wastes into Africa and on the Control of Their Transboundary Movements within Africa;

7. *Expresses the hope* that the effective implementation of the International Atomic Energy Agency Code of Practice on the International Transboundary Movement of Radioactive Waste will enhance the protection of all States from the dumping of radioactive wastes on their territories;

8. *Appeals* to all Member States that have not yet taken the necessary steps to become party to the Joint Convention on the Safety of Spent Fuel Management and on the Safety of Radioactive Waste Management[7] to do so as soon as possible;

9. *Decides* to include in the provisional agenda of its sixty-sixth session the item entitled "Prohibition of the dumping of radioactive wastes".

Action by the General Assembly

Date: 2 December 2009   Meeting: 55th plenary meeting
Vote: Adopted without a vote   Report: A/64/391

Sponsors

Nigeria,* on behalf of the States Members of the United Nations that are members of the Group of African States

Co-sponsors

Dominican Republic, Montenegro

Action by the First Committee

Date: 27 October 2009   Meeting: 19th meeting
Vote: Adopted without a vote   Draft resolution: A/C.1/64/L.34

---

* The draft decision was submitted by Nigeria.

Agenda item 96 (k)

64/46 Implementation of the Convention on the Prohibition of the Development, Production, Stockpiling and Use of Chemical Weapons and on Their Destruction

Text

The General Assembly,

Recalling its previous resolutions on the subject of chemical weapons, in particular resolution 63/48 of 2 December 2008, adopted without a vote, in which it noted with appreciation the ongoing work to achieve the objective and purpose of the Convention on the Prohibition of the Development, Production, Stockpiling and Use of Chemical Weapons and on Their Destruction,[1]

Determined to achieve the effective prohibition of the development, production, acquisition, transfer, stockpiling and use of chemical weapons and their destruction,

Noting with satisfaction that, since the adoption of resolution 63/48, four additional States have acceded to the Convention, bringing the total number of States parties to the Convention to one hundred and eighty-eight,

Reaffirming the importance of the outcome of the Second Special Session of the Conference of the States Parties to Review the Operation of the Chemical Weapons Convention (hereinafter "the Second Review Conference"), including the consensus final report,[2] which addressed all aspects of the Convention and made important recommendations on its continued implementation,

Emphasizing that the Second Review Conference welcomed the fact that, eleven years after its entry into force, the Convention remains a unique multilateral agreement banning an entire category of weapons of mass destruction in a non-discriminatory and verifiable manner under strict and effective international control,

1. *Emphasizes* that the universality of the Convention on the Prohibition of the Development, Production, Stockpiling and Use of Chemical Weapons and on Their Destruction[1] is fundamental to the achievement of its objective and purpose, acknowledges progress made in the implementation of the action plan for the universality of the Convention, and calls upon all States that have not yet done so to become parties to the Convention without delay;

2. *Underlines* that implementation of the Convention makes a major contribution to international peace and security through the elimination of

---

[1] United Nations, *Treaty Series*, vol. 1974, No. 33757.
[2] See Organization for the Prohibition of Chemical Weapons, document RC-2/4.

existing stockpiles of chemical weapons, the prohibition of the acquisition or use of chemical weapons, and provides for assistance and protection in the event of use, or threat of use, of chemical weapons and for international cooperation for peaceful purposes in the field of chemical activities;

3. *Stresses* the importance to the Convention that all possessors of chemical weapons, chemical weapons production facilities or chemical weapons development facilities, including previously declared possessor States, should be among the States parties to the Convention, and welcomes progress to that end;

4. *Reaffirms* the obligation of the States parties to the Convention to destroy chemical weapons and to destroy or convert chemical weapons production facilities within the time limits provided for by the Convention;

5. *Stresses* that the full and effective implementation of all provisions of the Convention, including those on national implementation (article VII) and assistance and protection (article X), constitutes an important contribution to the efforts of the United Nations in the global fight against terrorism in all its forms and manifestations;

6. *Notes* that the effective application of the verification system builds confidence in compliance with the Convention by States parties;

7. *Stresses* the importance of the Organization for the Prohibition of Chemical Weapons in verifying compliance with the provisions of the Convention as well as in promoting the timely and efficient accomplishment of all its objectives;

8. *Urges* all States parties to the Convention to meet in full and on time their obligations under the Convention and to support the Organization for the Prohibition of Chemical Weapons in its implementation activities;

9. *Welcomes* progress made in the national implementation of article VII obligations, commends the States parties and the Technical Secretariat for assisting other States parties, on request, with the implementation of the follow-up to the plan of action regarding article VII obligations, and urges States parties that have not fulfilled their obligations under article VII to do so without further delay, in accordance with their constitutional processes;

10. *Emphasizes* the continuing relevance and importance of the provisions of article X of the Convention, and welcomes the activities of the Organization for the Prohibition of Chemical Weapons in relation to assistance and protection against chemical weapons;

11. *Reaffirms* that the provisions of the Convention shall be implemented in a manner that avoids hampering the economic or technological development of States parties and international cooperation in the field of chemical activities for purposes not prohibited under the Convention, including the international

exchange of scientific and technical information, and chemicals and equipment for the production, processing or use of chemicals for purposes not prohibited under the Convention;

12. *Emphasizes* the importance of article XI provisions relating to the economic and technological development of States parties, recalls that the full, effective and non-discriminatory implementation of those provisions contributes to universality, and also reaffirms the undertaking of the States parties to foster international cooperation for peaceful purposes in the field of chemical activities of the States parties and the importance of that cooperation and its contribution to the promotion of the Convention as a whole;

13. *Notes with appreciation* the ongoing work of the Organization for the Prohibition of Chemical Weapons to achieve the objective and purpose of the Convention, to ensure the full implementation of its provisions, including those for international verification of compliance with it, and to provide a forum for consultation and cooperation among States parties, and also notes with appreciation the substantial contribution of the Technical Secretariat and the outgoing Director-General, Rogelio Pfirter, whose mandate expires in July 2010, to the continued development and success of the Organization;

14. *Welcomes* the cooperation between the United Nations and the Organization for the Prohibition of Chemical Weapons within the framework of the Relationship Agreement between the United Nations and the Organization, in accordance with the provisions of the Convention;

15. *Decides* to include in the provisional agenda of its sixty-fifth session the item entitled "Implementation of the Convention on the Prohibition of the Development, Production, Stockpiling and Use of Chemical Weapons and on Their Destruction".

Action by the General Assembly

Date: 2 December 2009　　　　Meeting: 55th plenary meeting
Vote: Adopted without a vote　　Report: A/64/391

Sponsors

Poland

Action by the First Committee

Date: 28 October 2009　　　　Meeting: 20th meeting
Vote: Adopted without a vote　Draft resolution: A/C.1/64/L.35

Agenda item 96 (y)

64/47 Renewed determination towards the total elimination of nuclear weapons

Text

The General Assembly,

Recalling the need for all States to take further practical steps and effective measures towards the total elimination of nuclear weapons, with a view to achieving a peaceful and safe world, without nuclear weapons, and renewing the determination to do so,

Noting that the ultimate objective of the efforts of States in the disarmament process is general and complete disarmament under strict and effective international control,

Recalling its resolution 63/73 of 2 December 2008,

Convinced that every effort should be made to avoid nuclear war and nuclear terrorism,

Reaffirming the crucial importance of the Treaty on the Non-Proliferation of Nuclear Weapons[1] as the cornerstone of the international nuclear non-proliferation regime and an essential foundation for the pursuit of nuclear disarmament and for the peaceful uses of nuclear energy, welcoming the results of the third session of the Preparatory Committee for the Review Conference of the Parties to the Treaty on the Non-Proliferation of Nuclear Weapons to be held in 2010, the year of the sixty-fifth anniversary of the atomic bombings in Hiroshima and Nagasaki, Japan, and noting the importance of achieving the success of the Review Conference,

Recalling the decisions and the resolution of the 1995 Review and Extension Conference of the Parties to the Treaty on the Non-Proliferation of Nuclear Weapons[2] and the Final Document of the 2000 Review Conference of the Parties to the Treaty,[3]

Recognizing that the enhancement of international peace and security and the promotion of nuclear disarmament are mutually reinforcing,

Reaffirming that further advancement in nuclear disarmament will contribute to consolidating the international regime for nuclear

---

[1] United Nations, *Treaty Series*, vol. 729, No. 10485.
[2] See *1995 Review and Extension Conference of the Parties to the Treaty on the Non-Proliferation of Nuclear Weapons, Final Document, Part I* (NPT/CONF.1995/32 (Part I) and Corr.2), annex.
[3] *2000 Review Conference of the Parties to the Treaty on the Non-Proliferation of Nuclear Weapons, Final Document*, vols. I-III (NPT/CONF.2000/28 (Parts I-IV)).

non-proliferation, which is, inter alia, essential to international peace and security,

Welcoming the recent global momentum of nuclear disarmament towards a world without nuclear weapons, which has been strengthened by concrete proposals and initiatives from political leaders of Member States, in particular by the Russian Federation and the United States of America, which currently together hold most of the nuclear weapons in the world,

Welcoming also the United Nations Security Council Summit on Nuclear Non-proliferation and Nuclear Disarmament, held on 24 September 2009, which confirmed the vision for a world without nuclear weapons,

Expressing deep concern regarding the growing dangers posed by the proliferation of weapons of mass destruction, inter alia, nuclear weapons, including that caused by proliferation networks,

Recognizing the importance of implementing Security Council resolution 1718 (2006) of 14 October 2006 with regard to the nuclear test proclaimed by the Democratic People's Republic of Korea on 9 October 2006 and Council resolution 1874 (2009) of 12 June 2009 with regard to the nuclear test conducted by the Democratic People's Republic of Korea on 25 May 2009, while calling upon the Democratic People's Republic of Korea to return immediately and without preconditions to the Six-Party Talks, and reiterating strong support for the early resumption of the Talks,

1. *Reaffirms* the importance of all States parties to the Treaty on the Non-Proliferation of Nuclear Weapons[1] complying with their obligations under all the articles of the Treaty;

2. *Stresses* the importance of an effective Treaty review process, and calls upon all States parties to the Treaty to work together so that the 2010 Review Conference of the Parties to the Treaty on the Non-Proliferation of Nuclear Weapons can successfully strengthen the Treaty regime and can establish effective and practical measures in all the Treaty's three pillars;

3. *Reaffirms* the importance of the universality of the Treaty, and calls upon States not parties to the Treaty to accede to it as non-nuclear-weapon States without delay and without conditions and, pending their accession to the Treaty, to adhere to its terms as well as to take practical steps in support of the Treaty;

4. *Encourages* further steps leading to nuclear disarmament, in accordance with article VI of the Treaty, including deeper reductions in all types of nuclear weapons, and emphasizes the importance of applying the principles of irreversibility and verifiability, as well as increased transparency, in a way that promotes international stability and undiminished security for all, in the process of working towards the elimination of nuclear weapons;

5.   *Calls upon* all nuclear-weapon States to undertake reductions of nuclear weapons in a transparent manner, and invites all nuclear-weapon States to agree on transparency and confidence-building measures, while noting in this regard the increased transparency demonstrated by nuclear-weapon States on their nuclear arsenals, including the current number of their nuclear warheads;

6.   *Encourages* the Russian Federation and the United States of America to fully implement the obligations under the Treaty on Strategic Offensive Reductions[4] and to undertake further steps in nuclear disarmament with greater transparency, including the conclusion of a legally binding successor to the Treaty on the Reduction and Limitation of Strategic Offensive Arms (START I),[5] which is due to expire in December 2009, while welcoming the progress that has been made recently;

7.   *Encourages* States to continue to pursue efforts, within the framework of international cooperation, contributing to the reduction of nuclear-weapons-related materials;

8.   *Calls upon* the nuclear-weapon States to take measures to reduce the risk of an accidental or unauthorized launch of nuclear weapons and to also consider further reducing the operational status of nuclear weapons systems in ways that promote international stability and security;

9.   *Stresses* the necessity of a diminishing role for nuclear weapons in security policies to minimize the risk that these weapons will ever be used and to facilitate the process of their total elimination, in a way that promotes international stability and based on the principle of undiminished security for all;

10.   *Urges* all States that have not yet done so to sign and ratify the Comprehensive Nuclear-Test-Ban Treaty[6] at the earliest opportunity with a view to its early entry into force and universalization, stresses the importance of maintaining existing moratoriums on nuclear-weapon test explosions or any other nuclear explosions pending the entry into force of the Treaty, and reaffirms the importance of the continued development of the Treaty verification regime, including the international monitoring system, which will be required to provide assurance of compliance with the Treaty;

11.   *Welcomes* the adoption by the Conference on Disarmament of a programme of work for its 2009 session,[7] and calls upon the Conference to start its substantive work when it convenes in January 2010, while taking into due consideration the increasing global momentum in favour of nuclear

---

[4] United Nations, *Treaty Series*, vol. 2350, No. 42195.
[5] *The United Nations Disarmament Yearbook*, vol. 16: 1991 (United Nations publication, Sales No. E.92.IX.1), appendix II.
[6] See resolution 50/245.
[7] See CD/1864.

disarmament as well as progress and active engagement in deliberations at the Conference;

12. *Calls for* the immediate commencement of negotiations on a fissile material cut-off treaty at the 2010 session of the Conference on Disarmament and its early conclusion, and calls upon all nuclear-weapon States and States not parties to the Treaty on the Non-Proliferation of Nuclear Weapons to declare and maintain moratoriums on the production of fissile material for any nuclear weapons or other nuclear explosive devices pending the entry into force of the treaty;

13. *Calls upon* all States to redouble their efforts to prevent and curb the proliferation of nuclear and other weapons of mass destruction and their means of delivery;

14. *Stresses* the importance of preventing nuclear terrorism, and encourages every effort to secure all vulnerable nuclear and radiological material;

15. *Also stresses* the importance of further efforts for non-proliferation, including the universalization of the comprehensive safeguards agreements of the International Atomic Energy Agency to include States which have not yet adopted and implemented such an agreement, while also strongly encouraging further works for achieving the universalization of the Model Protocol Additional to the Agreement(s) between State(s) and the International Atomic Energy Agency for the Application of Safeguards approved by the Board of Governors of the Agency on 15 May 1997,[8] and the full implementation of relevant Security Council resolutions, including resolution 1540 (2004) of 28 April 2004;

16. *Encourages* all States to undertake concrete activities to implement, as appropriate, the recommendations contained in the report of the Secretary-General on the United Nations study on disarmament and non-proliferation education, submitted to the General Assembly at its fifty-seventh session,[9] and to voluntarily share information on efforts they have been undertaking to that end;

17. *Commends and further encourages* the constructive role played by civil society, including the International Commission on Nuclear Non-Proliferation and Disarmament, in promoting nuclear non-proliferation and nuclear disarmament;

18. *Decides* to include in the provisional agenda of its sixty-fifth session the item entitled "Renewed determination towards the total elimination of nuclear weapons".

---

[8] International Atomic Energy Agency, INFCIRC/540 (Corrected).
[9] A/57/124.

Action by the General Assembly

Date: 2 December 2009
Vote: 171-2-8
Meeting: 55th plenary meeting
Report: A/64/391

Sponsors

Afghanistan, Andorra, Australia, Austria, Bangladesh, Belgium, Benin, Bulgaria, Burkina Faso, Canada, Croatia, Cyprus, Czech Republic, El Salvador, Finland, Germany, Haiti, Hungary, Iceland, Italy, **Japan**, Kazakhstan, Liechtenstein, Lithuania, Luxembourg, Madagascar, Nepal, Netherlands, Palau, Peru, Philippines, Senegal, Slovakia, Slovenia, Switzerland, the former Yugoslav Republic of Macedonia, Timor-Leste, Uganda, Ukraine, United Republic of Tanzania, United States, Zambia

Co-sponsors

Albania, Antigua and Barbuda, Bosnia and Herzegovina, Central African Republic, Chile, Colombia, Comoros, Congo, Costa Rica, Democratic Republic of the Congo, Denmark, Dominican Republic, Equatorial Guinea, Eritrea, Estonia, Greece, Grenada, Guatemala, Guyana, Iraq, Kyrgyzstan, Latvia, Malawi, Mali, Montenegro, Micronesia (Federated States of), Mozambique, Norway, Papua New Guinea, Paraguay, Poland, Portugal, Romania, Saint Lucia, Saint Vincent and the Grenadines, Samoa, San Marino, Serbia, Seychelles, Spain, Swaziland, Thailand, Turkey, Uruguay, Zimbabwe

Recorded vote*

In favour:

Afghanistan, Albania, Algeria, Andorra, Angola, Antigua and Barbuda, Argentina, Armenia, Australia, Austria, Azerbaijan, Bahamas, Bahrain, Bangladesh, Barbados, Belarus, Belgium, Belize, Benin, Bolivia (Plurinational State of), Bosnia and Herzegovina, Botswana, Brazil, Brunei Darussalam, Bulgaria, Burkina Faso, Burundi, Cambodia, Cameroon, Canada, Cape Verde, Chile, Colombia, Comoros, Congo, Costa Rica, Croatia, Cyprus, Czech Republic, Democratic Republic of the Congo, Denmark, Djibouti, Dominica, Dominican Republic, Ecuador, Egypt, El Salvador, Equatorial Guinea, Eritrea, Estonia, Fiji, Finland, Gambia, Georgia, Germany, Ghana, Greece, Grenada, Guatemala, Guinea, Guinea-Bissau, Guyana, Haiti, Honduras, Hungary, Iceland, Indonesia, Iraq, Ireland, Italy, Jamaica, Japan, Jordan, Kazakhstan, Kenya, Kiribati, Kuwait, Kyrgyzstan, Lao People's Democratic Republic, Latvia, Lebanon, Lesotho, Liberia, Libyan Arab Jamahiriya, Liechtenstein, Lithuania, Luxembourg, Madagascar, Malawi, Malaysia,

---

* Subsequently, the delegations of Côte d'Ivoire and Ethiopia advised the Secretariat that they had intended to vote in favour. The voting tally above does not reflect this information.

Maldives, Mali, Malta, Marshall Islands, Mauritania, Mauritius, Mexico, Micronesia (Federated States of), Monaco, Mongolia, Montenegro, Morocco, Mozambique, Namibia, Nepal, Netherlands, New Zealand, Nicaragua, Niger, Nigeria, Norway, Oman, Palau, Panama, Papua New Guinea, Paraguay, Peru, Philippines, Poland, Portugal, Qatar, Republic of Korea, Republic of Moldova, Romania, Russian Federation, Saint Kitts and Nevis, Saint Lucia, Saint Vincent and the Grenadines, Samoa, San Marino, Saudi Arabia, Senegal, Serbia, Seychelles, Sierra Leone, Singapore, Slovakia, Slovenia, Solomon Islands, Somalia, South Africa, Spain, Sri Lanka, Sudan, Suriname, Swaziland, Sweden, Switzerland, Syrian Arab Republic, Tajikistan, Thailand, the former Yugoslav Republic of Macedonia, Togo, Tonga, Trinidad and Tobago, Tunisia, Turkey, Turkmenistan, Uganda, Ukraine, United Arab Emirates, United Kingdom, United Republic of Tanzania, United States, Uruguay, Uzbekistan, Venezuela (Bolivarian Republic of), Viet Nam, Yemen, Zambia, Zimbabwe

Against:
Democratic People's Republic of Korea, India

Abstaining:
Bhutan, China, Cuba, France, Iran (Islamic Republic of), Israel, Myanmar, Pakistan

Action by the First Committee

Date: 29 October 2009   Meeting: 21st meeting
Vote: 161-2-8   Draft resolution: A/C.1/64/L.36

Agenda item 96 (z)

64/48   The arms trade treaty

Text

The General Assembly,

Guided by the purposes and principles enshrined in the Charter of the United Nations, and reaffirming its respect for and commitment to international law,

Recalling its resolutions 46/36 L of 9 December 1991, 51/45 N of 10 December 1996, 51/47 B of 10 December 1996, 56/24 V of 24 December 2001, 60/69 and 60/82 of 8 December 2005, 61/89 of 6 December 2006 and 63/240 of 24 December 2008,

Recognizing that arms control, disarmament and non-proliferation are essential for the maintenance of international peace and security,

Reaffirming the inherent right of all States to individual or collective self-defence in accordance with Article 51 of the Charter,

Recalling its commitment to the principles of political independence, sovereign equality and territorial integrity of all States, and acknowledging that peace and security, development and human rights are the foundations for collective security,

Acknowledging the right of all States to manufacture, import, export, transfer and retain conventional arms for self-defence and security needs and in order to participate in peace support operations,

Acknowledging also the right of States to regulate internal transfers of arms and national ownership, including through national constitutional protections on private ownership, exclusively within their territory,

Recalling the obligations of all States to fully comply with arms embargoes decided by the Security Council in accordance with the Charter,

Reaffirming its respect for international law, including international human rights law and international humanitarian law, and the rights and responsibilities of every State under the Charter,

Noting and encouraging relevant initiatives undertaken at the international, regional and subregional levels between States, including those of the United Nations,

Taking note of the role played by non-governmental organizations and civil society to enhance cooperation, improve information exchange and transparency and assist States in implementing confidence-building measures in the field of responsible arms trade,

Recognizing that the absence of commonly agreed international standards for the transfer of conventional arms that address, inter alia, the problems relating to the unregulated trade of conventional arms and their diversion to the illicit market is a contributory factor to armed conflict, the displacement of people, organized crime and terrorism, thereby undermining peace, reconciliation, safety, security, stability and sustainable social and economic development,

Acknowledging the growing support across all regions for concluding a legally binding instrument, negotiated on a non-discriminatory, transparent and multilateral basis, to establish the highest possible common international standards for the import, export and transfer of conventional arms, including through several regional and subregional workshops and seminars held in order to discuss the initiative launched by the General Assembly in its resolution 61/89, as well as those sponsored by the European Union and organized through the United Nations Institute for Disarmament Research in different regions around the world,

Taking due note of the views expressed by Member States on the feasibility, scope and draft parameters for a comprehensive, legally binding instrument establishing common international standards for the import, export and transfer of conventional arms, submitted to the Secretary-General at his request,[1]

Welcoming the report of the Group of Governmental Experts,[2] which states that, in view of the complexity of the issues of conventional arms transfers, further consideration of efforts within the United Nations to address the international trade in conventional arms is required on a step-by-step basis in an open and transparent manner to achieve, on the basis of consensus, a balance that will provide benefit to all, with the principles of the Charter at the centre of such efforts,

Mindful of the need to prevent the diversion of conventional arms, including small arms and light weapons, from the legal to the illicit market,

1. *Calls upon* all States to implement, on a national basis, the relevant recommendations contained in section VII of the report of the Group of Governmental Experts,[2] recommends that all States carefully consider how to achieve such implementation in order to ensure that their national import and export control systems are of the highest possible standard, and urges those States in a position to do so to render assistance in this regard upon request;

---

[1] See A/62/278 (Parts I and II) and Add.1-4.
[2] See A/63/334.

2. *Endorses* the report of the Open-ended Working Group[3] established by the General Assembly in its resolution 63/240 to further consider those elements in the report of the Group of Governmental Experts where consensus could be developed for their inclusion in an eventual legally binding treaty on the import, export and transfer of conventional arms, which provides a balance giving benefit to all, with the principles of the Charter of the United Nations and other existing international obligations at the centre of such considerations;

3. *Stresses* the need, as was underlined by consensus in the Open-ended Working Group, to address, inter alia, the problems relating to the unregulated trade in conventional weapons and their diversion to the illicit market, considering that such risks can fuel instability, transnational organized crime and terrorism, and that international action should be taken to address the problem;

4. *Decides*, therefore, to convene a United Nations Conference on the Arms Trade Treaty to meet for four consecutive weeks in 2012 to elaborate a legally binding instrument on the highest possible common international standards for the transfer of conventional arms;

5. *Also decides* that the United Nations Conference on the Arms Trade Treaty will be undertaken in an open and transparent manner, on the basis of consensus, to achieve a strong and robust treaty;

6. *Further decides* to consider the remaining sessions of the Open-ended Working Group in 2010 and 2011 as a preparatory committee for the United Nations Conference on the Arms Trade Treaty;

7. *Requests* the Preparatory Committee, at its four sessions in 2010 and 2011, to make recommendations to the United Nations Conference on the Arms Trade Treaty on the elements that would be needed to attain an effective and balanced legally binding instrument on the highest possible common international standards for the transfer of conventional arms, bearing in mind the views and recommendations expressed in the replies of Member States[1] and those contained in the report of the Group of Governmental Experts[2] and the report of the Open-ended Working Group,[3] and to present a report containing those elements to the General Assembly at its sixty-sixth session;

8. *Decides* to establish a fifth session of the Preparatory Committee in 2012 of up to three days' duration to decide on all relevant procedural matters, including the composition of the Bureau, the draft agenda and the submission of documents, for the United Nations Conference on the Arms Trade Treaty;

9. *Requests* the Secretary-General to seek the views of Member States on proposed treaty elements and other relevant issues relating to the United

---

[3] A/AC.277/2009/1.

Nations Conference on the Arms Trade Treaty, and to submit a report to the General Assembly at its sixty-sixth session;

10. *Decides* that intergovernmental organizations and specialized agencies, having received a standing invitation to participate as observers in the work of the General Assembly, may participate as observers in the sessions of the Preparatory Committee, and requests the Committee to take decisions on the modalities of attendance of non-governmental organizations at its sessions;

11. *Stresses* the need to ensure the widest possible and effective participation in the United Nations Conference on the Arms Trade Treaty in 2012;

12. *Requests* the Secretary-General to render the Preparatory Committee and the United Nations Conference on the Arms Trade Treaty all necessary assistance, including the provision of essential background information and relevant documents;

13. *Decides* to remain seized of the matter.

Action by the General Assembly

Date: 2 December 2009 Meeting: 55th plenary meeting
Vote: 151-1-20 Report: A/64/391

Sponsors

Argentina, Australia, Costa Rica, Finland, Japan, Kenya, **United Kingdom**

*Recorded vote**

In favour:

Afghanistan, Albania, Algeria, Andorra, Angola, Antigua and Barbuda, Argentina, Armenia, Australia, Austria, Azerbaijan, Bahamas, Bangladesh, Barbados, Belgium, Belize, Benin, Bhutan, Bosnia and Herzegovina, Botswana, Brazil, Brunei Darussalam, Bulgaria, Burkina Faso, Burundi, Cambodia, Cameroon, Canada, Cape Verde, Chile, Colombia, Comoros, Congo, Costa Rica, Côte d'Ivoire, Croatia, Cyprus, Czech Republic, Democratic Republic of the Congo, Denmark, Djibouti, Dominica, Dominican Republic, Ecuador, El Salvador, Equatorial Guinea, Eritrea, Estonia, Fiji, Finland, France, Gambia, Georgia, Germany, Ghana, Greece, Grenada, Guatemala, Guinea, Guinea-Bissau, Guyana, Haiti, Honduras, Hungary, Iceland, Indonesia, Iraq, Ireland, Israel, Italy, Jamaica, Japan, Jordan, Kazakhstan, Kenya, Latvia, Lebanon, Lesotho, Liberia, Liechtenstein, Lithuania, Luxembourg,

---

* Subsequently, the delegation of Ethiopia advised the Secretariat that it had intended to vote in favour. The voting tally above does not reflect this information.

Madagascar, Malawi, Malaysia, Maldives, Mali, Malta, Marshall Islands, Mauritania, Mauritius, Mexico, Micronesia (Federated States of), Monaco, Mongolia, Montenegro, Morocco, Mozambique, Myanmar, Namibia, Nepal, Netherlands, New Zealand, Niger, Nigeria, Norway, Oman, Palau, Panama, Papua New Guinea, Paraguay, Peru, Philippines, Poland, Portugal, Republic of Korea, Republic of Moldova, Romania, Saint Kitts and Nevis, Saint Lucia, Saint Vincent and the Grenadines, Samoa, San Marino, Senegal, Serbia, Sierra Leone, Singapore, Slovakia, Slovenia, Solomon Islands, Somalia, South Africa, Spain, Sri Lanka, Suriname, Swaziland, Sweden, Switzerland, Thailand, the former Yugoslav Republic of Macedonia, Togo, Tonga, Trinidad and Tobago, Tunisia, Turkey, Ukraine, United Kingdom, United Republic of Tanzania, United States, Uruguay, Zambia

Against:
Zimbabwe

Abstaining:
Bahrain, Belarus, Bolivia (Plurinational State of), China, Cuba, Egypt, India, Iran (Islamic Republic of), Kuwait, Libyan Arab Jamahiriya, Nicaragua, Pakistan, Qatar, Russian Federation, Saudi Arabia, Sudan, Syrian Arab Republic, United Arab Emirates, Venezuela (Bolivarian Republic of), Yemen

Action by the First Committee

Date: 30 October 2009   Meeting: 22nd meeting
Vote: 153-1-19   Draft resolution: A/C.1/64/L.38/Rev.1

Agenda item 96 (v)

64/49 Transparency and confidence-building measures in outer space activities

Text

The General Assembly,

Recalling its resolutions 60/66 of 8 December 2005, 61/75 of 6 December 2006, 62/43 of 5 December 2007 and 63/68 of 2 December 2008,

Reaffirming that the prevention of an arms race in outer space would avert a grave danger to international peace and security,

Conscious that further measures should be examined in the search for agreements to prevent an arms race in outer space, including the weaponization of outer space,

Recalling, in this context, its previous resolutions, including resolutions 45/55 B of 4 December 1990 and 48/74 B of 16 December 1993, which, inter alia, emphasize the need for increased transparency and confirm the importance of confidence-building measures as a means conducive to ensuring the attainment of the objective of the prevention of an arms race in outer space,

Recalling also the report of the Secretary-General of 15 October 1993 to the General Assembly at its forty-eighth session, the annex to which contains the study by governmental experts on the application of confidence-building measures in outer space,[1]

Noting the constructive debate which the Conference on Disarmament held on this subject in 2009, including the views expressed by Member States,

Noting also the introduction by China and the Russian Federation at the Conference on Disarmament of the draft treaty on the prevention of the placement of weapons in outer space and of the threat or use of force against outer space objects,[2]

Noting further the presentation by the European Union of a draft code of conduct for outer space activities,

Noting the contribution of Member States which have submitted to the Secretary-General concrete proposals on international outer space transparency and confidence-building measures pursuant to paragraph 1 of resolution 61/75, paragraph 2 of resolution 62/43 and paragraph 2 of resolution 63/68,

---

[1] A/48/305 and Corr.1.
[2] See CD/1839.

1. *Takes note* of the reports of the Secretary-General containing concrete proposals from Member States on international outer space transparency and confidence-building measures;[3]

2. *Invites* all Member States to continue to submit to the Secretary-General concrete proposals on international outer space transparency and confidence-building measures in the interest of maintaining international peace and security and promoting international cooperation and the prevention of an arms race in outer space;

3. *Requests* the Secretary-General to submit to the General Assembly at its sixty-fifth session a final report with an annex containing concrete proposals from Member States on international outer space transparency and confidence-building measures pursuant to resolutions 61/75, 62/43, 63/68 and the present resolution;

4. *Decides* to include in the provisional agenda of its sixty-fifth session the item entitled "Transparency and confidence-building measures in outer space activities".

Action by the General Assembly

Date: 2 December 2009 Meeting: 55th plenary meeting
Vote: Adopted without a vote Report: A/64/391

Sponsors

Armenia, Austria, Belarus, Belgium, Brazil, Bulgaria, Chile, China, Costa Rica, Croatia, Cuba, Cyprus, Czech Republic, Denmark, Estonia, Finland, France, Germany, Greece, Guatemala, Hungary, Iceland, Indonesia, Ireland, Italy, Kazakhstan, Kyrgyzstan, Lithuania, Luxembourg, Malta, Mongolia, Myanmar, Netherlands, New Zealand, Nicaragua, Norway, Pakistan, Poland, Portugal, Republic of Moldova, Romania, **Russian Federation**, Serbia, Slovakia, Slovenia, Spain, Sudan, Sweden, Switzerland, Syrian Arab Republic, the former Yugoslav Republic of Macedonia, Turkey, Turkmenistan, United Kingdom, Uruguay, Uzbekistan, Venezuela (Bolivarian Republic of), Viet Nam

Co-sponsors

Albania, Bolivia (Plurinational State of), Burkina Faso, Comoros, El Salvador, Fiji, Latvia, Madagascar, Philippines, Saint Lucia, Tajikistan

Action by the First Committee

Date: 29 October 2009 Meeting: 21st meeting
Vote: Adopted without a vote Draft resolution: A/C.1/64/L.40

---

[3] A/62/114 and Add.1, A/63/136 and Add.1 and A/64/138 and Add.1.

Agenda item 96 (x)

64/50 The illicit trade in small arms and light weapons in all its aspects

Text

The General Assembly,

Recalling its resolution 63/72 of 2 December 2008 as well as all previous resolutions entitled "The illicit trade in small arms and light weapons in all its aspects", including resolution 56/24 V of 24 December 2001,

Emphasizing the importance of the continued and full implementation of the Programme of Action to Prevent, Combat and Eradicate the Illicit Trade in Small Arms and Light Weapons in All Its Aspects, adopted by the United Nations Conference on the Illicit Trade in Small Arms and Light Weapons in All Its Aspects,[1]

Emphasizing also the importance of the continued and full implementation of the International Instrument to Enable States to Identify and Trace, in a Timely and Reliable Manner, Illicit Small Arms and Light Weapons (the International Tracing Instrument),[2]

Recalling the commitment of States to the Programme of Action as the main framework for measures within the activities of the international community to prevent, combat and eradicate the illicit trade in small arms and light weapons in all its aspects,

Underlining the need for States to enhance their efforts to build national capacity for the effective implementation of the Programme of Action and the International Tracing Instrument,

Welcoming the early designation of Mexico as the Chair of the fourth biennial meeting of States to consider the implementation of the Programme of Action,

Welcoming also the efforts by Member States to submit, on a voluntary basis, national reports on their implementation of the Programme of Action,

Bearing in mind the importance of regular national reporting, which could greatly facilitate the rendering of international cooperation and assistance to affected States,

Noting the analysis of national reports prepared for the biennial meetings of States to consider the implementation of the Programme of Action by the United Nations Institute for Disarmament Research,

---

[1] See *Report of the United Nations Conference on the Illicit Trade in Small Arms and Light Weapons in All Its Aspects, New York, 9–20 July 2001* (A/CONF.192/15), chap. IV, para. 24.

[2] A/60/88 and Corr.2, annex; see also decision 60/519.

Taking into account the importance of regional approaches to the implementation of the Programme of Action,

Noting with satisfaction regional and subregional efforts being undertaken in support of the implementation of the Programme of Action, and commending the progress that has already been made in this regard, including tackling both supply and demand factors that are relevant to addressing the illicit trade in small arms and light weapons,

Welcoming the holding of such regional meetings in Australia, Nepal, Peru and Rwanda,

Recognizing that illicit brokering in small arms and light weapons is a serious problem that the international community should address urgently,

Recognizing also the efforts undertaken by non-governmental organizations in the provision of assistance to States for the implementation of the Programme of Action,

Welcoming the coordinated efforts within the United Nations to implement the Programme of Action, including through developing the Programme of Action Implementation Support System, which forms an integrated clearing house for international cooperation and assistance for capacity-building in the area of small arms and light weapons,

Taking note of the report of the Secretary-General on the implementation of resolution 63/72,[3]

1. *Underlines* the fact that the issue of the illicit trade in small arms and light weapons in all its aspects requires concerted efforts at the national, regional and international levels to prevent, combat and eradicate the illicit manufacture, transfer and circulation of small arms and light weapons and that their uncontrolled spread in many regions of the world has a wide range of humanitarian and socio-economic consequences and poses a serious threat to peace, reconciliation, safety, security, stability and sustainable development at the individual, local, national, regional and international levels;

2. *Encourages* all initiatives, including those of the United Nations, other international organizations, regional and subregional organizations, non-governmental organizations and civil society, for the successful implementation of the Programme of Action to Prevent, Combat and Eradicate the Illicit Trade in Small Arms and Light Weapons in All Its Aspects,[1] and calls upon all Member States to contribute towards the continued implementation of the Programme of Action at the national, regional and global levels;

3. *Encourages* States to implement the recommendations contained in the report of the Group of Governmental Experts established pursuant to resolution 60/81 to consider further steps to enhance international cooperation

---

[3] See A/64/173.

in preventing, combating and eradicating illicit brokering in small arms and light weapons;[4]

4. *Recalls* its endorsement of the report adopted at the third biennial meeting of States to consider the implementation of the Programme of Action, and encourages all States to implement the measures highlighted in the section of the report entitled "The way forward";[5]

5. *Encourages* all efforts to build national capacity for the effective implementation of the Programme of Action, including those highlighted in the report of the third biennial meeting of States;

6. *Decides* that, in conformity with the follow-up to the Programme of Action, the fourth biennial meeting of States to consider the national, regional and global implementation of the Programme of Action shall be held in New York from 14 to 18 June 2010;

7. *Recalls* that the meeting of States to consider the implementation of the International Instrument to Enable States to Identify and Trace, in a Timely and Reliable Manner, Illicit Small Arms and Light Weapons[2] shall be held within the framework of the biennial meeting of States;

8. *Encourages* States at the fourth biennial meeting of States to promote substantive discussions on possible practical measures by sharing lessons learned in the implementation of practical measures highlighted in the report of the third biennial meeting of States;

9. *Encourages* States, as appropriate and where applicable, to develop common positions on issues relevant to the implementation of the Programme of Action and to present such common positions to the fourth biennial meeting of States;

10. *Encourages* States that have not yet done so to submit their national reports and, for those in a position to do so, to use the reporting template prepared by the United Nations Development Programme, and to include therein information on progress made in the implementation of the measures highlighted in the report of the third biennial meeting of States;

11. *Encourages* States to also submit, well in advance of the fourth biennial meeting of States, their national reports on the implementation of the International Tracing Instrument;

12. *Calls upon* all States to implement the International Tracing Instrument by, inter alia, including in their national reports the name and contact information of the national points of contact and information on national marking practices used to indicate country of manufacture and/or country of import, as applicable;

---

[4] See A/62/163 and Corr.1.
[5] See A/CONF.192/BMS/2008/3.

13. *Encourages* States, on a voluntary basis, to make increasing use of their national reports as another tool for communicating assistance needs and information on the resources and mechanisms available to address such needs, and encourages States in a position to render such assistance to make use of these national reports;

14. *Also encourages* States to identify, in cooperation with the Chair-designate, well in advance of the fourth biennial meeting of States, priority issues or topics of relevance in the illicit trade in small arms and light weapons in all its aspects, including their implementation challenges and opportunities, as well as any follow-up to the third biennial meeting of States;

15. *Recalls* its decision to convene an open-ended meeting of governmental experts for a period of one week, no later than in 2011, to address key implementation challenges and opportunities relating to particular issues and themes, including international cooperation and assistance;

16. *Also recalls* its decision to convene a conference to review progress made in the implementation of the Programme of Action, for a period of two weeks in New York, no later than in 2012;

17. *Encourages* interested States and international, regional and other relevant organizations in a position to do so, to convene regional meetings to consider and advance the implementation of the Programme of Action as well as the International Tracing Instrument in preparation for the fourth biennial meeting of States;

18. *Encourages* States to make use of the Programme of Action Implementation Support System and the United Nations Institute for Disarmament Research clearing house for matching assistance needs with potential donors as additional tools to facilitate global action on small arms and light weapons;

19. *Emphasizes* the need to facilitate the implementation at the national level of the Programme of Action through the strengthening of national coordination agencies or bodies and institutional infrastructure;

20. *Also emphasizes* the fact that initiatives by the international community with respect to international cooperation and assistance remain essential and complementary to national implementation efforts, as well as to those at the regional and global levels;

21. *Recognizes* the necessity for interested States to develop effective coordination mechanisms, where they do not exist, in order to match the needs of States with existing resources to enhance the implementation of the Programme of Action and to make international cooperation and assistance more effective;

22. *Encourages* States to consider, among other mechanisms, the coherent identification of needs, priorities, national plans and programmes that

may require international cooperation and assistance from States and regional and international organizations in a position to do so;

23. *Encourages* civil society and relevant organizations to strengthen their cooperation and work with States at the respective national and regional levels to achieve the implementation of the Programme of Action;

24. *Requests* the Secretary-General to report to the General Assembly at its sixty-fifth session on the implementation of the present resolution;

25. *Decides* to include in the provisional agenda of its sixty-fifth session the item entitled "The illicit trade in small arms and light weapons in all its aspects".

Action by the General Assembly

Date: 2 December 2009
Vote: 180-0-0, as a whole
177-0-1, o.p. 4
176-0-1, o.p. 15
Meeting: 55th plenary meeting
Report: A/64/391

Sponsors

Afghanistan, Albania, Antigua and Barbuda, Argentina, Armenia, Australia, Austria, Bangladesh, Belgium, Belize, Bulgaria, Central African Republic, Colombia, Comoros, Costa Rica, Czech Republic, Democratic Republic of the Congo, Denmark, Dominican Republic, Estonia, Finland, France, Gabon, Germany, Guatemala, Honduras, Hungary, Iceland, Ireland, Israel, Italy, Jamaica, Japan, Latvia, Liechtenstein, Lithuania, Luxembourg, Mali, Malta, Morocco, Netherlands, Panama, Peru, Poland, Portugal, Republic of Korea, Republic of Moldova, Romania, Saint Kitts and Nevis, Saint Lucia, Serbia, Slovakia, Slovenia, **South Africa**, Spain, Sri Lanka, Sweden, Switzerland, Thailand, the former Yugoslav Republic of Macedonia, Togo, Trinidad and Tobago, Ukraine, United Kingdom

Co-sponsors

Azerbaijan, Benin, Bolivia (Plurinational State of), Bosnia and Herzegovina, Brazil, Burkina Faso, Congo, Croatia, Cyprus, Dominica, Ecuador, El Salvador, Greece, Guyana, India, Kazakhstan, Kyrgyzstan, Liberia, Papua New Guinea, Philippines, Samoa, San Marino, Sierra Leone, Suriname, Turkey, United States, Uruguay

Recorded vote

As a whole*

In favour:
Afghanistan, Albania, Algeria, Andorra, Angola, Antigua and Barbuda, Argentina, Armenia, Australia, Austria, Azerbaijan, Bahamas, Bahrain, Bangladesh, Barbados, Belarus, Belgium, Belize, Benin, Bhutan, Bolivia (Plurinational State of), Bosnia and Herzegovina, Botswana, Brazil, Brunei Darussalam, Bulgaria, Burkina Faso, Burundi, Cambodia, Cameroon, Canada, Cape Verde, Chile, China, Colombia, Comoros, Congo, Costa Rica, Côte d'Ivoire, Croatia, Cuba, Cyprus, Czech Republic, Democratic Republic of the Congo, Denmark, Djibouti, Dominica, Dominican Republic, Ecuador, Egypt, El Salvador, Equatorial Guinea, Eritrea, Estonia, Fiji, Finland, France, Gambia, Georgia, Germany, Ghana, Greece, Grenada, Guatemala, Guinea, Guinea-Bissau, Guyana, Haiti, Honduras, Hungary, Iceland, India, Indonesia, Iran (Islamic Republic of), Iraq, Ireland, Israel, Italy, Jamaica, Japan, Jordan, Kazakhstan, Kenya, Kuwait, Kyrgyzstan, Lao People's Democratic Republic, Latvia, Lebanon, Lesotho, Liberia, Libyan Arab Jamahiriya, Liechtenstein, Lithuania, Luxembourg, Madagascar, Malawi, Malaysia, Maldives, Mali, Malta, Marshall Islands, Mauritania, Mauritius, Mexico, Micronesia (Federated States of), Monaco, Mongolia, Montenegro, Morocco, Mozambique, Myanmar, Namibia, Nepal, Netherlands, New Zealand, Nicaragua, Niger, Nigeria, Norway, Oman, Pakistan, Palau, Panama, Papua New Guinea, Paraguay, Peru, Philippines, Poland, Portugal, Qatar, Republic of Korea, Republic of Moldova, Romania, Russian Federation, Saint Kitts and Nevis, Saint Lucia, Saint Vincent and the Grenadines, Samoa, San Marino, Saudi Arabia, Senegal, Serbia, Seychelles, Sierra Leone, Singapore, Slovakia, Slovenia, Solomon Islands, Somalia, South Africa, Spain, Sri Lanka, Sudan, Suriname, Swaziland, Sweden, Switzerland, Syrian Arab Republic, Tajikistan, Thailand, the former Yugoslav Republic of Macedonia, Togo, Tonga, Trinidad and Tobago, Tunisia, Turkey, Turkmenistan, Uganda, Ukraine, United Arab Emirates, United Kingdom, United Republic of Tanzania, United States, Uruguay, Uzbekistan, Venezuela (Bolivarian Republic of), Viet Nam, Yemen, Zambia, Zimbabwe

Against:
None

Abstaining:
None

---

* Subsequently, the delegation of Ethiopia advised the Secretariat that it had intended to vote in favour. The voting tally above does not reflect this information.

Operative paragraph 4*

In favour:
Afghanistan, Albania, Algeria, Andorra, Angola, Antigua and Barbuda, Argentina, Armenia, Australia, Austria, Azerbaijan, Bahamas, Bahrain, Bangladesh, Barbados, Belarus, Belgium, Belize, Benin, Bhutan, Bolivia (Plurinational State of), Bosnia and Herzegovina, Botswana, Brazil, Brunei Darussalam, Bulgaria, Burkina Faso, Burundi, Cambodia, Cameroon, Canada, Cape Verde, Chile, China, Colombia, Comoros, Congo, Costa Rica, Côte d'Ivoire, Croatia, Cuba, Cyprus, Czech Republic, Democratic Republic of the Congo, Denmark, Djibouti, Dominica, Dominican Republic, Ecuador, Egypt, El Salvador, Equatorial Guinea, Eritrea, Estonia, Fiji, Finland, France, Gambia, Georgia, Germany, Ghana, Greece, Grenada, Guatemala, Guinea, Guinea-Bissau, Guyana, Haiti, Honduras, Hungary, Iceland, India, Indonesia, Iraq, Ireland, Israel, Italy, Jamaica, Japan, Jordan, Kazakhstan, Kenya, Kuwait, Kyrgyzstan, Lao People's Democratic Republic, Latvia, Lebanon, Lesotho, Liberia, Libyan Arab Jamahiriya, Liechtenstein, Lithuania, Luxembourg, Madagascar, Malawi, Malaysia, Maldives, Mali, Malta, Marshall Islands, Mauritania, Mauritius, Mexico, Micronesia (Federated States of), Monaco, Mongolia, Montenegro, Morocco, Mozambique, Myanmar, Namibia, Nepal, Netherlands, New Zealand, Nicaragua, Niger, Nigeria, Norway, Oman, Pakistan, Panama, Papua New Guinea, Paraguay, Peru, Philippines, Poland, Portugal, Qatar, Republic of Korea, Republic of Moldova, Romania, Russian Federation, Saint Kitts and Nevis, Saint Lucia, Saint Vincent and the Grenadines, Samoa, San Marino, Saudi Arabia, Senegal, Serbia, Sierra Leone, Singapore, Slovakia, Slovenia, Solomon Islands, Somalia, South Africa, Spain, Sri Lanka, Sudan, Suriname, Swaziland, Sweden, Switzerland, Syrian Arab Republic, Tajikistan, Thailand, the former Yugoslav Republic of Macedonia, Togo, Tonga, Trinidad and Tobago, Tunisia, Turkey, Turkmenistan, Uganda, Ukraine, United Arab Emirates, United Kingdom, United Republic of Tanzania, United States, Uruguay, Uzbekistan, Venezuela (Bolivarian Republic of), Viet Nam, Yemen, Zambia, Zimbabwe

Against:
None

Abstaining:
Iran (Islamic Republic of)

---

* Subsequently, the delegation of Ethiopia advised the Secretariat that it had intended to vote in favour. The voting tally above does not reflect this information.

Operative paragraph 15*

In favour:
Afghanistan, Albania, Algeria, Andorra, Angola, Antigua and Barbuda, Argentina, Armenia, Australia, Austria, Azerbaijan, Bahamas, Bahrain, Bangladesh, Barbados, Belarus, Belgium, Belize, Benin, Bhutan, Bolivia (Plurinational State of), Bosnia and Herzegovina, Botswana, Brazil, Brunei Darussalam, Bulgaria, Burkina Faso, Burundi, Cambodia, Cameroon, Canada, Cape Verde, Chile, China, Colombia, Comoros, Congo, Costa Rica, Côte d'Ivoire, Croatia, Cuba, Cyprus, Czech Republic, Democratic Republic of the Congo, Denmark, Djibouti, Dominica, Dominican Republic, Ecuador, Egypt, El Salvador, Equatorial Guinea, Eritrea, Estonia, Fiji, Finland, France, Georgia, Germany, Ghana, Greece, Grenada, Guatemala, Guinea, Guinea-Bissau, Guyana, Haiti, Honduras, Hungary, Iceland, India, Indonesia, Iraq, Ireland, Israel, Italy, Jamaica, Japan, Jordan, Kazakhstan, Kenya, Kuwait, Kyrgyzstan, Lao People's Democratic Republic, Latvia, Lebanon, Lesotho, Liberia, Libyan Arab Jamahiriya, Liechtenstein, Lithuania, Luxembourg, Madagascar, Malawi, Malaysia, Maldives, Mali, Malta, Marshall Islands, Mauritania, Mauritius, Mexico, Micronesia (Federated States of), Monaco, Mongolia, Montenegro, Morocco, Mozambique, Myanmar, Namibia, Nepal, Netherlands, New Zealand, Nicaragua, Niger, Nigeria, Norway, Oman, Pakistan, Panama, Papua New Guinea, Paraguay, Peru, Philippines, Poland, Portugal, Qatar, Republic of Korea, Republic of Moldova, Romania, Russian Federation, Saint Kitts and Nevis, Saint Lucia, Saint Vincent and the Grenadines, Samoa, San Marino, Saudi Arabia, Senegal, Serbia, Sierra Leone, Singapore, Slovakia, Slovenia, Solomon Islands, Somalia, South Africa, Spain, Sri Lanka, Sudan, Suriname, Swaziland, Sweden, Switzerland, Syrian Arab Republic, Tajikistan, Thailand, the former Yugoslav Republic of Macedonia, Togo, Tonga, Trinidad and Tobago, Tunisia, Turkey, Turkmenistan, Uganda, Ukraine, United Arab Emirates, United Kingdom, United Republic of Tanzania, United States, Uruguay, Uzbekistan, Venezuela (Bolivarian Republic of), Viet Nam, Yemen, Zambia, Zimbabwe

Against:
None

Abstaining:
Iran (Islamic Republic of)

---

* Subsequently, the delegation of Ethiopia advised the Secretariat that it had intended to vote in favour. The voting tally above does not reflect this information.

Action by the First Committee

Date: 29 October 2009 Meeting: 21st meeting
Vote: 179-0-0, as a whole Draft resolution: A/C.1/64/L.42/Rev.1
177-0-1, o.p. 4
177-0-1, o.p. 15

Agenda item 96 (r)

64/51 Problems arising from the accumulation of conventional ammunition stockpiles in surplus

Text

The General Assembly,

Mindful of contributing to the process initiated within the framework of the United Nations reform to make the Organization more effective in maintaining peace and security by giving it the resources and tools it needs for conflict prevention, peaceful resolution of disputes, peacekeeping, post-conflict peacebuilding and reconstruction,

Underlining the importance of a comprehensive and integrated approach to disarmament through the development of practical measures,

Taking note of the report of the Group of Experts on the problem of ammunition and explosives,[1]

Recalling the recommendation contained in paragraph 27 of the report submitted by the Chairman of the Open-ended Working Group to Negotiate an International Instrument to Enable States to Identify and Trace, in a Timely and Reliable Manner, Illicit Small Arms and Light Weapons, namely, to address the issue of small arms and light weapons ammunition in a comprehensive manner as part of a separate process conducted within the framework of the United Nations,[2]

Noting with satisfaction the work and measures pursued at the regional and subregional levels with regard to the issue of conventional ammunition,

Recalling its decision 59/515 of 3 December 2004 and its resolutions 60/74 of 8 December 2005 and 61/72 of 6 December 2006, as well as its resolution 63/61 of 2 December 2008, by which it welcomed the report of the Group of Governmental Experts established pursuant to resolution 61/72 to consider further steps to enhance cooperation with regard to the issue of conventional ammunition stockpiles in surplus[3] and decided to include the issue of conventional ammunition stockpiles in surplus in the agenda of its sixty-fourth session,

    1. *Encourages* all interested States to assess, on a voluntary basis, whether, in conformity with their legitimate security needs, parts of their stockpiles of conventional ammunition should be considered to be in surplus, and recognizes that the security of such stockpiles must be taken into consideration and that appropriate controls with regard to the security

---

[1] See A/54/155.
[2] A/60/88 and Corr.2.
[3] See A/63/182.

and safety of stockpiles of conventional ammunition are indispensable at the national level in order to eliminate the risk of explosion, pollution or diversion;

2. *Appeals* to all interested States to determine the size and nature of their surplus stockpiles of conventional ammunition, whether they represent a security risk, their means of destruction, if appropriate, and whether external assistance is needed to eliminate this risk;

3. *Encourages* States in a position to do so to assist interested States within a bilateral framework or through international or regional organizations, on a voluntary and transparent basis, in elaborating and implementing programmes to eliminate surplus stockpiles or to improve their management;

4. *Encourages* all Member States to examine the possibility of developing and implementing, within a national, regional or subregional framework, measures to address accordingly the illicit trafficking related to the accumulation of such stockpiles;

5. *Takes note* of the replies submitted by Member States in response to the Secretary-General's request for views regarding the risks arising from the accumulation of conventional ammunition stockpiles in surplus and regarding national ways of strengthening controls on conventional ammunition;[4]

6. *Strongly encourages* States to implement the recommendations of the report of the Group of Governmental Experts established pursuant to resolution 61/72 to consider further steps to enhance cooperation with regard to the issue of conventional ammunition stockpiles in surplus;[3]

7. *Continues to encourage* States in a position to do so to contribute, on a voluntary and transparent basis, to the development within the United Nations of technical guidelines for the stockpile management of conventional ammunition, which would be available for States to use on a voluntary basis, in order to assist States in improving their national stockpile management capacity, preventing the growth of conventional ammunition surpluses and addressing wider risk mitigation;[5]

8. *Reiterates its decision* to address the issue of conventional ammunition stockpiles in surplus in a comprehensive manner;

9. *Decides* to include in the provisional agenda of its sixty-sixth session the item entitled "Problems arising from the accumulation of conventional ammunition stockpiles in surplus".

Action by the General Assembly

Date: 2 December 2009 Meeting: 55th plenary meeting
Vote: Adopted without a vote Report: A/64/391

---

[4] A/61/118 and Add.1 and A/62/166 and Add.1.
[5] See A/63/182, para. 72.

Sponsors

Andorra, Australia, Austria, Belgium, Bulgaria, Chile, Croatia, Cyprus, Czech Republic, Denmark, Ecuador, Estonia, Finland, France, Georgia, **Germany**, Ghana, Greece, Hungary, Iceland, Ireland, Italy, Latvia, Lesotho, Liberia, Liechtenstein, Lithuania, Luxembourg, Madagascar, Netherlands, Norway, Peru, Poland, Portugal, Republic of Moldova, Romania, Serbia, Slovakia, Slovenia, Spain, Sweden, Switzerland, the former Yugoslav Republic of Macedonia, Ukraine, United Kingdom, United States, Zambia

Co-sponsors

Albania, Cameroon, Canada, Central African Republic, Congo, El Salvador, Fiji, Japan, Malta, Montenegro, Philippines

Action by the First Committee

Date: 28 October 2009 Meeting: 20th meeting
Vote: Adopted without a vote Draft resolution: A/C.1/64/L.44

Agenda item 96

64/52 Second Conference of States Parties and Signatories of Treaties that Establish Nuclear-Weapon-Free Zones and Mongolia

Text

The General Assembly,

Recognizing the right of any group of States to conclude regional treaties in order to ensure the total absence of nuclear weapons in their respective territories, under article VII of the Treaty on the Non-Proliferation of Nuclear Weapons,[1]

Recognizing also the important contribution of the treaties of Tlatelolco,[2] Rarotonga,[3] Bangkok,[4] Pelindaba[5] and Central Asia,[6] as well as the Antarctic Treaty,[7] to the achievement of the objectives of nuclear non-proliferation and nuclear disarmament,

Recalling its resolution 63/56 of 2 December 2008 on Mongolia's international security and nuclear-weapon-free status,

Urging regions that have not yet established nuclear-weapon-free zone treaties to accelerate efforts in this direction, particularly in the Middle East, through agreements freely arrived at among the States of the region concerned, in accordance with the provisions of the Final Document of the First Special Session of the General Assembly devoted to disarmament[8] and the principles adopted by the United Nations Disarmament Commission in 1999,[9]

Taking note of paragraph 122 of the Final Document of the Fifteenth Summit Conference of Heads of State and Government of the Movement of Non-Aligned Countries, held in Sharm el-Sheikh, Egypt, from 11 to 16 July 2009,[10] in which the Heads of State and Government stated their belief that those nuclear-weapon-free zones were positive steps and important measures towards strengthening global nuclear disarmament and nuclear non-proliferation,

---

[1] United Nations, *Treaty Series*, vol. 729, No. 10485.
[2] Ibid., vol. 634, No. 9068.
[3] See *The United Nations Disarmament Yearbook*, vol. 10: 1985 (United Nations publication, Sales No. E.86.IX.7), appendix VII.
[4] United Nations, *Treaty Series*, vol. 1981, No. 33873.
[5] A/50/426, annex.
[6] Treaty on a Nuclear-Weapon-Free Zone in Central Asia.
[7] United Nations, *Treaty Series*, vol. 402, No. 5778.
[8] Resolution S-10/2.
[9] See *Official Records of the General Assembly, Fifty-fourth session, Supplement No. 42* (A/54/42), annex I, sect. C.
[10] See A/63/965-S/2009/514, annex.

Recognizing the progress made on increased collaboration within and between zones at the first Conference of States Parties and Signatories to Treaties that Establish Nuclear-Weapon-Free Zones, held in Tlatelolco, Mexico, from 26 to 28 April 2005, at which States reaffirmed their need to cooperate in order to achieve their common objectives,

Recalling the adoption of the Declaration of Santiago de Chile by the Governments of the States members of the Agency for the Prohibition of Nuclear Weapons in Latin America and the Caribbean and the States parties to the Treaty of Tlatelolco, during the nineteenth regular session of the General Conference of the Agency, held in Santiago on 7 and 8 November 2005,[11]

Recalling also the support for nuclear-weapon-free zones expressed by the Security Council summit on nuclear non-proliferation and nuclear disarmament, held on 24 September 2009, and for the convening of the second Conference of States Parties and Signatories to Treaties that Establish Nuclear-Weapon-Free Zones and Mongolia, to be held in New York on 30 April 2010,

1. *Decides* to convene the second Conference of States Parties and Signatories to Treaties that Establish Nuclear-Weapon-Free Zones and Mongolia in New York on 30 April 2010;

2. *Notes* that the objective of the Conference will be to consider ways and means to enhance consultations and cooperation among States parties and signatories, the treaty agencies and other interested States, with the purpose of promoting coordination and convergence in the implementation of the provisions of the treaties and in strengthening the regime of nuclear disarmament and non-proliferation;

3. *Urges* the States parties and signatories to treaties that have established nuclear-weapon-free zones to develop activities of cooperation and coordination in order to promote their common objectives in the framework of the Conference;

4. *Requests* the Secretary-General to provide the necessary assistance and services as may be required for the second Conference of States Parties and Signatories to Treaties that Establish Nuclear-Weapon-Free Zones and Mongolia.

Action by the General Assembly

Date: 2 December 2009 Meeting: 55th plenary meeting
Vote: 166-3-6   Report: A/64/391

Sponsors

Antigua and Barbuda, Argentina, Australia, Belize, Brazil, Burkina Faso, Cambodia, **Chile**, Comoros, Congo, Colombia, Costa Rica, Cuba,

---

[11] See A/60/678.

Dominican Republic, El Salvador, Fiji, Guatemala, Guyana, Haiti, Honduras, Jamaica, Kazakhstan, Kyrgyzstan, Malawi, Malaysia, Mexico, Mongolia, Myanmar, New Zealand, Nicaragua, Panama, Paraguay, Peru, Philippines, Samoa, Sierra Leone, Thailand, Uruguay, Venezuela (Bolivarian Republic of), Viet Nam, Zambia

Co-sponsors

Ecuador, Egypt, Grenada, Tajikistan, Uzbekistan

Recorded vote*

In favour:

Afghanistan, Albania, Algeria, Andorra, Angola, Antigua and Barbuda, Argentina, Armenia, Australia, Austria, Azerbaijan, Bahamas, Bahrain, Bangladesh, Barbados, Belarus, Belgium, Belize, Benin, Bhutan, Bolivia (Plurinational State of), Bosnia and Herzegovina, Botswana, Brazil, Brunei Darussalam, Bulgaria, Burkina Faso, Burundi, Cambodia, Cameroon, Canada, Cape Verde, Chile, China, Colombia, Comoros, Congo, Costa Rica, Côte d'Ivoire, Croatia, Cuba, Cyprus, Czech Republic, Democratic Republic of the Congo, Denmark, Djibouti, Dominica, Dominican Republic, Ecuador, Egypt, El Salvador, Equatorial Guinea, Eritrea, Estonia, Fiji, Finland, Gambia, Georgia, Germany, Ghana, Greece, Grenada, Guatemala, Guinea, Guinea-Bissau, Guyana, Haiti, Honduras, Hungary, Iceland, India, Indonesia, Iran (Islamic Republic of), Iraq, Ireland, Italy, Jamaica, Japan, Jordan, Kazakhstan, Kenya, Kuwait, Kyrgyzstan, Lao People's Democratic Republic, Latvia, Lebanon, Lesotho, Liberia, Libyan Arab Jamahiriya, Liechtenstein, Luxembourg, Madagascar, Malawi, Malaysia, Maldives, Mali, Malta, Mauritania, Mauritius, Mexico, Monaco, Mongolia, Montenegro, Morocco, Mozambique, Myanmar, Namibia, Nepal, Netherlands, Nicaragua, Niger, Nigeria, Norway, Oman, Pakistan, Panama, Papua New Guinea, Paraguay, Peru, Philippines, Portugal, Qatar, Republic of Korea, Republic of Moldova, Romania, Saint Kitts and Nevis, Saint Lucia, Saint Vincent and the Grenadines, Samoa, San Marino, Saudi Arabia, Senegal, Serbia, Singapore, Slovakia, Slovenia, Solomon Islands, Somalia, South Africa, Spain, Sri Lanka, Sudan, Suriname, Swaziland, Sweden, Switzerland, Syrian Arab Republic, Tajikistan, Thailand, the former Yugoslav Republic of Macedonia, Togo, Tonga, Trinidad and Tobago, Tunisia, Turkey, Uganda, Ukraine, United Arab Emirates, United Republic of Tanzania, Uruguay, Uzbekistan, Venezuela (Bolivarian Republic of), Viet Nam, Yemen, Zambia, Zimbabwe

---

* Subsequently, the delegations of Ethiopia, Lithuania, New Zealand and Poland advised the Secretariat that they had intended to vote in favour. The voting tally above does not reflect this information.

Against:
> Lithuania, New Zealand, Poland

Abstaining:
> France, Israel, Marshall Islands, Russian Federation, United Kingdom, United States

Action by the First Committee

> Date: 2 Nov. Meeting: 23rd meeting
> Vote: 159-0-6* Draft resolution: A/C.1/64/L.46/Rev.1

---

* At the 23rd meeting of the First Committee on 2 November 2009, an amendment to the fourth preambular paragraph of draft resolution A/C.1/64/L.46/Rev.1 contained in document A/C.1/64/L.55 was rejected by a recorded vote of 103 to 4, with 22 abstentions (see A/64/391, para. 64 (a)).

Agenda item 96 (i)

64/53   Nuclear disarmament

Text

The General Assembly,

Recalling its resolution 49/75 E of 15 December 1994 on a step-by-step reduction of the nuclear threat, and its resolutions 50/70 P of 12 December 1995, 51/45 O of 10 December 1996, 52/38 L of 9 December 1997, 53/77 X of 4 December 1998, 54/54 P of 1 December 1999, 55/33 T of 20 November 2000, 56/24 R of 29 November 2001, 57/79 of 22 November 2002, 58/56 of 8 December 2003, 59/77 of 3 December 2004, 60/70 of 8 December 2005, 61/78 of 6 December 2006, 62/42 of 5 December 2007 and 63/46 of 2 December 2008 on nuclear disarmament,

Reaffirming the commitment of the international community to the goal of the total elimination of nuclear weapons and the establishment of a nuclear-weapon-free world,

Bearing in mind that the Convention on the Prohibition of the Development, Production and Stockpiling of Bacteriological (Biological) and Toxin Weapons and on Their Destruction of 1972[1] and the Convention on the Prohibition of the Development, Production, Stockpiling and Use of Chemical Weapons and on Their Destruction of 1993[2] have already established legal regimes on the complete prohibition of biological and chemical weapons, respectively, and determined to achieve a nuclear weapons convention on the prohibition of the development, testing, production, stockpiling, loan, transfer, use and threat of use of nuclear weapons and on their destruction, and to conclude such an international convention at an early date,

Recognizing that there now exist conditions for the establishment of a world free of nuclear weapons, and stressing the need to take concrete practical steps towards achieving this goal,

Bearing in mind paragraph 50 of the Final Document of the Tenth Special Session of the General Assembly, the first special session devoted to disarmament,[3] which called for the urgent negotiation of agreements for the cessation of the qualitative improvement and development of nuclear-weapon systems, and for a comprehensive and phased programme with agreed time frames, wherever feasible, for the progressive and balanced reduction of nuclear weapons and their means of delivery, leading to their ultimate and complete elimination at the earliest possible time,

---

[1] United Nations, *Treaty Series*, vol. 1015, No. 14860.
[2] Ibid., vol. 1974, No. 33757.
[3] Resolution S-10/2.

Reaffirming the conviction of the States parties to the Treaty on the Non-Proliferation of Nuclear Weapons[4] that the Treaty is a cornerstone of nuclear non-proliferation and nuclear disarmament, and the importance of the decision on strengthening the review process for the Treaty, the decision on principles and objectives for nuclear non-proliferation and disarmament, the decision on the extension of the Treaty and the resolution on the Middle East, adopted by the 1995 Review and Extension Conference of the Parties to the Treaty on the Non-Proliferation of Nuclear Weapons,[5]

Stressing the importance of the thirteen steps for the systematic and progressive efforts to achieve the objective of nuclear disarmament leading to the total elimination of nuclear weapons, as agreed to by the States parties in the Final Document of the 2000 Review Conference of the Parties to the Treaty on the Non-Proliferation of Nuclear Weapons,[6]

Reiterating the highest priority accorded to nuclear disarmament in the Final Document of the Tenth Special Session of the General Assembly and by the international community,

Reiterating its call for an early entry into force of the Comprehensive Nuclear-Test-Ban Treaty,[7]

Taking note of the positive signals by the Russian Federation and the United States of America regarding their negotiations on the replacement for the Treaty on the Reduction and Limitation of Strategic Offensive Arms (START I),[8] which is due to expire by the end of 2009,

Urging the Russian Federation and the United States of America to conclude such negotiations urgently in order to achieve further deep cuts in their strategic and tactical nuclear weapons, and stressing that such cuts should be irreversible, verifiable and transparent,

Recalling the entry into force of the Treaty on Strategic Offensive Reductions ("the Moscow Treaty") between the United States of America and the Russian Federation[9] as a significant step towards reducing their deployed strategic nuclear weapons, while calling for further irreversible deep cuts in their nuclear arsenals,

---

[4] United Nations, *Treaty Series*, vol. 729, No. 10485.
[5] See *1995 Review and Extension Conference of the Parties to the Treaty on the Non-Proliferation of Nuclear Weapons, Final Document, Part I* (NPT/CONF.1995/32 (Part I) and Corr.2), annex.
[6] See *2000 Review Conference of the Parties to the Treaty on the Non-Proliferation of Nuclear Weapons, Final Document,* vol. I (NPT/CONF.2000/28 (Parts I and II)), part I, section entitled "Article VI and eighth to twelfth preambular paragraphs", para. 15.
[7] See resolution 50/245.
[8] *The United Nations Disarmament Yearbook*, vol. 16: 1991 (United Nations publication, Sales No. E.92.IX.1), appendix II.
[9] See CD/1674.

Noting the recent positive statements by nuclear-weapon States regarding their intention to pursue actions to achieve a world free of nuclear weapons, while reaffirming the need for urgent concrete actions by nuclear-weapon States to achieve this goal within a specified framework of time, and urging them to take further measures for progress on nuclear disarmament,

Recognizing the complementarity of bilateral, plurilateral and multilateral negotiations on nuclear disarmament, and that bilateral negotiations can never replace multilateral negotiations in this respect,

Noting the support expressed in the Conference on Disarmament and in the General Assembly for the elaboration of an international convention to assure non-nuclear-weapon States against the use or threat of use of nuclear weapons, and the multilateral efforts in the Conference on Disarmament to reach agreement on such an international convention at an early date,

Recalling the advisory opinion of the International Court of Justice on the *Legality of the Threat or Use of Nuclear Weapons*, issued on 8 July 1996,[10] and welcoming the unanimous reaffirmation by all Judges of the Court that there exists an obligation for all States to pursue in good faith and bring to a conclusion negotiations leading to nuclear disarmament in all its aspects under strict and effective international control,

Mindful of paragraph 102 of the Final Document of the Coordinating Bureau of the Non-Aligned Movement at its Ministerial Meeting, held in Havana from 27 to 30 April 2009,[11]

Recalling paragraph 112 and other relevant recommendations in the Final Document of the Fifteenth Summit Conference of Heads of State and Government of the Movement of Non-Aligned Countries, held in Sharm el-Sheikh, Egypt, on 15 and 16 July 2009,[12] which called upon the Conference on Disarmament to establish, as soon as possible and as the highest priority, an ad hoc committee on nuclear disarmament and to commence negotiations on a phased programme for the complete elimination of nuclear weapons within a specified framework of time, including a nuclear weapons convention,

Noting the adoption of the programme of work for the 2009 session by the Conference on Disarmament on 29 May 2009,[13] after years of stalemate, while reaffirming the importance of the Conference as the sole multilateral negotiating forum on disarmament,

Reaffirming the specific mandate conferred upon the Disarmament Commission by the General Assembly, in its decision 52/492 of 8 September

---

[10] A/51/218, annex; see also *Legality of the Threat or Use of Nuclear Weapons, Advisory Opinion, I.C.J. Reports 1996*, p. 226.
[11] See A/63/858.
[12] See A/63/965-S/2009/514, annex.
[13] See CD/1864.

1998, to discuss the subject of nuclear disarmament as one of its main substantive agenda items,

Recalling the United Nations Millennium Declaration,[14] in which Heads of State and Government resolved to strive for the elimination of weapons of mass destruction, in particular nuclear weapons, and to keep all options open for achieving this aim, including the possibility of convening an international conference to identify ways of eliminating nuclear dangers,

Reaffirming that, in accordance with the Charter of the United Nations, States should refrain from the use or threat of use of nuclear weapons in settling their disputes in international relations,

Seized of the danger of the use of weapons of mass destruction, particularly nuclear weapons, in terrorist acts and the urgent need for concerted international efforts to control and overcome it,

1. *Recognizes* that the time is now opportune for all the nuclear-weapon States to take effective disarmament measures to achieve the total elimination of these weapons at the earliest possible time;

2. *Reaffirms* that nuclear disarmament and nuclear non-proliferation are substantively interrelated and mutually reinforcing, that the two processes must go hand in hand and that there is a genuine need for a systematic and progressive process of nuclear disarmament;

3. *Welcomes and encourages* the efforts to establish new nuclear-weapon-free zones in different parts of the world on the basis of agreements or arrangements freely arrived at among the States of the regions concerned, which is an effective measure for limiting the further spread of nuclear weapons geographically and contributes to the cause of nuclear disarmament;

4. *Recognizes* that there is a genuine need to diminish the role of nuclear weapons in strategic doctrines and security policies to minimize the risk that these weapons will ever be used and to facilitate the process of their total elimination;

5. *Urges* the nuclear-weapon States to stop immediately the qualitative improvement, development, production and stockpiling of nuclear warheads and their delivery systems;

6. *Also urges* the nuclear-weapon States, as an interim measure, to de-alert and deactivate immediately their nuclear weapons and to take other concrete measures to reduce further the operational status of their nuclear-weapon systems, while stressing that reductions in deployments and in operational status cannot substitute for irreversible cuts in, and the total elimination of, nuclear weapons;

---

[14] See resolution 55/2.

7. *Reiterates its call* upon the nuclear-weapon States to undertake the step-by-step reduction of the nuclear threat and to carry out effective nuclear disarmament measures with a view to achieving the total elimination of these weapons within a specified framework of time;

8. *Calls upon* the nuclear-weapon States, pending the achievement of the total elimination of nuclear weapons, to agree on an internationally and legally binding instrument on a joint undertaking not to be the first to use nuclear weapons, and calls upon all States to conclude an internationally and legally binding instrument on security assurances of non-use and non-threat of use of nuclear weapons against non-nuclear-weapon States;

9. *Urges* the nuclear-weapon States to commence plurilateral negotiations among themselves at an appropriate stage on further deep reductions of nuclear weapons as an effective measure of nuclear disarmament;

10. *Underlines* the importance of applying the principles of transparency, irreversibility and verifiability to the process of nuclear disarmament and to nuclear and other related arms control and reduction measures;

11. *Underscores* the importance of the unequivocal undertaking by the nuclear-weapon States, in the Final Document of the 2000 Review Conference of the Parties to the Treaty on the Non-Proliferation of Nuclear Weapons,[6] to accomplish the total elimination of their nuclear arsenals leading to nuclear disarmament, to which all States parties are committed under article VI of the Treaty,[15] and the reaffirmation by the States parties that the total elimination of nuclear weapons is the only absolute guarantee against the use or threat of use of nuclear weapons;[16]

12. *Calls for* the full and effective implementation of the thirteen practical steps for nuclear disarmament contained in the Final Document of the 2000 Review Conference;

13. *Urges* the nuclear-weapon States to carry out further reductions of non-strategic nuclear weapons, based on unilateral initiatives and as an integral part of the nuclear arms reduction and disarmament process;

14. *Calls for* the immediate commencement of negotiations in the Conference on Disarmament on a non-discriminatory, multilateral and internationally and effectively verifiable treaty banning the production of fissile material for nuclear weapons or other nuclear explosive devices on the basis of the report of the Special Coordinator[17] and the mandate contained therein;

---

[15] *2000 Review Conference of the Parties to the Treaty on the Non-Proliferation of Nuclear Weapons, Final Document*, vol. I (NPT/CONF.2000/28 (Parts I and II)), part I, section entitled "Article VI and eighth to twelfth preambular paragraphs", para. 15:6.
[16] Ibid., section entitled "Article VII and the security of non-nuclear-weapon States", para. 2.
[17] CD/1299.

15. *Urges* the Conference on Disarmament to commence as early as possible its substantive work during its 2010 session, on the basis of a comprehensive and balanced programme of work that takes into consideration all the real and existing priorities in the field of disarmament and arms control, including the immediate commencement of negotiations on such a treaty with a view to their conclusion within five years;

16. *Calls for* the conclusion of an international legal instrument or instruments on adequate security assurances to non-nuclear-weapon States;

17. *Also calls for* the early entry into force and strict observance of the Comprehensive Nuclear-Test-Ban Treaty;[7]

18. *Expresses its regret* that the 2005 Review Conference of the Parties to the Treaty on the Non-Proliferation of Nuclear Weapons was unable to achieve any substantive result and that the 2005 World Summit Outcome adopted by the General Assembly[18] failed to make any reference to nuclear disarmament and nuclear non-proliferation;

19. *Also expresses its regret* that the Conference on Disarmament was unable to establish an ad hoc committee to deal with nuclear disarmament early in 2009, as called for by the General Assembly in its resolution 63/46;

20. *Reiterates its call upon* the Conference on Disarmament to establish, as soon as possible and as the highest priority, an ad hoc committee on nuclear disarmament early in 2010, and to commence negotiations on a phased programme of nuclear disarmament leading to the total elimination of nuclear weapons within a specified framework of time;

21. *Calls for* the convening of an international conference on nuclear disarmament in all its aspects at an early date to identify and deal with concrete measures of nuclear disarmament;

22. *Requests* the Secretary-General to submit to the General Assembly at its sixty-fifth session a report on the implementation of the present resolution;

23. *Decides* to include in the provisional agenda of its sixty-fifth session the item entitled "Nuclear disarmament".

Action by the General Assembly

Date: 2 December 2009   Meeting: 55th plenary meeting
Vote: 111-45-19   Report: A/64/391

Sponsors

Algeria, Bangladesh, Bhutan, Burundi, Cambodia, Congo, Cuba, Indonesia, Iran (Islamic Republic of), Jordan, Kenya, Kuwait, Lao

---

[18] See resolution 60/1.

People's Democratic Republic, Mongolia, **Myanmar**, Nepal, Philippines, Samoa, Saudi Arabia, Senegal, Sierra Leone, Singapore, Sri Lanka, Sudan, Suriname, Thailand, Timor-Leste, Uganda, Venezuela (Bolivarian Republic of), Viet Nam, Zambia, Zimbabwe

Co-sponsors

Bolivia (Plurinational State of), Brunei Darussalam, Central African Republic, Comoros, Dominican Republic, Fiji, Malaysia

*Recorded vote**

In favour:

Afghanistan, Algeria, Angola, Antigua and Barbuda, Argentina, Bahamas, Bahrain, Bangladesh, Barbados, Belize, Benin, Bhutan, Botswana, Brazil, Brunei Darussalam, Burkina Faso, Burundi, Cambodia, Cameroon, Cape Verde, Chile, China, Colombia, Congo, Costa Rica, Cuba, Democratic People's Republic of Korea, Democratic Republic of the Congo, Djibouti, Dominica, Dominican Republic, Ecuador, Egypt, El Salvador, Equatorial Guinea, Eritrea, Fiji, Gambia, Ghana, Grenada, Guatemala, Guinea, Guinea-Bissau, Guyana, Haiti, Honduras, Indonesia, Iran (Islamic Republic of), Iraq, Jamaica, Jordan, Kenya, Kuwait, Lao People's Democratic Republic, Lebanon, Lesotho, Liberia, Libyan Arab Jamahiriya, Madagascar, Malawi, Malaysia, Maldives, Mali, Mauritania, Mexico, Mongolia, Morocco, Mozambique, Myanmar, Namibia, Nepal, New Zealand, Nicaragua, Niger, Nigeria, Oman, Panama, Papua New Guinea, Paraguay, Peru, Philippines, Qatar, Saint Kitts and Nevis, Saint Lucia, Saint Vincent and the Grenadines, Samoa, Saudi Arabia, Senegal, Singapore, Solomon Islands, Somalia, South Africa, Sri Lanka, Sudan, Suriname, Swaziland, Syrian Arab Republic, Thailand, Togo, Tonga, Trinidad and Tobago, Tunisia, Uganda, United Arab Emirates, United Republic of Tanzania, Uruguay, Venezuela (Bolivarian Republic of), Viet Nam, Yemen, Zambia, Zimbabwe

Against:

Albania, Andorra, Australia, Belgium, Bosnia and Herzegovina, Bulgaria, Canada, Croatia, Cyprus, Czech Republic, Denmark, Estonia, Finland, France, Georgia, Germany, Greece, Hungary, Iceland, Israel, Italy, Latvia, Liechtenstein, Lithuania, Luxembourg, Micronesia (Federated States of), Monaco, Montenegro, Netherlands, Norway, Palau, Poland, Portugal, Republic of Moldova, Romania, San Marino, Slovakia, Slovenia, Spain, Switzerland, the former Yugoslav Republic of Macedonia, Turkey, Ukraine, United Kingdom, United States

---

* Subsequently, the delegation of Ethiopia advised the Secretariat that it had intended to vote in favour. The voting tally above does not reflect this information.

Abstaining:
>Armenia, Austria, Azerbaijan, Belarus, India, Ireland, Japan, Kazakhstan, Kyrgyzstan, Malta, Marshall Islands, Mauritius, Pakistan, Republic of Korea, Russian Federation, Serbia, Sweden, Tajikistan, Uzbekistan

Action by the First Committee

Date: 27 October 2009   Meeting: 19th meeting
Vote: 112-43-21   Draft resolution: A/C.1/64/L.48

Agenda item 96 (w)

64/54   Transparency in armaments

Text

The General Assembly,

Recalling its resolutions 46/36 L of 9 December 1991, 47/52 L of 15 December 1992, 48/75 E of 16 December 1993, 49/75 C of 15 December 1994, 50/70 D of 12 December 1995, 51/45 H of 10 December 1996, 52/38 R of 9 December 1997, 53/77 V of 4 December 1998, 54/54 O of 1 December 1999, 55/33 U of 20 November 2000, 56/24 Q of 29 November 2001, 57/75 of 22 November 2002, 58/54 of 8 December 2003, 60/226 of 23 December 2005, 61/77 of 6 December 2006 and 63/69 of 2 December 2008, entitled "Transparency in armaments",

Continuing to take the view that an enhanced level of transparency in armaments contributes greatly to confidence-building and security among States and that the establishment of the United Nations Register of Conventional Arms[1] constitutes an important step forward in the promotion of transparency in military matters,

Welcoming the consolidated report of the Secretary-General on the Register, which includes the returns of Member States for 2008,[2]

Welcoming also the response of Member States to the request contained in paragraphs 9 and 10 of resolution 46/36 L to provide data on their imports and exports of arms, as well as available background information regarding their military holdings, procurement through national production and relevant policies,

Welcoming further the inclusion by some Member States of their transfers of small arms and light weapons in their annual report to the Register as part of their additional background information,

Noting the focused discussions on transparency in armaments that took place in the Conference on Disarmament in 2009,

Noting with concern the reduction in reporting to the United Nations Register of Conventional Arms in the last two years,

Stressing that the continuing operation of the Register and its further development should be reviewed in order to secure a Register that is capable of attracting the widest possible participation,

---

[1] See resolution 46/36 L.
[2] A/64/135 and Add.1.

1. *Reaffirms its determination* to ensure the effective operation of the United Nations Register of Conventional Arms,[1] as provided for in paragraphs 7 to 10 of resolution 46/36 L;

2. *Endorses* the report of the Secretary-General on the continuing operation of the Register and its further development[3] and the recommendations contained in the consensus report of the 2009 group of governmental experts;

3. *Calls upon* Member States, with a view to achieving universal participation, to provide the Secretary-General, by 31 May annually, with the requested data and information for the Register, including nil reports if appropriate, on the basis of resolutions 46/36 L and 47/52 L, the recommendations contained in paragraph 64 of the 1997 report of the Secretary-General on the continuing operation of the Register and its further development,[4] the recommendations contained in paragraph 94 of the 2000 report of the Secretary-General and the appendices and annexes thereto,[5] the recommendations contained in paragraphs 112 to 114 of the 2003 report of the Secretary-General,[6] the recommendations contained in paragraphs 123 to 127 of the 2006 report of the Secretary-General[7] and the recommendations contained in paragraphs 71 to 75 of the 2009 report of the Secretary-General;[3]

4. *Invites* Member States in a position to do so, pending further development of the Register, to provide additional information on procurement through national production and military holdings and to make use of the "Remarks" column in the standardized reporting form to provide additional information such as types or models;

5. *Also invites* Member States in a position to do so to provide additional information on transfers of small arms and light weapons on the basis of the optional standardized reporting form, as adopted by the 2006 group of governmental experts,[8] or by any other methods they deem appropriate;

6. *Reaffirms its decision*, with a view to further development of the Register, to keep the scope of and participation in the Register under review and, to that end:

(*a*) *Recalls* its request to Member States to provide the Secretary-General with their views on the continuing operation of the Register and its further development and on transparency measures related to weapons of mass destruction;

(*b*) *Requests* the Secretary-General to seek the views of Member States, including whether the absence of small arms and light weapons as a

---

[3] A/64/296.
[4] A/52/316 and Corr.2.
[5] A/55/281.
[6] A/58/274.
[7] See A/61/261.
[8] Ibid., annex I.

main category in the Register has limited its relevance and directly affected decisions on participation;

(*c*) Requests the Secretary-General to continue to assist Member States to build capacity to submit meaningful reports, including capacity to report on small arms and light weapons;

(*d*) Requests the Secretary-General, with a view to the three-year review cycle of the Register, to ensure that sufficient resources are made available for a group of governmental experts to be convened in 2012 to review the continuing operation of the Register and its further development, taking into account the work of the Conference on Disarmament, the views expressed by Member States and the reports of the Secretary-General on the continuing operation of the Register and its further development;

7. *Requests* the Secretary-General to implement the recommendations contained in his 2000, 2003, 2006 and 2009 reports on the continuing operation of the Register and its further development and to ensure that sufficient resources are made available for the Secretariat to operate and maintain the Register;

8. *Invites* the Conference on Disarmament to consider continuing its work undertaken in the field of transparency in armaments;

9. *Reiterates its call upon* all Member States to cooperate at the regional and subregional levels, taking fully into account the specific conditions prevailing in the region or subregion, with a view to enhancing and coordinating international efforts aimed at increased openness and transparency in armaments;

10. *Requests* the Secretary-General to report to the General Assembly at its sixty-fifth session on progress made in implementing the present resolution;

11. *Decides* to include in the provisional agenda of its sixty-sixth session the item entitled "Transparency in armaments".

Action by the General Assembly

Date: 2 December 2009
Vote: 153-0-23, as a whole
      149-0-24, o.p. 3
      152-0-22, o.p. 4
      151-0-22, o.p. 5
      151-0-22, o.p. 6 (d)
      149-0-24, o.p. 6
      152-0-22, o.p. 8

Meeting: 55th plenary meeting
Report: A/64/391

Sponsors

Albania, Andorra, Argentina, Armenia, Australia, Austria, Belgium, Belize, Benin, Bhutan, Brazil, Bulgaria, Burkina Faso, Colombia, Costa Rica, Croatia, Cyprus, Czech Republic, Denmark, Dominican Republic, Estonia, Finland, France, Germany, Greece, Guatemala, Haiti, Honduras, Hungary, Iceland, Ireland, Israel, Italy, Japan, Kazakhstan, Latvia, Liberia, Liechtenstein, Lithuania, Luxembourg, Malta, Monaco, Montenegro, Nepal, **Netherlands**, New Zealand, Nigeria, Norway, Paraguay, Peru, Philippines, Poland, Portugal, Republic of Korea, Republic of Moldova, Romania, Senegal, Serbia, Slovakia, Slovenia, South Africa, Spain, Sweden, Switzerland, the former Yugoslav Republic of Macedonia, Timor-Leste, Turkey, Ukraine, United Kingdom, United Republic of Tanzania, United States, Uruguay, Zambia

Co-sponsors

Antigua and Barbuda, Bangladesh, Bolivia (Plurinational State of), Bosnia and Herzegovina, Burundi, Canada, Chile, Comoros, Ecuador, Gabon, Ghana, Grenada, Guyana, Jamaica, Lesotho, Madagascar, Malaysia, Mali, Micronesia (Federated States of), Mongolia, Niger, Panama, Saint Kitts and Nevis, Saint Lucia, San Marino, Sierra Leone, Singapore, Suriname, Swaziland, Trinidad and Tobago

Recorded vote

As a whole*

In favour:
Afghanistan, Albania, Andorra, Angola, Antigua and Barbuda, Argentina, Armenia, Australia, Austria, Azerbaijan, Bahamas, Bangladesh, Barbados, Belarus, Belgium, Belize, Benin, Bhutan, Bolivia (Plurinational State of), Bosnia and Herzegovina, Botswana, Brazil, Brunei Darussalam, Bulgaria, Burkina Faso, Burundi, Cambodia, Canada, Cape Verde, Chile, China, Colombia, Comoros, Congo, Costa Rica, Côte d'Ivoire, Croatia, Cyprus, Czech Republic, Democratic Republic of the Congo, Denmark, Dominica, Dominican Republic, Ecuador, El Salvador, Equatorial Guinea, Eritrea, Estonia, Fiji, Finland, France, Gambia, Georgia, Germany, Ghana, Greece, Grenada, Guatemala, Guinea, Guinea-Bissau, Guyana, Haiti, Honduras, Hungary, Iceland, India, Indonesia, Ireland, Israel, Italy, Jamaica, Japan, Kazakhstan, Kenya, Kyrgyzstan, Lao People's Democratic Republic, Latvia, Lesotho, Liberia, Liechtenstein, Lithuania, Luxembourg, Madagascar, Malawi, Malaysia, Maldives, Mali, Malta, Marshall Islands, Mauritius, Mexico, Micronesia (Federated States of), Monaco, Mongolia, Montenegro, Mozambique,

---

* Subsequently, the delegations of Cameroon and Ethiopia advised the Secretariat that they had intended to vote in favour. The voting tally above does not reflect this information.

Namibia, Nepal, Netherlands, New Zealand, Nicaragua, Niger, Nigeria, Norway, Pakistan, Palau, Panama, Papua New Guinea, Paraguay, Peru, Philippines, Poland, Portugal, Republic of Korea, Republic of Moldova, Romania, Russian Federation, Saint Kitts and Nevis, Saint Lucia, Saint Vincent and the Grenadines, Samoa, San Marino, Senegal, Serbia, Sierra Leone, Singapore, Slovakia, Slovenia, Solomon Islands, South Africa, Spain, Sri Lanka, Suriname, Swaziland, Sweden, Switzerland, Tajikistan, Thailand, the former Yugoslav Republic of Macedonia, Togo, Tonga, Trinidad and Tobago, Turkey, Turkmenistan, Ukraine, United Kingdom, United Republic of Tanzania, United States, Uruguay, Uzbekistan, Venezuela (Bolivarian Republic of), Zambia, Zimbabwe

Against:
None

Abstaining:
Algeria, Bahrain, Cuba, Djibouti, Egypt, Iran (Islamic Republic of), Iraq, Jordan, Kuwait, Lebanon, Libyan Arab Jamahiriya, Mauritania, Morocco, Myanmar, Oman, Qatar, Saudi Arabia, Somalia, Sudan, Syrian Arab Republic, Tunisia, United Arab Emirates, Yemen

Operative paragraph 3*

In favour:
Afghanistan, Albania, Andorra, Angola, Antigua and Barbuda, Argentina, Armenia, Australia, Austria, Azerbaijan, Bahamas, Bangladesh, Barbados, Belarus, Belgium, Belize, Benin, Bhutan, Bolivia (Plurinational State of), Bosnia and Herzegovina, Botswana, Brazil, Brunei Darussalam, Bulgaria, Burkina Faso, Burundi, Cambodia, Cameroon, Canada, Cape Verde, Chile, China, Colombia, Comoros, Congo, Costa Rica, Côte d'Ivoire, Croatia, Cyprus, Czech Republic, Democratic Republic of the Congo, Denmark, Dominica, Dominican Republic, Ecuador, El Salvador, Equatorial Guinea, Eritrea, Estonia, Fiji, Finland, France, Gambia, Georgia, Germany, Ghana, Greece, Grenada, Guatemala, Guinea, Guinea-Bissau, Guyana, Haiti, Honduras, Hungary, Iceland, India, Indonesia, Ireland, Israel, Italy, Jamaica, Japan, Kazakhstan, Kenya, Kyrgyzstan, Lao People's Democratic Republic, Latvia, Lesotho, Liberia, Liechtenstein, Lithuania, Luxembourg, Madagascar, Malawi, Malaysia, Maldives, Mali, Malta, Marshall Islands, Mauritius, Mexico, Micronesia (Federated States of), Monaco, Mongolia, Montenegro, Mozambique, Namibia, Nepal, Netherlands, New Zealand, Niger, Nigeria, Norway, Pakistan, Panama, Papua New Guinea, Paraguay, Peru, Philippines, Poland, Portugal, Republic of Korea, Republic of Moldova, Romania, Russian Federation, Saint Kitts and Nevis, Saint Lucia, Saint

---

* Subsequently, the delegation of Ethiopia advised the Secretariat that it had intended to vote in favour. The voting tally above does not reflect this information.

Vincent and the Grenadines, Samoa, San Marino, Senegal, Serbia, Singapore, Slovakia, Slovenia, Solomon Islands, South Africa, Spain, Sri Lanka, Suriname, Swaziland, Sweden, Switzerland, Thailand, the former Yugoslav Republic of Macedonia, Tonga, Trinidad and Tobago, Turkey, Turkmenistan, Ukraine, United Kingdom, United Republic of Tanzania, United States, Uruguay, Uzbekistan, Venezuela (Bolivarian Republic of), Zambia, Zimbabwe

Against:
None

Abstaining:
Algeria, Bahrain, Cuba, Djibouti, Egypt, Iran (Islamic Republic of), Iraq, Jordan, Kuwait, Lebanon, Libyan Arab Jamahiriya, Mauritania, Morocco, Myanmar, Nicaragua, Oman, Qatar, Saudi Arabia, Somalia, Sudan, Syrian Arab Republic, Tunisia, United Arab Emirates, Yemen

Operative paragraph 4*

In favour:
Afghanistan, Albania, Andorra, Angola, Antigua and Barbuda, Argentina, Armenia, Australia, Austria, Azerbaijan, Bahamas, Bangladesh, Barbados, Belarus, Belgium, Belize, Benin, Bhutan, Bolivia (Plurinational State of), Bosnia and Herzegovina, Botswana, Brazil, Brunei Darussalam, Bulgaria, Burkina Faso, Burundi, Cambodia, Cameroon, Canada, Cape Verde, Chile, China, Colombia, Comoros, Congo, Costa Rica, Côte d'Ivoire, Croatia, Cuba, Cyprus, Czech Republic, Democratic Republic of the Congo, Denmark, Dominica, Dominican Republic, Ecuador, El Salvador, Equatorial Guinea, Eritrea, Estonia, Fiji, Finland, France, Gambia, Georgia, Germany, Ghana, Greece, Grenada, Guatemala, Guinea, Guinea-Bissau, Guyana, Haiti, Honduras, Hungary, Iceland, India, Indonesia, Ireland, Israel, Italy, Jamaica, Japan, Kazakhstan, Kenya, Kyrgyzstan, Lao People's Democratic Republic, Latvia, Lesotho, Liberia, Liechtenstein, Lithuania, Luxembourg, Madagascar, Malawi, Malaysia, Maldives, Mali, Malta, Marshall Islands, Mauritius, Mexico, Micronesia (Federated States of), Monaco, Mongolia, Montenegro, Mozambique, Namibia, Nepal, Netherlands, New Zealand, Nicaragua, Niger, Nigeria, Norway, Pakistan, Panama, Papua New Guinea, Paraguay, Peru, Philippines, Poland, Portugal, Republic of Korea, Republic of Moldova, Romania, Russian Federation, Saint Kitts and Nevis, Saint Lucia, Saint Vincent and the Grenadines, Samoa, San Marino, Senegal, Serbia, Singapore, Slovakia, Slovenia, Solomon Islands, South Africa, Spain, Sri Lanka, Suriname, Swaziland, Sweden, Switzerland, Thailand, the former Yugoslav Republic of Macedonia, Togo, Tonga, Trinidad

---

* Subsequently, the delegation of Ethiopia advised the Secretariat that it had intended to vote in favour. The voting tally above does not reflect this information.

and Tobago, Turkey, Turkmenistan, Ukraine, United Kingdom, United Republic of Tanzania, United States, Uruguay, Uzbekistan, Venezuela (Bolivarian Republic of), Zambia, Zimbabwe

Against:
None

Abstaining:
Algeria, Bahrain, Djibouti, Egypt, Iran (Islamic Republic of), Iraq, Jordan, Kuwait, Lebanon, Libyan Arab Jamahiriya, Mauritania, Morocco, Myanmar, Oman, Qatar, Saudi Arabia, Somalia, Sudan, Syrian Arab Republic, Tunisia, United Arab Emirates, Yemen

Operative paragraph 5*

In favour:
Afghanistan, Albania, Andorra, Angola, Antigua and Barbuda, Argentina, Armenia, Australia, Austria, Azerbaijan, Bahamas, Bangladesh, Barbados, Belarus, Belgium, Belize, Benin, Bhutan, Bolivia (Plurinational State of), Bosnia and Herzegovina, Botswana, Brazil, Brunei Darussalam, Bulgaria, Burkina Faso, Burundi, Cambodia, Cameroon, Canada, Cape Verde, Chile, China, Colombia, Congo, Costa Rica, Côte d'Ivoire, Croatia, Cuba, Cyprus, Czech Republic, Democratic Republic of the Congo, Denmark, Dominica, Dominican Republic, Ecuador, El Salvador, Equatorial Guinea, Eritrea, Estonia, Fiji, Finland, France, Gambia, Georgia, Germany, Ghana, Greece, Grenada, Guatemala, Guinea, Guinea-Bissau, Guyana, Haiti, Honduras, Hungary, Iceland, India, Indonesia, Ireland, Israel, Italy, Jamaica, Japan, Kazakhstan, Kenya, Kyrgyzstan, Lao People's Democratic Republic, Latvia, Lesotho, Liberia, Liechtenstein, Lithuania, Luxembourg, Madagascar, Malawi, Malaysia, Maldives, Mali, Malta, Marshall Islands, Mauritius, Mexico, Micronesia (Federated States of), Monaco, Mongolia, Montenegro, Mozambique, Namibia, Nepal, Netherlands, New Zealand, Nicaragua, Niger, Nigeria, Norway, Pakistan, Panama, Papua New Guinea, Paraguay, Peru, Philippines, Poland, Portugal, Republic of Korea, Republic of Moldova, Romania, Russian Federation, Saint Kitts and Nevis, Saint Lucia, Saint Vincent and the Grenadines, Samoa, San Marino, Senegal, Serbia, Singapore, Slovakia, Slovenia, Solomon Islands, South Africa, Spain, Sri Lanka, Suriname, Swaziland, Sweden, Switzerland, Thailand, the former Yugoslav Republic of Macedonia, Togo, Tonga, Trinidad and Tobago, Turkey, Turkmenistan, Ukraine, United Kingdom, United Republic of Tanzania, United States, Uruguay, Uzbekistan, Venezuela (Bolivarian Republic of), Zambia, Zimbabwe

---

* Subsequently, the delegation of Ethiopia advised the Secretariat that it had intended to vote in favour. The voting tally above does not reflect this information.

Against:
   None

Abstaining:
   Algeria, Bahrain, Djibouti, Egypt, Iran (Islamic Republic of), Iraq, Jordan, Kuwait, Lebanon, Libyan Arab Jamahiriya, Mauritania, Morocco, Myanmar, Oman, Qatar, Saudi Arabia, Somalia, Sudan, Syrian Arab Republic, Tunisia, United Arab Emirates, Yemen

Operative paragraph 6 (d)*

In favour:
   Afghanistan, Albania, Andorra, Angola, Antigua and Barbuda, Argentina, Armenia, Australia, Austria, Azerbaijan, Bahamas, Bangladesh, Barbados, Belarus, Belgium, Belize, Benin, Bhutan, Bolivia (Plurinational State of), Bosnia and Herzegovina, Botswana, Brazil, Brunei Darussalam, Bulgaria, Burkina Faso, Burundi, Cambodia, Cameroon, Canada, Cape Verde, Chile, China, Colombia, Congo, Costa Rica, Côte d'Ivoire, Croatia, Cuba, Cyprus, Czech Republic, Democratic Republic of the Congo, Denmark, Dominica, Dominican Republic, Ecuador, El Salvador, Equatorial Guinea, Eritrea, Estonia, Fiji, Finland, France, Gambia, Georgia, Germany, Ghana, Greece, Grenada, Guatemala, Guinea, Guinea-Bissau, Guyana, Haiti, Honduras, Hungary, Iceland, India, Indonesia, Ireland, Israel, Italy, Jamaica, Japan, Kazakhstan, Kenya, Kyrgyzstan, Lao People's Democratic Republic, Latvia, Lesotho, Liberia, Liechtenstein, Lithuania, Luxembourg, Madagascar, Malawi, Malaysia, Maldives, Mali, Malta, Marshall Islands, Mauritius, Mexico, Micronesia (Federated States of), Monaco, Mongolia, Montenegro, Mozambique, Namibia, Nepal, Netherlands, New Zealand, Nicaragua, Niger, Nigeria, Norway, Pakistan, Panama, Papua New Guinea, Paraguay, Peru, Philippines, Poland, Portugal, Republic of Korea, Republic of Moldova, Romania, Russian Federation, Saint Kitts and Nevis, Saint Lucia, Saint Vincent and the Grenadines, Samoa, San Marino, Senegal, Serbia, Singapore, Slovakia, Slovenia, Solomon Islands, South Africa, Spain, Sri Lanka, Suriname, Swaziland, Sweden, Switzerland, Thailand, the former Yugoslav Republic of Macedonia, Togo, Tonga, Trinidad and Tobago, Turkey, Turkmenistan, Ukraine, United Kingdom, United Republic of Tanzania, United States, Uruguay, Uzbekistan, Venezuela (Bolivarian Republic of), Zambia, Zimbabwe

Against:
   None

---

  * Subsequently, the delegation of Ethiopia advised the Secretariat that it had intended to vote in favour. The voting tally above does not reflect this information.

Abstaining:
   Algeria, Bahrain, Djibouti, Egypt, Iran (Islamic Republic of), Iraq, Jordan, Kuwait, Lebanon, Libyan Arab Jamahiriya, Mauritania, Morocco, Myanmar, Oman, Qatar, Saudi Arabia, Somalia, Sudan, Syrian Arab Republic, Tunisia, United Arab Emirates, Yemen

Operative paragraph 6*

In favour:
   Afghanistan, Albania, Andorra, Angola, Antigua and Barbuda, Argentina, Armenia, Australia, Austria, Azerbaijan, Bahamas, Bangladesh, Barbados, Belarus, Belgium, Belize, Benin, Bhutan, Bolivia (Plurinational State of), Bosnia and Herzegovina, Botswana, Brazil, Brunei Darussalam, Bulgaria, Burkina Faso, Burundi, Cambodia, Cameroon, Canada, Cape Verde, Chile, China, Colombia, Congo, Costa Rica, Côte d'Ivoire, Croatia, Cyprus, Czech Republic, Democratic Republic of the Congo, Denmark, Dominica, Dominican Republic, Ecuador, El Salvador, Equatorial Guinea, Eritrea, Estonia, Fiji, Finland, France, Gambia, Georgia, Germany, Ghana, Greece, Grenada, Guatemala, Guinea, Guinea-Bissau, Guyana, Haiti, Honduras, Hungary, Iceland, India, Indonesia, Ireland, Israel, Italy, Jamaica, Japan, Kazakhstan, Kenya, Kyrgyzstan, Lao People's Democratic Republic, Latvia, Lesotho, Liberia, Liechtenstein, Lithuania, Luxembourg, Madagascar, Malawi, Malaysia, Maldives, Mali, Malta, Marshall Islands, Mauritius, Mexico, Micronesia (Federated States of), Monaco, Mongolia, Montenegro, Mozambique, Namibia, Nepal, Netherlands, New Zealand, Niger, Nigeria, Norway, Pakistan, Panama, Papua New Guinea, Paraguay, Peru, Philippines, Poland, Portugal, Republic of Korea, Republic of Moldova, Romania, Russian Federation, Saint Kitts and Nevis, Saint Lucia, Saint Vincent and the Grenadines, Samoa, San Marino, Senegal, Serbia, Singapore, Slovakia, Slovenia, Solomon Islands, South Africa, Spain, Sri Lanka, Suriname, Swaziland, Sweden, Switzerland, Thailand, the former Yugoslav Republic of Macedonia, Togo, Tonga, Trinidad and Tobago, Turkey, Turkmenistan, Ukraine, United Kingdom, United Republic of Tanzania, United States, Uruguay, Uzbekistan, Venezuela (Bolivarian Republic of), Zambia, Zimbabwe

Against:
   None

Abstaining:
   Algeria, Bahrain, Cuba, Djibouti, Egypt, Iran (Islamic Republic of), Iraq, Jordan, Kuwait, Lebanon, Libyan Arab Jamahiriya, Mauritania,

---

   * Subsequently, the delegation of Ethiopia advised the Secretariat that it had intended to vote in favour. The voting tally above does not reflect this information.

Morocco, Myanmar, Nicaragua, Oman, Qatar, Saudi Arabia, Somalia, Sudan, Syrian Arab Republic, Tunisia, United Arab Emirates, Yemen

Operative paragraph 8*

In favour:
Afghanistan, Albania, Andorra, Angola, Antigua and Barbuda, Argentina, Armenia, Australia, Austria, Azerbaijan, Bahamas, Bangladesh, Barbados, Belarus, Belgium, Belize, Benin, Bhutan, Bolivia (Plurinational State of), Bosnia and Herzegovina, Botswana, Brazil, Brunei Darussalam, Bulgaria, Burkina Faso, Burundi, Cambodia, Cameroon, Canada, Cape Verde, Chile, China, Colombia, Congo, Costa Rica, Côte d'Ivoire, Croatia, Cuba, Cyprus, Czech Republic, Democratic Republic of the Congo, Denmark, Dominica, Dominican Republic, Ecuador, El Salvador, Equatorial Guinea, Eritrea, Estonia, Fiji, Finland, France, Gambia, Georgia, Germany, Ghana, Greece, Grenada, Guatemala, Guinea, Guinea-Bissau, Guyana, Haiti, Honduras, Hungary, Iceland, India, Indonesia, Ireland, Israel, Italy, Jamaica, Japan, Kazakhstan, Kenya, Kyrgyzstan, Lao People's Democratic Republic, Latvia, Lesotho, Liberia, Liechtenstein, Lithuania, Luxembourg, Madagascar, Malawi, Malaysia, Maldives, Mali, Malta, Marshall Islands, Mauritius, Mexico, Micronesia (Federated States of), Monaco, Mongolia, Montenegro, Mozambique, Namibia, Nepal, Netherlands, New Zealand, Nicaragua, Niger, Nigeria, Norway, Pakistan, Panama, Papua New Guinea, Paraguay, Peru, Philippines, Poland, Portugal, Republic of Korea, Republic of Moldova, Romania, Russian Federation, Saint Kitts and Nevis, Saint Lucia, Saint Vincent and the Grenadines, Samoa, San Marino, Senegal, Serbia, Sierra Leone, Singapore, Slovakia, Slovenia, Solomon Islands, South Africa, Spain, Sri Lanka, Suriname, Swaziland, Sweden, Switzerland, Thailand, the former Yugoslav Republic of Macedonia, Togo, Tonga, Trinidad and Tobago, Turkey, Turkmenistan, Ukraine, United Kingdom, United Republic of Tanzania, United States, Uruguay, Uzbekistan, Venezuela (Bolivarian Republic of), Zambia, Zimbabwe

Against:
None

Abstaining:
Algeria, Bahrain, Djibouti, Egypt, Iran (Islamic Republic of), Iraq, Jordan, Kuwait, Lebanon, Libyan Arab Jamahiriya, Mauritania, Morocco, Myanmar, Oman, Qatar, Saudi Arabia, Somalia, Sudan, Syrian Arab Republic, Tunisia, United Arab Emirates, Yemen

---

* Subsequently, the delegation of Ethiopia advised the Secretariat that it had intended to vote in favour. The voting tally above does not reflect this information.

Action by the First Committee

Date: 29 October 2009 Meeting: 21st meeting
Vote: 150-0-22, as a whole Draft resolution: A/C.1/64/L.50
  147-0-24, o.p. 3
  147-0-24, o.p. 4
  149-0-22, o.p. 5
  147-0-23, o.p. 6 (d)
  148-0-22, o.p. 6
  146-0-23, o.p. 8

Agenda item 96 (l)

64/55 Follow-up to the advisory opinion of the International Court of Justice on the *Legality of the Threat or Use of Nuclear Weapons*

Text

The General Assembly,

Recalling its resolutions 49/75 K of 15 December 1994, 51/45 M of 10 December 1996, 52/38 O of 9 December 1997, 53/77 W of 4 December 1998, 54/54 Q of 1 December 1999, 55/33 X of 20 November 2000, 56/24 S of 29 November 2001, 57/85 of 22 November 2002, 58/46 of 8 December 2003, 59/83 of 3 December 2004, 60/76 of 8 December 2005, 61/83 of 6 December 2006, 62/39 of 5 December 2007 and 63/49 of 2 December 2008,

Convinced that the continuing existence of nuclear weapons poses a threat to all humanity and that their use would have catastrophic consequences for all life on Earth, and recognizing that the only defence against a nuclear catastrophe is the total elimination of nuclear weapons and the certainty that they will never be produced again,

Reaffirming the commitment of the international community to the goal of the total elimination of nuclear weapons and the creation of a nuclear-weapon-free world,

Mindful of the solemn obligations of States parties, undertaken in article VI of the Treaty on the Non-Proliferation of Nuclear Weapons,[1] particularly to pursue negotiations in good faith on effective measures relating to cessation of the nuclear arms race at an early date and to nuclear disarmament,

Recalling the principles and objectives for nuclear non-proliferation and disarmament adopted at the 1995 Review and Extension Conference of the Parties to the Treaty on the Non-Proliferation of Nuclear Weapons,[2]

Emphasizing the unequivocal undertaking by the nuclear-weapon States to accomplish the total elimination of their nuclear arsenals leading to nuclear disarmament, adopted at the 2000 Review Conference of the Parties to the Treaty on the Non-Proliferation of Nuclear Weapons,[3]

---

[1] United Nations, *Treaty Series*, vol. 729, No. 10485.
[2] *1995 Review and Extension Conference of the Parties to the Treaty on the Non-Proliferation of Nuclear Weapons, Final Document, Part I* (NPT/CONF.1995/32 (Part I) and Corr.2), annex, decision 2.
[3] *2000 Review Conference of the Parties to the Treaty on the Non-Proliferation of Nuclear Weapons, Final Document*, vol. I (NPT/CONF.2000/28 (Parts I and II)), part I, section entitled "Article VI and eighth to twelfth preambular paragraphs", para. 15:6.

Recalling the adoption of the Comprehensive Nuclear-Test-Ban Treaty in its resolution 50/245 of 10 September 1996, and expressing its satisfaction at the increasing number of States that have signed and ratified the Treaty,

Recognizing with satisfaction that the Antarctic Treaty[4] and the treaties of Tlatelolco,[5] Rarotonga,[6] Bangkok,[7] Pelindaba[8] and Central Asia,[9] as well as Mongolia's nuclear-weapon-free status, are gradually freeing the entire southern hemisphere and adjacent areas covered by those treaties from nuclear weapons,

Stressing the importance of strengthening all existing nuclear-related disarmament and arms control and reduction measures,

Recognizing the need for a multilaterally negotiated and legally binding instrument to assure non-nuclear-weapon States against the threat or use of nuclear weapons,

Reaffirming the central role of the Conference on Disarmament as the sole multilateral disarmament negotiating forum,

Emphasizing the need for the Conference on Disarmament to commence negotiations on a phased programme for the complete elimination of nuclear weapons with a specified framework of time,

Expressing its regret over the failure of the 2005 Review Conference of the Parties to the Treaty on the Non-Proliferation of Nuclear Weapons to reach agreement on any substantive issues,

Expressing its deep concern at the lack of progress in the implementation of the thirteen steps to implement article VI of the Treaty on the Non-Proliferation of Nuclear Weapons agreed to at the 2000 Review Conference of the Parties to the Treaty,[10]

Desiring to achieve the objective of a legally binding prohibition of the development, production, testing, deployment, stockpiling, threat or use of nuclear weapons and their destruction under effective international control,

Recalling the advisory opinion of the International Court of Justice on the *Legality of the Threat or Use of Nuclear Weapons*, issued on 8 July 1996,[11]

---

[4] United Nations, *Treaty Series*, vol. 402, No. 5778.
[5] Ibid., vol. 634, No. 9068.
[6] See *The United Nations Disarmament Yearbook*, vol. 10: 1985 (United Nations publication, Sales No. E.86.IX.7), appendix VII.
[7] United Nations, *Treaty Series*, vol. 1981, No. 33873.
[8] A/50/426, annex.
[9] Treaty on a Nuclear-Weapon-Free Zone in Central Asia.
[10] See *2000 Review Conference of the Parties to the Treaty on the Non-Proliferation of Nuclear Weapons, Final Document*, vol. I (NPT/CONF.2000/28 (Parts I and II)), part I, section entitled "Article VI and eighth to twelfth preambular paragraphs", para. 15.
[11] A/51/218, annex; see also *Legality of the Threat or Use of Nuclear Weapons, Advisory Opinion, I.C.J. Reports 1996*, p. 226.

Taking note of the relevant portions of the report of the Secretary-General relating to the implementation of resolution 63/49,[12]

1. *Underlines once again* the unanimous conclusion of the International Court of Justice that there exists an obligation to pursue in good faith and bring to a conclusion negotiations leading to nuclear disarmament in all its aspects under strict and effective international control;

2. *Calls once again upon* all States immediately to fulfil that obligation by commencing multilateral negotiations leading to an early conclusion of a nuclear weapons convention prohibiting the development, production, testing, deployment, stockpiling, transfer, threat or use of nuclear weapons and providing for their elimination;

3. *Requests* all States to inform the Secretary-General of the efforts and measures they have taken on the implementation of the present resolution and nuclear disarmament, and requests the Secretary-General to apprise the General Assembly of that information at its sixty-fifth session;

4. *Decides* to include in the provisional agenda of its sixty-fifth session the item entitled "Follow-up to the advisory opinion of the International Court of Justice on the *Legality of the Threat or Use of Nuclear Weapons*".

Action by the General Assembly

Date: 2 December 2009
Vote: 124-31-21
Meeting: 55th plenary meeting
Report: A/64/391

Sponsors

Algeria, Bangladesh, Belize, Benin, Brunei Darussalam, Cambodia, Colombia, Congo, Costa Rica, Cuba, Egypt, Fiji, Guatemala, India, Indonesia, Iran (Islamic Republic of), Iraq, Jamaica, Jordan, Kenya, Kuwait, Lao People's Democratic Republic, Libyan Arab Jamahiriya, Madagascar, **Malaysia**, Mexico, Myanmar, Nicaragua, Pakistan, Peru, Philippines, Qatar, Singapore, Solomon Islands, Sri Lanka, Sudan, Syrian Arab Republic, Thailand, Timor-Leste, Uganda, United Republic of Tanzania, Uruguay, Venezuela (Bolivarian Republic of), Viet Nam, Zimbabwe

Co-sponsors

Bolivia (Plurinational State of), Burkina Faso, Central African Republic, Chile, Democratic People's Republic of Korea, Dominican Republic, Ecuador, Gabon, Ghana, Honduras, Mali, Mauritania, Nepal, Samoa, Senegal, Trinidad and Tobago

---

[12] A/64/139.

*Recorded vote**

In favour:
Afghanistan, Algeria, Angola, Antigua and Barbuda, Argentina, Austria, Bahamas, Bahrain, Bangladesh, Barbados, Belize, Benin, Bhutan, Bolivia (Plurinational State of), Bosnia and Herzegovina, Botswana, Brazil, Brunei Darussalam, Burkina Faso, Burundi, Cambodia, Cameroon, Cape Verde, Chile, China, Colombia, Congo, Costa Rica, Côte d'Ivoire, Cuba, Democratic People's Republic of Korea, Democratic Republic of the Congo, Djibouti, Dominica, Dominican Republic, Ecuador, Egypt, El Salvador, Equatorial Guinea, Eritrea, Fiji, Gambia, Ghana, Grenada, Guatemala, Guinea, Guinea-Bissau, Guyana, Haiti, Honduras, India, Indonesia, Iran (Islamic Republic of), Iraq, Ireland, Jamaica, Jordan, Kenya, Kuwait, Lao People's Democratic Republic, Lebanon, Lesotho, Liberia, Libyan Arab Jamahiriya, Madagascar, Malawi, Malaysia, Maldives, Mali, Malta, Mauritania, Mauritius, Mexico, Mongolia, Morocco, Mozambique, Myanmar, Namibia, Nepal, New Zealand, Nicaragua, Niger, Nigeria, Oman, Pakistan, Panama, Papua New Guinea, Paraguay, Peru, Philippines, Qatar, Saint Kitts and Nevis, Saint Lucia, Saint Vincent and the Grenadines, Samoa, San Marino, Saudi Arabia, Senegal, Serbia, Singapore, Solomon Islands, Somalia, South Africa, Sri Lanka, Sudan, Suriname, Swaziland, Sweden, Switzerland, Syrian Arab Republic, Thailand, Togo, Trinidad and Tobago, Tunisia, Turkmenistan, Uganda, United Arab Emirates, United Republic of Tanzania, Uruguay, Venezuela (Bolivarian Republic of), Viet Nam, Yemen, Zambia, Zimbabwe

Against:
Albania, Belgium, Bulgaria, Czech Republic, Denmark, Estonia, France, Georgia, Germany, Greece, Hungary, Iceland, Israel, Italy, Latvia, Lithuania, Luxembourg, Montenegro, Netherlands, Norway, Palau, Poland, Portugal, Russian Federation, Slovakia, Slovenia, Spain, the former Yugoslav Republic of Macedonia, Turkey, United Kingdom, United States

Abstaining:
Andorra, Armenia, Australia, Azerbaijan, Belarus, Canada, Croatia, Cyprus, Finland, Japan, Kazakhstan, Kyrgyzstan, Liechtenstein, Marshall Islands, Micronesia (Federated States of), Republic of Korea, Republic of Moldova, Romania, Tajikistan, Ukraine, Uzbekistan

Action by the First Committee

Date: 30 October 2009   Meeting: 22nd meeting
Vote: 126-29-22   Draft resolution: A/C.1/64/L.51

---

* Subsequently, the delegation of Ethiopia advised the Secretariat that it had intended to vote in favour. The voting tally above does not reflect this information.

Agenda item 96

64/56 Implementation of the Convention on the Prohibition of the Use, Stockpiling, Production and Transfer of Anti-personnel Mines and on Their Destruction

Text

The General Assembly,

Recalling its resolutions 54/54 B of 1 December 1999, 55/33 V of 20 November 2000, 56/24 M of 29 November 2001, 57/74 of 22 November 2002, 58/53 of 8 December 2003, 59/84 of 3 December 2004, 60/80 of 8 December 2005, 61/84 of 6 December 2006, 62/41 of 5 December 2007 and 63/42 of 2 December 2008,

Reaffirming its determination to put an end to the suffering and casualties caused by anti-personnel mines, which kill or maim hundreds of people every week, mostly innocent and defenceless civilians, including children, obstruct economic development and reconstruction, inhibit the repatriation of refugees and internally displaced persons and have other severe consequences for years after emplacement,

Believing it necessary to do the utmost to contribute in an efficient and coordinated manner to facing the challenge of removing anti-personnel mines placed throughout the world and to assure their destruction,

Wishing to do the utmost in ensuring assistance for the care and rehabilitation, including the social and economic reintegration, of mine victims,

Recalling that 2009 marks the tenth anniversary of the entry into force of the Convention on the Prohibition of the Use, Stockpiling, Production and Transfer of Anti-personnel Mines and on Their Destruction,[1]

Noting with satisfaction the work undertaken to implement the Convention and the substantial progress made towards addressing the global anti-personnel landmine problem,

Recalling the first to ninth meetings of the States parties to the Convention, held in Maputo (1999),[2] Geneva (2000),[3] Managua (2001),[4]

---

[1] United Nations, *Treaty Series*, vol. 2056, No. 35597.
[2] See APLC/MSP.1/1999/1.
[3] See APLC/MSP.2/2000/1.
[4] See APLC/MSP.3/2001/1.

Geneva (2002),[5] Bangkok (2003),[6] Zagreb (2005),[7] Geneva (2006),[8] the Dead Sea (2007)[9] and Geneva (2008)[10] and the First Review Conference of the States Parties to the Convention, held in Nairobi (2004),[11]

Recalling also the ninth meeting of the States parties to the Convention, held in Geneva from 24 to 28 November 2008, at which the international community monitored progress on implementation of the Convention, supported continued application of the Nairobi Action Plan 2005–2009,[12] and established priorities to achieve further progress towards ending, for all people and for all time, the suffering caused by anti-personnel mines,

Recalling further the preparatory process for the Second Review Conference of the States Parties to the Convention on the Prohibition of the Use, Stockpiling, Production and Transfer of Anti-personnel Mines and on Their Destruction, entitled "The Cartagena Summit on a Mine-Free World", to be held in Cartagena, Colombia, from 29 November to 4 December 2009, and the two preparatory meetings held in 2009 pursuant to the decisions of the ninth meeting of the States parties,

Noting with satisfaction that one hundred and fifty-six States have ratified or acceded to the Convention and have formally accepted the obligations of the Convention,

Emphasizing the desirability of attracting the adherence of all States to the Convention, and determined to work strenuously towards the promotion of its universalization,

Noting with regret that anti-personnel mines continue to be used in conflicts around the world, causing human suffering and impeding post-conflict development,

1. *Invites* all States that have not signed the Convention on the Prohibition of the Use, Stockpiling, Production and Transfer of Anti-personnel Mines and on Their Destruction[1] to accede to it without delay;

2. *Urges* all States that have signed but have not ratified the Convention to ratify it without delay;

3. *Stresses* the importance of the full and effective implementation of and compliance with the Convention, including through the continued implementation of the Nairobi Action Plan 2005–2009;[12]

---

[5] See APLC/MSP.4/2002/1.
[6] See APLC/MSP.5/2003/5.
[7] See APLC/MSP.6/2005/5.
[8] See APLC/MSP.7/2006/5.
[9] See APLC/MSP.8/2007/6.
[10] See APLC/MSP.9/2008/5.
[11] See APLC/CONF/2004/5 and Corr.1.
[12] Ibid., part III.

4. *Urges* all States parties to provide the Secretary-General with complete and timely information as required under article 7 of the Convention in order to promote transparency and compliance with the Convention;

5. *Invites* all States that have not ratified the Convention or acceded to it to provide, on a voluntary basis, information to make global mine action efforts more effective;

6. *Renews its call* upon all States and other relevant parties to work together to promote, support and advance the care, rehabilitation and social and economic reintegration of mine victims, mine risk education programmes and the removal and destruction of anti-personnel mines placed or stockpiled throughout the world;

7. *Urges* all States to remain seized of the issue at the highest political level and, where in a position to do so, to promote adherence to the Convention through bilateral, subregional, regional and multilateral contacts, outreach, seminars and other means;

8. *Reiterates its invitation and encouragement* to all interested States, the United Nations, other relevant international organizations or institutions, regional organizations, the International Committee of the Red Cross and relevant non-governmental organizations to attend the Second Review Conference of the States Parties to the Convention, entitled "The Cartagena Summit on a Mine-Free World", at the highest possible level and, pending a decision to be taken at the Second Review Conference, to participate in the future meetings programme;

9. *Requests* the Secretary-General, in accordance with article 11, paragraph 2, of the Convention, to undertake the preparations necessary to convene the next meeting of the States parties, pending a decision to be taken at the Second Review Conference, and on behalf of the States parties and in accordance with article 11, paragraph 4, of the Convention, to invite States not parties to the Convention, as well as the United Nations, other relevant international organizations or institutions, regional organizations, the International Committee of the Red Cross and relevant non-governmental organizations, to attend the Second Review Conference and future meetings as observers;

10. *Decides* to remain seized of the matter.

Action by the General Assembly

Date: 2 December 2009 Meeting: 55th plenary meeting
Vote: 160-0-18 Report: A/64/391

Sponsors

Jordan, Norway, **Switzerland**

*Recorded vote**

In favour:
Afghanistan, Albania, Algeria, Andorra, Angola, Antigua and Barbuda, Argentina, Armenia, Australia, Austria, Azerbaijan, Bahamas, Bahrain, Bangladesh, Barbados, Belarus, Belgium, Belize, Benin, Bhutan, Bolivia (Plurinational State of), Bosnia and Herzegovina, Botswana, Brazil, Brunei Darussalam, Bulgaria, Burkina Faso, Burundi, Cambodia, Cameroon, Canada, Cape Verde, Chile, China, Colombia, Comoros, Congo, Costa Rica, Côte d'Ivoire, Croatia, Cyprus, Czech Republic, Democratic Republic of the Congo, Denmark, Djibouti, Dominica, Dominican Republic, Ecuador, El Salvador, Equatorial Guinea, Eritrea, Estonia, Fiji, Finland, France, Gambia, Georgia, Germany, Ghana, Greece, Grenada, Guatemala, Guinea, Guinea-Bissau, Guyana, Haiti, Honduras, Hungary, Iceland, Indonesia, Iraq, Ireland, Italy, Jamaica, Japan, Jordan, Kazakhstan, Kenya, Kuwait, Lao People's Democratic Republic, Latvia, Lesotho, Liberia, Liechtenstein, Lithuania, Luxembourg, Madagascar, Malawi, Malaysia, Maldives, Mali, Malta, Marshall Islands, Mauritania, Mauritius, Mexico, Micronesia (Federated States of), Monaco, Mongolia, Montenegro, Morocco, Mozambique, Namibia, Netherlands, New Zealand, Niger, Nigeria, Norway, Oman, Palau, Panama, Papua New Guinea, Paraguay, Peru, Philippines, Poland, Portugal, Qatar, Republic of Moldova, Romania, Saint Kitts and Nevis, Saint Lucia, Saint Vincent and the Grenadines, Samoa, San Marino, Senegal, Serbia, Sierra Leone, Singapore, Slovakia, Slovenia, Solomon Islands, Somalia, South Africa, Spain, Sri Lanka, Sudan, Suriname, Swaziland, Sweden, Switzerland, Tajikistan, Thailand, the former Yugoslav Republic of Macedonia, Togo, Tonga, Trinidad and Tobago, Tunisia, Turkey, Turkmenistan, Uganda, Ukraine, United Arab Emirates, United Kingdom, United Republic of Tanzania, Uruguay, Venezuela (Bolivarian Republic of), Yemen, Zambia, Zimbabwe

Against:
None

Abstaining:
Cuba, Democratic People's Republic of Korea, Egypt, India, Iran (Islamic Republic of), Israel, Kyrgyzstan, Lebanon, Libyan Arab Jamahiriya, Myanmar, Nepal, Pakistan, Republic of Korea, Russian Federation, Syrian Arab Republic, United States, Uzbekistan, Viet Nam

Action by the First Committee

Date: 29 October 2009   Meeting: 21st meeting
Vote: 158-0-18   Draft resolution: A/C.1/64/L.53

---

* Subsequently, the delegations of Côte d'Ivoire and Ethiopia advised the Secretariat that they had intended to vote in favour. The voting tally above does not reflect this information.

Agenda item 96 (p)

64/57   Towards a nuclear-weapon-free world: accelerating the implementation of nuclear disarmament commitments

Text

The General Assembly,

Recalling its resolution 63/58 of 2 December 2008,

Reiterating its grave concern at the danger to humanity posed by the possibility that nuclear weapons could be used,

Noting with satisfaction the renewed interest in nuclear disarmament on the part of international leaders expressed, inter alia, during the Security Council summit on nuclear non-proliferation and nuclear disarmament held on 24 September 2009, and underlining in this regard the urgent need for concrete, transparent, verifiable and irreversible steps to realize the goal of a world free of nuclear weapons,

Reaffirming that nuclear disarmament and nuclear non-proliferation are mutually reinforcing processes requiring urgent irreversible progress on both fronts,

Recognizing the continued vital importance of the early entry into force of the Comprehensive Nuclear-Test-Ban Treaty[1] to the advancement of nuclear disarmament and nuclear non-proliferation objectives, and welcoming the recent ratifications of the Treaty by Lebanon, Liberia, Malawi, Mozambique and Saint Vincent and the Grenadines,

Recalling that the 2000 Review Conference of the Parties to the Treaty on the Non-Proliferation of Nuclear Weapons in its final document, inter alia, reaffirmed the conviction that the establishment of nuclear-weapon-free zones enhances global and regional peace and security, strengthens the nuclear non-proliferation regime and contributes towards realizing the objectives of nuclear disarmament,[2]

Welcoming the entry into force, on 21 March 2009, of the Treaty on a Nuclear-Weapon-Free Zone in Central Asia and the entry into force, on 15 July 2009, of the Treaty of Pelindaba,[3] which establishes a nuclear-weapon-free zone in Africa, and expressing the hope that these important steps will be

---

[1] See resolution 50/245.
[2] See *2000 Review Conference of the Parties to the Treaty on the Non-Proliferation of Nuclear Weapons, Final Document*, vols. I–III (NPT/CONF.2000/28 (Parts I–IV)), vol. I, part I.
[3] A/50/426, annex.

followed by concerted international efforts to create nuclear-weapon-free zones in other areas in the world, especially in the Middle East,

Recalling the decisions entitled "Strengthening the review process for the Treaty", "Principles and objectives for nuclear non-proliferation and disarmament" and "Extension of the Treaty on the Non-Proliferation of Nuclear Weapons" and the resolution on the Middle East, all of which were adopted at the 1995 Review and Extension Conference of the Parties to the Treaty on the Non-Proliferation of Nuclear Weapons[4] and the Final Document of the 2000 Review Conference of the Parties to the Treaty on the Non-Proliferation of Nuclear Weapons,[5]

Recalling also the unequivocal undertaking by the nuclear-weapon States to accomplish the total elimination of their nuclear arsenals, leading to nuclear disarmament, in accordance with commitments made under article VI of the Treaty on the Non-Proliferation of Nuclear Weapons,[6]

Welcoming the progress towards a follow-up agreement to the Strategic Arms Reduction Treaty,[7] as reflected in recent statements made by the Presidents of the Russian Federation and of the United States of America,

Welcoming also the outcome of the third session of the Preparatory Committee for the 2010 Review Conference of the Parties to the Treaty on the Non-Proliferation of Nuclear Weapons,[8] at which the Committee adopted the provisional agenda and decisions relating to the organization of the work of the Review Conference,

Welcoming further the recent positive developments in the Conference on Disarmament, which led to the adoption of a programme of work on 29 May 2009,

1. *Continues to emphasize* the central role of the Treaty on the Non-Proliferation of Nuclear Weapons[6] and its universality in achieving nuclear disarmament and nuclear non-proliferation, and calls upon all States parties to respect their obligations;

2. *Calls upon* all States to comply fully with all commitments made regarding nuclear disarmament and nuclear non-proliferation and not to act in any way that may compromise either cause or that may lead to a new nuclear arms race;

---

[4] See *1995 Review and Extension Conference of the Parties to the Treaty on the Non-Proliferation of Nuclear Weapons, Final Document, Part I* (NPT/CONF.1995/32 (Part I) and Corr.2), annex.

[5] *2000 Review Conference of the Parties to the Treaty on the Non-Proliferation of Nuclear Weapons, Final Document*, vols. I-III (NPT/CONF.2000/28 (Parts I–IV)).

[6] United Nations, *Treaty Series*, vol. 729, No. 10485.

[7] *The United Nations Disarmament Yearbook*, vol. 16: 1991 (United Nations publication, Sales No. E.92.IX.1), appendix II.

[8] NPT/CONF.2010/1.

3. *Reaffirms* that the outcome of the 2000 Review Conference of the Parties to the Treaty on the Non-Proliferation of Nuclear Weapons[5] sets out the agreed process for systematic and progressive efforts towards nuclear disarmament, and in this regard renews its call upon the nuclear-weapon States to accelerate the implementation of the practical steps towards nuclear disarmament that were agreed upon at the 2000 Review Conference, thereby contributing to a safer world for all;

4. *Reiterates its call* upon all States parties to spare no effort to achieve the universality of the Treaty on the Non-Proliferation of Nuclear Weapons, and in this regard urges India, Israel and Pakistan to accede to the Treaty as non-nuclear-weapon States promptly and without conditions;

5. *Urges* the Democratic People's Republic of Korea to rescind its announced withdrawal from the Treaty on the Non-Proliferation of Nuclear Weapons, to re-establish cooperation with the International Atomic Energy Agency and to rejoin the Six-Party Talks, with a view to achieving the denuclearization of the Korean Peninsula in a peaceful manner;

6. *Calls upon* all Parties to the Treaty on the Non-Proliferation of Nuclear Weapons to spare no effort to ensure a successful and constructive outcome of the 2010 Review Conference;

7. *Stresses* that the outcome of the 2010 Review Conference should build upon the positive results reached at the 1995 and 2000 Conferences, contribute significantly to the concrete implementation of the outcomes of both Conferences, advance the objective of a nuclear-weapon-free world, strengthen the Treaty on the Non-Proliferation of Nuclear Weapons in all its aspects and contribute to achieving its full implementation and universality;

8. *Calls upon* all States parties to the Treaty on the Non-Proliferation of Nuclear Weapons to work towards the full implementation of the resolution on the Middle East adopted at the 1995 Review Conference;

9. *Calls upon* the States members of the Conference on Disarmament to pursue continued positive developments in that forum, in order to maintain the momentum that led to the adoption of a programme of work on 29 May 2009, and spare no efforts to ensure an early start to the substantive work of the Conference at the beginning of its 2010 session;

10. *Decides* to include in the provisional agenda of its sixty-fifth session the item entitled "Towards a nuclear-weapon-free world: accelerating the implementation of nuclear disarmament commitments" and to review the implementation of the present resolution at that session.

Action by the General Assembly

Date: 2 December 2009 Meeting: 55th plenary meeting
Vote: 169-5-5, as a whole Report: A/64/391
 162-4-2, o.p. 4

Sponsors

Brazil, Egypt, Ireland, Mexico, New Zealand, South Africa, Sweden

Co-sponsors

Austria, Comoros, Costa Rica, Fiji, Guyana, Malta, Norway

Recorded vote

As a whole*

In favour:
Afghanistan, Albania, Algeria, Andorra, Angola, Antigua and Barbuda, Argentina, Armenia, Australia, Austria, Azerbaijan, Bahamas, Bahrain, Bangladesh, Barbados, Belarus, Belgium, Belize, Benin, Bolivia (Plurinational State of), Bosnia and Herzegovina, Botswana, Brazil, Brunei Darussalam, Bulgaria, Burkina Faso, Burundi, Cambodia, Cameroon, Canada, Cape Verde, Chile, China, Colombia, Comoros, Congo, Costa Rica, Côte d'Ivoire, Croatia, Cuba, Cyprus, Czech Republic, Democratic Republic of the Congo, Denmark, Djibouti, Dominica, Dominican Republic, Ecuador, Egypt, El Salvador, Equatorial Guinea, Eritrea, Estonia, Fiji, Finland, Gambia, Georgia, Germany, Ghana, Greece, Grenada, Guatemala, Guinea, Guinea-Bissau, Guyana, Haiti, Honduras, Hungary, Iceland, Indonesia, Iran (Islamic Republic of), Iraq, Ireland, Italy, Jamaica, Japan, Jordan, Kazakhstan, Kenya, Kuwait, Kyrgyzstan, Lao People's Democratic Republic, Latvia, Lebanon, Lesotho, Liberia, Libyan Arab Jamahiriya, Liechtenstein, Lithuania, Luxembourg, Madagascar, Malawi, Malaysia, Maldives, Mali, Malta, Marshall Islands, Mauritania, Mauritius, Mexico, Mongolia, Montenegro, Morocco, Mozambique, Myanmar, Namibia, Nepal, Netherlands, New Zealand, Nicaragua, Niger, Nigeria, Norway, Oman, Panama, Papua New Guinea, Paraguay, Peru, Philippines, Poland, Portugal, Qatar, Republic of Korea, Republic of Moldova, Romania, Russian Federation, Saint Kitts and Nevis, Saint Lucia, Saint Vincent and the Grenadines, Samoa, San Marino, Saudi Arabia, Senegal, Serbia, Seychelles, Sierra Leone, Singapore, Slovakia, Slovenia, Solomon Islands, Somalia, South Africa, Spain, Sri Lanka, Sudan, Suriname, Swaziland, Sweden, Switzerland, Syrian Arab Republic, Tajikistan, Thailand, the former Yugoslav Republic of Macedonia, Togo, Tonga, Trinidad and Tobago, Tunisia, Turkey, Uganda, Ukraine, United Arab Emirates, United Republic of Tanzania, Uruguay, Uzbekistan, Venezuela (Bolivarian Republic of), Viet Nam, Yemen, Zambia, Zimbabwe

---

* Subsequently, the delegation of Ethiopia advised the Secretariat that it had intended to vote in favour. The voting tally above does not reflect this information.

Against:
Democratic People's Republic of Korea, France, India, Israel, United States

Abstaining:
Bhutan, Micronesia (Federated States of), Pakistan, Palau, United Kingdom

Operative paragraph 4*

In favour:
Afghanistan, Albania, Algeria, Andorra, Angola, Antigua and Barbuda, Argentina, Armenia, Australia, Austria, Azerbaijan, Bahamas, Bahrain, Bangladesh, Barbados, Belarus, Belgium, Belize, Benin, Bolivia (Plurinational State of), Bosnia and Herzegovina, Botswana, Brazil, Brunei Darussalam, Bulgaria, Burkina Faso, Burundi, Cambodia, Cameroon, Canada, Cape Verde, Chile, China, Colombia, Comoros, Congo, Costa Rica, Côte d'Ivoire, Croatia, Cuba, Cyprus, Czech Republic, Democratic Republic of the Congo, Denmark, Djibouti, Dominica, Dominican Republic, Ecuador, Egypt, El Salvador, Equatorial Guinea, Eritrea, Estonia, Fiji, Finland, Gambia, Georgia, Germany, Ghana, Greece, Grenada, Guatemala, Guinea, Guinea-Bissau, Guyana, Haiti, Honduras, Hungary, Iceland, Indonesia, Iran (Islamic Republic of), Iraq, Ireland, Italy, Jamaica, Japan, Jordan, Kazakhstan, Kenya, Kuwait, Kyrgyzstan, Latvia, Lebanon, Lesotho, Liberia, Libyan Arab Jamahiriya, Liechtenstein, Lithuania, Luxembourg, Madagascar, Malawi, Malaysia, Maldives, Mali, Malta, Mauritania, Mexico, Mongolia, Montenegro, Morocco, Mozambique, Myanmar, Nepal, Netherlands, New Zealand, Nicaragua, Niger, Nigeria, Norway, Oman, Panama, Papua New Guinea, Paraguay, Peru, Philippines, Poland, Portugal, Qatar, Republic of Korea, Republic of Moldova, Romania, Russian Federation, Saint Kitts and Nevis, Saint Lucia, Saint Vincent and the Grenadines, Samoa, San Marino, Saudi Arabia, Senegal, Serbia, Singapore, Slovakia, Slovenia, Solomon Islands, Somalia, South Africa, Spain, Sri Lanka, Sudan, Suriname, Swaziland, Sweden, Switzerland, Syrian Arab Republic, Thailand, the former Yugoslav Republic of Macedonia, Togo, Trinidad and Tobago, Tunisia, Turkey, Uganda, Ukraine, United Arab Emirates, United Kingdom, United Republic of Tanzania, Uruguay, Uzbekistan, Venezuela (Bolivarian Republic of), Viet Nam, Yemen, Zambia, Zimbabwe

Against:
India, Israel, Pakistan, United States

---

* Subsequently, the delegation of Ethiopia advised the Secretariat that it had intended to vote in favour. The voting tally above does not reflect this information.

Abstaining:
Bhutan, France

Action by the First Committee

Date: 27 October 2009 Meeting: 19th meeting
Vote: 165-5-4 Draft resolution: A/C.1/64/L.54
159-4-2, o.p. 4

Agenda item 97 (c)

64/58 United Nations regional centres for peace and disarmament

Text

The General Assembly,

Recalling its resolutions 60/83 of 8 December 2005, 61/90 of 6 December 2006, 62/50 of 5 December 2007 and 63/76 of 2 December 2008 regarding the maintenance and revitalization of the three United Nations regional centres for peace and disarmament,

Recalling also the reports of the Secretary-General on the United Nations Regional Centre for Peace and Disarmament in Africa,[1] the United Nations Regional Centre for Peace and Disarmament in Asia and the Pacific[2] and the United Nations Regional Centre for Peace, Disarmament and Development in Latin America and the Caribbean,[3]

Reaffirming its decision, taken in 1982 at its twelfth special session, to establish the United Nations Disarmament Information Programme, the purpose of which is to inform, educate and generate public understanding and support for the objectives of the United Nations in the field of arms control and disarmament,[4]

Bearing in mind its resolutions 40/151 G of 16 December 1985, 41/60 J of 3 December 1986, 42/39 D of 30 November 1987 and 44/117 F of 15 December 1989 on the regional centres for peace and disarmament in Nepal, Peru and Togo,

Recognizing that the changes that have taken place in the world have created new opportunities as well as posed new challenges for the pursuit of disarmament, and, in this regard, bearing in mind that the regional centres for peace and disarmament can contribute substantially to understanding and cooperation among States in each particular region in the areas of peace, disarmament and development,

Noting that in paragraph 127 of the Final Document of the Fifteenth Summit Conference of Heads of State and Government of the Movement of Non-Aligned Countries, held in Sharm el-Sheikh, Egypt, from 11 to 16 July 2009, the Heads of State and Government emphasized the importance of the United Nations activities at the regional level to increase the stability and security of its Member States, which could be promoted in a substantive

---
[1] A/64/112.
[2] A/64/111.
[3] A/64/116.
[4] See *Official Records of the General Assembly, Twelfth Special Session, Plenary Meetings*, 1st meeting, paras. 110 and 111.

manner by the maintenance and revitalization of the three regional centres for peace and disarmament,[5]

1. *Reiterates* the importance of the United Nations activities at the regional level to advancement in disarmament and to increase the stability and security of its Member States, which could be promoted in a substantive manner by the maintenance and revitalization of the three regional centres for peace and disarmament;

2. *Reaffirms* that, in order to achieve positive results, it is useful for the three regional centres to carry out dissemination and educational programmes that promote regional peace and security that are aimed at changing basic attitudes with respect to peace and security and disarmament so as to support the achievement of the purposes and principles of the United Nations;

3. *Appeals* to Member States in each region and those that are able to do so, as well as to international governmental and non-governmental organizations and foundations, to make voluntary contributions to the regional centres in their respective regions to strengthen their activities and initiatives;

4. *Emphasizes* the importance of the activities of the Regional Disarmament Branch of the Office for Disarmament Affairs of the Secretariat;

5. *Requests* the Secretary-General to provide all necessary support, within existing resources, to the regional centres in carrying out their programmes of activities;

6. *Decides* to include in the provisional agenda of its sixty-fifth session the item entitled "United Nations regional centres for peace and disarmament".

Action by the General Assembly

Date: 2 December 2009   Meeting: 55th plenary meeting
Vote: Adopted without a vote   Report: A/64/392

Sponsors

Indonesia, on behalf of the States Members of the United Nations that are members of the Movement of Non-Aligned Countries

Action by the First Committee

Date: 28 October 2009   Meeting: 20th meeting
Vote: Adopted without a vote   Draft resolution: A/C.1/64/L.11

---

[5] See A/63/965-S/2009/514, annex.

Agenda item 97 (b)

64/59 Convention on the Prohibition of the Use of Nuclear Weapons

Text

The General Assembly,

Convinced that the use of nuclear weapons poses the most serious threat to the survival of mankind,

Bearing in mind the advisory opinion of the International Court of Justice of 8 July 1996 on the *Legality of the Threat or Use of Nuclear Weapons*,[1]

Convinced that a multilateral, universal and binding agreement prohibiting the use or threat of use of nuclear weapons would contribute to the elimination of the nuclear threat and to the climate for negotiations leading to the ultimate elimination of nuclear weapons, thereby strengthening international peace and security,

Conscious that some steps taken by the Russian Federation and the United States of America towards a reduction of their nuclear weapons and the improvement in the international climate can contribute towards the goal of the complete elimination of nuclear weapons,

Recalling that paragraph 58 of the Final Document of the Tenth Special Session of the General Assembly[2] states that all States should actively participate in efforts to bring about conditions in international relations among States in which a code of peaceful conduct of nations in international affairs could be agreed upon and that would preclude the use or threat of use of nuclear weapons,

Reaffirming that any use of nuclear weapons would be a violation of the Charter of the United Nations and a crime against humanity, as declared in its resolutions 1653 (XVI) of 24 November 1961, 33/71 B of 14 December 1978, 34/83 G of 11 December 1979, 35/152 D of 12 December 1980 and 36/92 I of 9 December 1981,

Determined to achieve an international convention prohibiting the development, production, stockpiling and use of nuclear weapons, leading to their ultimate destruction,

Stressing that an international convention on the prohibition of the use of nuclear weapons would be an important step in a phased programme towards the complete elimination of nuclear weapons, with a specified framework of time,

---

[1] A/51/218, annex; see also *Legality of the Threat or Use of Nuclear Weapons, Advisory Opinion, I.C.J. Reports 1996*, p. 226.

[2] See resolution S-10/2.

Noting with regret that the Conference on Disarmament, during its 2009 session, was unable to undertake negotiations on this subject as called for in General Assembly resolution 63/75 of 2 December 2008,

1. *Reiterates its request* to the Conference on Disarmament to commence negotiations in order to reach agreement on an international convention prohibiting the use or threat of use of nuclear weapons under any circumstances;

2. *Requests* the Conference on Disarmament to report to the General Assembly on the results of those negotiations.

Action by the General Assembly

Date: 2 December 2009   Meeting: 55th plenary meeting
Vote: 116-50-12   Report: A/64/392

Sponsors

Bangladesh, Bhutan, Brunei Darussalam, Cambodia, Cuba, Democratic Republic of the Congo, Egypt, El Salvador, Fiji, Haiti, **India**, Indonesia, Iran (Islamic Republic of), Jamaica, Jordan, Kuwait, Libyan Arab Jamahiriya, Madagascar, Malaysia, Mauritius, Myanmar, Nepal, Nicaragua, Philippines, Sudan, Viet Nam, Zambia

Co-sponsors

Bolivia (Plurinational State of), Comoros, Congo

Recorded vote*

In favour:

Afghanistan, Algeria, Angola, Antigua and Barbuda, Argentina, Bahamas, Bahrain, Bangladesh, Barbados, Belize, Benin, Bhutan, Bolivia (Plurinational State of), Botswana, Brazil, Brunei Darussalam, Burkina Faso, Burundi, Cambodia, Cameroon, Cape Verde, Chile, China, Colombia, Congo, Costa Rica, Côte d'Ivoire, Cuba, Democratic People's Republic of Korea, Democratic Republic of the Congo, Djibouti, Dominica, Dominican Republic, Ecuador, Egypt, El Salvador, Equatorial Guinea, Eritrea, Fiji, Gambia, Ghana, Grenada, Guatemala, Guinea, Guinea-Bissau, Guyana, Haiti, Honduras, India, Indonesia, Iran (Islamic Republic of), Iraq, Jamaica, Jordan, Kenya, Kuwait, Lao People's Democratic Republic, Lebanon, Lesotho, Liberia, Libyan Arab Jamahiriya, Madagascar, Malawi, Malaysia, Maldives, Mali, Mauritania, Mauritius, Mexico, Mongolia, Morocco, Mozambique, Myanmar, Namibia, Nepal, Nicaragua, Niger, Nigeria, Oman, Pakistan, Panama, Papua New Guinea, Paraguay, Peru, Philippines, Qatar, Saint Kitts and

---

* Subsequently, the delegation of Ethiopia advised the Secretariat that it had intended to vote in favour. The voting tally above does not reflect this information.

Nevis, Saint Lucia, Saint Vincent and the Grenadines, Samoa, Saudi Arabia, Senegal, Singapore, Solomon Islands, South Africa, Sri Lanka, Sudan, Suriname, Swaziland, Syrian Arab Republic, Tajikistan, Thailand, Togo, Tonga, Trinidad and Tobago, Tunisia, Turkmenistan, Uganda, United Arab Emirates, United Republic of Tanzania, Uruguay, Venezuela (Bolivarian Republic of), Viet Nam, Yemen, Zambia, Zimbabwe

Against:
Albania, Andorra, Australia, Austria, Belgium, Bosnia and Herzegovina, Bulgaria, Canada, Croatia, Cyprus, Czech Republic, Denmark, Estonia, Finland, France, Georgia, Germany, Greece, Hungary, Iceland, Ireland, Israel, Italy, Latvia, Liechtenstein, Lithuania, Luxembourg, Malta, Micronesia (Federated States of), Monaco, Montenegro, Netherlands, New Zealand, Norway, Palau, Poland, Portugal, Republic of Moldova, Romania, San Marino, Slovakia, Slovenia, Spain, Sweden, Switzerland, the former Yugoslav Republic of Macedonia, Turkey, Ukraine, United Kingdom, United States

Abstaining:
Armenia, Azerbaijan, Belarus, Comoros, Japan, Kazakhstan, Kyrgyzstan, Marshall Islands, Republic of Korea, Russian Federation, Serbia, Uzbekistan

Action by the First Committee

Date: 27 October 2009   Meeting: 19th meeting
Vote: 116-50-11   Draft resolution: A/C.1/64/L.20

Agenda item 97 (a)

64/60 United Nations Regional Centre for Peace, Disarmament and Development in Latin America and the Caribbean

Text

The General Assembly,

Recalling its resolutions 41/60 J of 3 December 1986, 42/39 K of 30 November 1987 and 43/76 H of 7 December 1988 on the United Nations Regional Centre for Peace, Disarmament and Development in Latin America and the Caribbean, with headquarters in Lima,

Recalling also its resolutions 46/37 F of 9 December 1991, 48/76 E of 16 December 1993, 49/76 D of 15 December 1994, 50/71 C of 12 December 1995, 52/220 of 22 December 1997, 53/78 F of 4 December 1998, 54/55 F of 1 December 1999, 55/34 E of 20 November 2000, 56/25 E of 29 November 2001, 57/89 of 22 November 2002, 58/60 of 8 December 2003, 59/99 of 3 December 2004, 60/84 of 8 December 2005, 61/92 of 6 December 2006, 62/49 of 5 December 2007 and 63/74 of 2 December 2008,

Recognizing that the Regional Centre has continued to provide substantive support for the implementation of regional and subregional initiatives and has intensified its contribution to the coordination of United Nations efforts towards peace and disarmament and for the promotion of economic and social development,

Reaffirming the mandate of the Regional Centre to provide, on request, substantive support for the initiatives and other activities of the Member States of the region for the implementation of measures for peace and disarmament and for the promotion of economic and social development,

Taking note of the report of the Secretary-General,[1] and expressing its appreciation for the important assistance provided by the Regional Centre to many countries in the region for the development of plans to reduce and prevent armed violence from an arms control perspective and for promoting the implementation of relevant agreements and treaties,

Emphasizing the need for the Regional Centre to develop and strengthen its activities and programmes in a comprehensive and balanced manner, in accordance with its mandate,

Recalling the report of the Group of Governmental Experts on the relationship between disarmament and development,[2] referred to in General Assembly resolution 59/78 of 3 December 2004, which is of utmost interest

---

[1] A/64/116.
[2] See A/59/119.

with regard to the role that the Regional Centre plays in promoting the issue in the region in pursuit of its mandate to promote economic and social development related to peace and disarmament,

Noting that security and disarmament issues have always been recognized as significant topics in Latin America and the Caribbean, the first inhabited region in the world to be declared a nuclear-weapon-free zone,

Welcoming the support provided by the Regional Centre to strengthening the nuclear-weapon-free zone established by the Treaty for the Prohibition of Nuclear Weapons in Latin America and the Caribbean (Treaty of Tlatelolco),[3] as well as to promoting and assisting the ratification and implementation of existing multilateral agreements related to weapons of mass destruction and to promoting peace and disarmament education projects during the period under review,

Bearing in mind the important role of the Regional Centre in promoting confidence-building measures, arms control and limitation, disarmament and development at the regional level,

Bearing in mind also the importance of information, research, education and training for peace, disarmament and development in order to achieve understanding and cooperation among States,

1. *Reiterates its strong support* for the role of the United Nations Regional Centre for Peace, Disarmament and Development in Latin America and the Caribbean in the promotion of United Nations activities at the regional level to strengthen peace, disarmament, stability, security and development among its member States;

2. *Expresses its satisfaction* for the activities carried out in the past year by the Regional Centre, and requests the Centre to take into account the proposals to be submitted by the countries of the region in promoting confidence-building measures, arms control and limitation, transparency, disarmament and development at the regional level;

3. *Expresses its appreciation* for the political support and financial contributions to the Regional Centre, which are essential for its continued operation;

4. *Appeals* to Member States, in particular those within the Latin American and Caribbean region, and to international governmental and non-governmental organizations and foundations to make and to increase voluntary contributions to strengthen the Regional Centre, its programme of activities and the implementation thereof;

5. *Invites* all States of the region to continue to take part in the activities of the Regional Centre, proposing items for inclusion in its

---

[3] United Nations, *Treaty Series*, vol. 634, No. 9068.

programme of activities and making greater and better use of the potential of the Centre to meet the current challenges facing the international community with a view to fulfilling the aims of the Charter of the United Nations in the areas of peace, disarmament and development;

6. *Recognizes* that the Regional Centre has an important role in the promotion and development of regional initiatives agreed upon by the countries of Latin America and the Caribbean in the field of weapons of mass destruction, in particular nuclear weapons, and conventional arms, including small arms and light weapons, as well as in the relationship between disarmament and development;

7. *Encourages* the Regional Centre to further develop activities in all countries of the region in the important areas of peace, disarmament and development;

8. *Requests* the Secretary-General to report to the General Assembly at its sixty-fifth session on the implementation of the present resolution;

9. *Decides* to include in the provisional agenda of its sixty-fifth session the item entitled "United Nations Regional Centre for Peace, Disarmament and Development in Latin America and the Caribbean".

Action by the General Assembly

Date: 2 December 2009　　　Meeting: 55th plenary meeting
Vote: Adopted without a vote　Report: A/64/392

Sponsors

Peru, on behalf of the States Members of the United Nations that are members of the Group of Latin American and Caribbean States

Action by the First Committee

Date: 28 October 2009　　　Meeting: 20th meeting
Vote: Adopted without a vote　Draft resolution: A/C.1/64/L.22

Agenda item 97 (e)

64/61 Regional confidence-building measures: activities of the United Nations Standing Advisory Committee on Security Questions in Central Africa

Text

The General Assembly,

Recalling its previous relevant resolutions, in particular resolution 63/78 of 2 December 2008,

Recalling also the guidelines for general and complete disarmament adopted at its tenth special session, the first special session devoted to disarmament,

Bearing in mind the establishment by the Secretary-General on 28 May 1992 of the United Nations Standing Advisory Committee on Security Questions in Central Africa, the purpose of which is to encourage arms limitation, disarmament, non-proliferation and development in the subregion,

Reaffirming that the purpose of the Standing Advisory Committee is to conduct reconstruction and confidence-building activities in Central Africa among its member States, including through confidence-building and arms limitation measures,

Convinced that the resources released by disarmament, including regional disarmament, can be devoted to economic and social development and to the protection of the environment for the benefit of all peoples, in particular those of the developing countries,

Considering the importance and effectiveness of confidence-building measures taken on the initiative and with the participation of all States concerned and taking into account the specific characteristics of each region, since such measures can contribute to regional stability and to international peace and security,

Convinced that development can be achieved only in a climate of peace, security and mutual confidence both within and among States,

Recalling the Brazzaville Declaration on Cooperation for Peace and Security in Central Africa,[1] the Bata Declaration for the Promotion of Lasting Democracy, Peace and Development in Central Africa[2] and the Yaoundé Declaration on Peace, Security and Stability in Central Africa,[3]

---

[1] A/50/474, annex I.
[2] A/53/258-S/1998/763, annex II, appendix I.
[3] A/53/868-S/1999/303, annex II.

Bearing in mind resolutions 1196 (1998) and 1197 (1998), adopted by the Security Council on 16 and 18 September 1998 respectively, following its consideration of the report of the Secretary-General on the causes of conflict and the promotion of durable peace and sustainable development in Africa,[4]

Emphasizing the need to strengthen the capacity for conflict prevention and peacekeeping in Africa, and welcoming the close cooperation established between the United Nations and the Economic Community of Central African States for that purpose,

1. *Reaffirms its support* for efforts aimed at promoting confidence-building measures at the regional and subregional levels in order to ease tensions and conflicts in Central Africa and to further sustainable peace, stability and development in the subregion;

2. *Reaffirms* the importance of disarmament and arms limitation programmes in Central Africa carried out by the States of the subregion with the support of the United Nations, the African Union and other international partners;

3. *Welcomes* the adoption by the States members of the United Nations Standing Advisory Committee on Security Questions in Central Africa on 8 May 2009 of the Code of Conduct for the Defence and Security Forces in Central Africa[5] and the major strides made by States in the drafting of a legal instrument on the control of small arms and light weapons in Central Africa, and encourages interested countries to provide their financial support to the implementation of the "Sao Tome Initiative";

4. *Encourages* the States members of the Standing Advisory Committee to carry out the programmes of activities adopted at their ministerial meetings;

5. *Also encourages* the States members of the Standing Advisory Committee to continue their efforts to render the early-warning mechanism for Central Africa fully operational as an instrument for analysing and monitoring the political situation in the subregion within the framework of the prevention of crises and armed conflicts, and requests the Secretary-General to provide the necessary assistance for its smooth functioning;

6. *Appeals* to the international community to support the efforts undertaken by the States concerned to implement disarmament, demobilization and reintegration programmes;

7. *Requests* the Secretary-General and the Office of the United Nations High Commissioner for Refugees to continue their assistance to the countries of Central Africa in tackling the problems of refugees and displaced persons in their territories;

---

[4] A/52/871-S/1998/318.
[5] A/64/85-S/2009/288, annex II.

8. *Requests* the Secretary-General and the United Nations High Commissioner for Human Rights to continue to provide their full assistance for the proper functioning of the Subregional Centre for Human Rights and Democracy in Central Africa;

9. *Welcomes* the adoption on 8 May 2009 of the Libreville Declaration calling upon States members of the Standing Advisory Committee to contribute to the Trust Fund for the United Nations Standing Advisory Committee on Security Questions in Central Africa;[6]

10. *Urges* other Member States and intergovernmental and non-governmental organizations to support the activities of the Standing Advisory Committee effectively through voluntary contributions to the Trust Fund;

11. *Expresses its satisfaction* to the Secretary-General for his support for the revitalization of the activities of the Standing Advisory Committee, and requests him to continue to provide the assistance needed to ensure the success of its regular biannual meetings;

12. *Calls upon* the Secretary-General to submit to the General Assembly at its sixty-fifth session a report on the implementation of the present resolution;

13. *Decides* to include in the provisional agenda of its sixty-fifth session the item entitled "Regional confidence-building measures: activities of the United Nations Standing Advisory Committee on Security Questions in Central Africa".

Action by the General Assembly

Date: 2 December 2009   Meeting: 55th plenary meeting
Vote: Adopted without a vote   Report: A/64/392

Sponsors

Gabon

Co-sponsors

Angola, Benin, Cameroon, Central African Republic, Comoros, Congo, Montenegro, Togo

Action by the First Committee

Date: 29 October 2009   Meeting: 21st meeting
Vote: Adopted without a vote   Draft resolution: A/C.1/64/L.27

---

[6] Ibid., annex I.

Agenda item 97 (f)

64/62 United Nations Regional Centre for Peace and Disarmament in Africa

Text

The General Assembly,

Mindful of the provisions of Article 11, paragraph 1, of the Charter of the United Nations stipulating that a function of the General Assembly is to consider the general principles of cooperation in the maintenance of international peace and security, including the principles governing disarmament and arms limitation,

Recalling its resolutions 40/151 G of 16 December 1985, 41/60 D of 3 December 1986, 42/39 J of 30 November 1987 and 43/76 D of 7 December 1988 on the United Nations Regional Centre for Peace and Disarmament in Africa and its resolutions 46/36 F of 6 December 1991 and 47/52 G of 9 December 1992 on regional disarmament, including confidence-building measures,

Recalling also its resolutions 48/76 E of 16 December 1993, 49/76 D of 15 December 1994, 50/71 C of 12 December 1995, 51/46 E of 10 December 1996, 52/220 of 22 December 1997, 53/78 C of 4 December 1998, 54/55 B of 1 December 1999, 55/34 D of 20 November 2000, 56/25 D of 29 November 2001, 57/91 of 22 November 2002, 58/61 of 8 December 2003, 59/101 of 3 December 2004, 60/86 of 8 December 2005, 61/93 of 6 December 2006, 62/216 of 22 December 2007 and 63/80 of 2 December 2008,

Reaffirming the role of the Regional Centre in promoting peace, security and disarmament at the regional level,

Taking into account the need to strengthen the existing cooperation between the Regional Centre and the African Union, in particular its institutions in the fields of peace, security and disarmament, as well as with relevant United Nations bodies and programmes in Africa for greater effectiveness, and considering the focus of its resolution 63/310 of 14 September 2009 on cooperation between the United Nations and the African Union, and in particular the need to address the problems related to peace and disarmament, and the communiqué adopted by the Peace and Security Council of the African Union at its two-hundredth meeting, held in Addis Ababa on 21 August 2009, in which the Council welcomes the increased collaboration between the Regional Centre and the African Union and regional organizations in the areas of peace, security and disarmament,

Recalling the report of the Secretary-General,[1] in which he stated that an increase in the Regional Centre's human and operational capacity would enable it to discharge its mandate in full and to respond more effectively to requests for assistance from African States,

Taking note of the revitalization of the Regional Centre and the progress made in covering all of Africa and widening its scope of activities related to peace and disarmament in implementation of the recommendations made by the Consultative Mechanism for the Reorganization of the United Nations Regional Centre for Peace and Disarmament in Africa established by resolution 60/86 of 8 December 2005,[2]

Noting the timely implementation by the Secretary-General of its resolution 62/216 of 22 December 2007 concerning the future work programme of the Regional Centre, as well as its staffing and funding,

Deeply concerned that, as noted in the report of the Secretary-General,[1] despite the decision taken in Khartoum in January 2006 by the Executive Council of the African Union,[3] in which the Council called upon member States to make voluntary contributions to the Regional Centre to maintain its operations, no such funds have been received to ensure its operations,

1. *Takes note* of the report of the Secretary-General;[4]

2. *Notes* the successful conclusion of the process of revitalization of the United Nations Regional Centre for Peace and Disarmament in Africa through the strengthening of its financial and human capacities;

3. *Notes with appreciation* the efforts of the Regional Centre to align its actions with the priorities identified in the recommendations of the Consultative Mechanism for the Reorganization of the United Nations Regional Centre for Peace and Disarmament in Africa;[2]

4. *Welcomes* the undertaking by the Regional Centre of new initiatives and projects in the fields of security sector reform and practical disarmament measures, as detailed in the report of the Secretary-General;[4]

5. *Also welcomes* the efforts made by the Regional Centre to revitalize its activities and extend its operations to cover all of Africa, in order to respond to the evolving needs of the continent in the areas of peace, security and disarmament;

6. *Urges* all States, as well as international governmental and non-governmental organizations and foundations, to make voluntary contributions to support the programmes and activities of the Regional Centre and facilitate their implementation;

---

[1] A/63/163.
[2] See A/62/167.
[3] A/60/693, annex II, decision EX.CL/Dec.263 (VIII).
[4] A/64/112.

7. *Urges*, in particular, States members of the African Union to make voluntary contributions to the Regional Centre's trust fund in conformity with the decision taken by the Executive Council of the African Union in Khartoum in January 2006;[3]

8. *Requests* the Secretary-General to facilitate closer cooperation between the Regional Centre and the African Union, in particular in the areas of peace, security and disarmament;

9. *Also requests* the Secretary-General to continue to provide the necessary support to the Regional Centre for greater achievements and results;

10. *Further requests* the Secretary-General to report to the General Assembly at its sixty-sixth session on the implementation of the present resolution;

11. *Decides* to include in the provisional agenda of its sixty-sixth session the item entitled "United Nations Regional Centre for Peace and Disarmament in Africa".

Action by the General Assembly

Date: 2 December 2009 Meeting: 55th plenary meeting
Vote: Adopted without a vote Report: A/64/392

Sponsors

Nigeria, on behalf of the States Members of the United Nations that are members of the group of African States

Action by the First Committee

Date: 30 October 2009 Meeting: 22nd meeting
Vote: Adopted without a vote Draft resolution: A/C.1/64/L.32/Rev.2

Agenda item 97 (d)

64/63   United Nations Regional Centre for Peace and Disarmament in Asia and the Pacific

Text

The General Assembly,

Recalling its resolutions 42/39 D of 30 November 1987 and 44/117 F of 15 December 1989, by which it established the United Nations Regional Centre for Peace and Disarmament in Asia and renamed it the United Nations Regional Centre for Peace and Disarmament in Asia and the Pacific, with headquarters in Kathmandu and with the mandate of providing, on request, substantive support for the initiatives and other activities mutually agreed upon by the Member States of the Asia-Pacific region for the implementation of measures for peace and disarmament, through appropriate utilization of available resources,

Welcoming the physical operation of the Regional Centre from Kathmandu in accordance with General Assembly resolution 62/52 of 5 December 2007,

Recalling the Regional Centre's mandate of providing, on request, substantive support for the initiatives and other activities mutually agreed upon by the Member States of the Asia-Pacific region for the implementation of measures for peace and disarmament,

Expressing its appreciation to the Regional Centre for its important work in promoting confidence-building measures through the organization of meetings, conferences and workshops in the region, including conferences held on Jeju Island, Republic of Korea, from 24 to 26 November 2008 and in Niigata, Japan, from 26 to 28 August 2009,

Concerned by the report of the Secretary-General, in which he indicates that in order to be able to carry out its mandate fully and effectively, the Regional Centre needs to rely on a stable core team of skilled professional and support staff,[1]

Appreciating the timely execution by Nepal of its financial commitments for the physical operation of the Regional Centre,

1.   *Welcomes* the physical operation of the United Nations Regional Centre for Peace and Disarmament in Asia and the Pacific from Kathmandu in close cooperation with Member States;

---

[1]   See A/64/111, para. 24.

2. *Expresses its gratitude* to the Government of Nepal for its cooperation and financial support, which has allowed the new office of the Regional Centre to operate from Kathmandu;

3. *Expresses its appreciation* to the Secretary-General and the Office for Disarmament Affairs of the Secretariat for providing necessary support with a view to ensuring the smooth operation of the Regional Centre from Kathmandu and to enabling the Centre to function effectively;

4. *Appeals* to Member States, in particular those within the Asia-Pacific region, as well as to international governmental and non-governmental organizations and foundations, to make voluntary contributions, the only resources of the Regional Centre, to strengthen the programme of activities of the Centre and the implementation thereof;

5. *Reaffirms its strong support* for the role of the Regional Centre in the promotion of United Nations activities at the regional level to strengthen peace, stability and security among its Member States;

6. *Underlines* the importance of the Kathmandu process for the development of the practice of region-wide security and disarmament dialogues;

7. *Requests* the Secretary-General to report to the General Assembly at its sixty-fifth session on the implementation of the present resolution;

8. *Decides* to include in the provisional agenda of its sixty-fifth session the item entitled "United Nations Regional Centre for Peace and Disarmament in Asia and the Pacific".

Action by the General Assembly

Date: 2 December 2009 Meeting: 55th plenary meeting
Vote: Adopted without a vote Report: A/64/392

Sponsors

Afghanistan, Australia, Bangladesh, Bhutan, China, India, Indonesia, Japan, Kazakhstan, Maldives, Micronesia (Federated States of), Mongolia, Myanmar, Nauru, **Nepal**, New Zealand, Pakistan, Sri Lanka, Thailand, Viet Nam

Co-sponsors

Comoros, Kyrgyzstan, Papua New Guinea, Samoa, Timor-Leste

Action by the First Committee

Date: 28 October 2009 Meeting: 20th meeting
Vote: Adopted without a vote Draft resolution: A/C.1/64/L.45

Agenda item 98 (a)

64/64   Report of the Conference on Disarmament

Text

The General Assembly,

Having considered the report of the Conference on Disarmament,[1]

Convinced that the Conference on Disarmament, as the sole multilateral disarmament negotiating forum of the international community, has the primary role in substantive negotiations on priority questions of disarmament,

Recognizing the address by the Secretary-General of the United Nations, as well as the addresses by Ministers for Foreign Affairs and other high-level officials in the Conference on Disarmament, as expressions of support for the endeavours of the Conference and its role as the sole multilateral disarmament negotiating forum,

Recognizing also the need to conduct multilateral negotiations with the aim of reaching agreement on concrete issues,

Recalling, in this respect, that the Conference on Disarmament has a number of urgent and important issues for negotiation,

Considering that the present international climate should give additional impetus to multilateral negotiations with the aim of reaching concrete agreements,

Acknowledging the support of the United Nations Security Council summit on nuclear non-proliferation and nuclear disarmament, held on 24 September 2009, for the work of the Conference on Disarmament,

Bearing in mind the decision of the Conference on Disarmament of 29 May 2009[2] to establish four working groups and appoint three special coordinators, including one working group under agenda item 1 entitled "Cessation of the nuclear arms race and nuclear disarmament", which shall negotiate a treaty banning the production of fissile material for nuclear weapons or other nuclear explosive devices, on the basis of the report of the Special Coordinator of 1995[3] and the mandate contained therein, without prescribing or precluding any outcome of discussions in the other three working groups, with a view to enabling future compromise and including the possibility of future negotiations under any agenda item, thus upholding the nature of the Conference,

---

[1] *Official Records of the General Assembly, Sixty-fourth Session, Supplement No. 27* (A/64/27).
[2] Ibid., sect. II.D; see also CD/1864.
[3] CD/1299.

Appreciating the continued cooperation among the States members of the Conference on Disarmament as well as the six successive Presidents of the Conference at its 2009 session,

Recognizing the importance of continuing consultations on the question of the expansion of the membership of the Conference on Disarmament,

Taking note of significant contributions made during the 2009 session to promote substantive discussions on issues on the agenda, as well as of discussions held on other issues that could also be relevant to the current international security environment,

Welcoming the enhanced engagement between civil society and the Conference on Disarmament at its 2009 session according to decisions taken by the Conference,

Stressing the urgent need for the Conference on Disarmament to commence its substantive work at the beginning of its 2010 session,

1. *Reaffirms* the role of the Conference on Disarmament as the sole multilateral disarmament negotiating forum of the international community;

2. *Welcomes* the consensus adoption of a programme of work for the 2009 session of the Conference on Disarmament,[2] including the establishment of four working groups and the appointment of three special coordinators;

3. *Takes note* of the active discussions held on the implementation of the programme of work at the 2009 session of the Conference on Disarmament, as duly reflected in the report[1] and the records of the plenary meetings;

4. *Welcomes* the decision of the Conference on Disarmament to request the current President and the incoming President to conduct consultations during the intersessional period and, if possible, make recommendations, taking into account all relevant proposals, past, present and future, including those submitted as documents of the Conference on Disarmament, views presented and discussions held, and to endeavour to keep the membership of the Conference informed, as appropriate, of their consultations;

5. *Requests* all States members of the Conference on Disarmament to cooperate with the current President and successive Presidents in their efforts to guide the Conference to the early commencement of substantive work, including negotiations, in its 2010 session;

6. *Requests* the Secretary-General to continue to ensure and strengthen, if needed, the provision to the Conference on Disarmament of all necessary administrative, substantive and conference support services;

7. *Requests* the Conference on Disarmament to submit a report on its work to the General Assembly at its sixty-fifth session;

8. *Decides* to include in the provisional agenda of its sixty-fifth session the item entitled "Report of the Conference on Disarmament".

Action by the General Assembly

Date: 2 December 2009　　　Meeting: 55th plenary meeting
Vote: Adopted without a vote　　Report: A/64/393

Sponsors

Algeria, Argentina, Australia, **Austria**, Viet Nam, Zimbabwe

Action by the First Committee

Date: 30 October 2009　　　Meeting: 22nd meeting
Vote: Adopted without a vote　　Draft resolution: A/C.1/64/L.41

Agenda item 98 (b)

64/65   Report of the Disarmament Commission

Text

The General Assembly,

Having considered the report of the Disarmament Commission,[1]

Recalling its resolutions 47/54 A of 9 December 1992, 47/54 G of 8 April 1993, 48/77 A of 16 December 1993, 49/77 A of 15 December 1994, 50/72 D of 12 December 1995, 51/47 B of 10 December 1996, 52/40 B of 9 December 1997, 53/79 A of 4 December 1998, 54/56 A of 1 December 1999, 55/35 C of 20 November 2000, 56/26 A of 29 November 2001, 57/95 of 22 November 2002, 58/67 of 8 December 2003, 59/105 of 3 December 2004, 60/91 of 8 December 2005, 61/98 of 6 December 2006, 62/54 of 5 December 2007 and 63/83 of 2 December 2008,

Considering the role that the Disarmament Commission has been called upon to play and the contribution that it should make in examining and submitting recommendations on various problems in the field of disarmament and in the promotion of the implementation of the relevant decisions adopted by the General Assembly at its tenth special session,

1.   *Takes note* of the report of the Disarmament Commission;[1]

2.   *Reaffirms* the validity of its decision 52/492 of 8 September 1998, concerning the efficient functioning of the Disarmament Commission;

3.   *Recalls* its resolution 61/98, by which it adopted additional measures for improving the effectiveness of the Commission's methods of work;

4.   *Reaffirms* the mandate of the Disarmament Commission as the specialized, deliberative body within the United Nations multilateral disarmament machinery that allows for in-depth deliberations on specific disarmament issues, leading to the submission of concrete recommendations on those issues;

5.   *Also reaffirms* the importance of further enhancing the dialogue and cooperation among the First Committee, the Disarmament Commission and the Conference on Disarmament;

6.   *Requests* the Disarmament Commission to continue its work in accordance with its mandate, as set forth in paragraph 118 of the Final Document of the Tenth Special Session of the General Assembly,[2] and with

---

[1]   *Official Records of the General Assembly, Sixty-fourth Session, Supplement No. 42* (A/64/42).
[2]   Resolution S-10/2.

paragraph 3 of Assembly resolution 37/78 H of 9 December 1982, and to that end to make every effort to achieve specific recommendations on the items on its agenda, taking into account the adopted "Ways and means to enhance the functioning of the Disarmament Commission";[3]

7. *Recommends* that the Disarmament Commission continue the consideration of the following items at its substantive session of 2010:

(*a*) Recommendations for achieving the objective of nuclear disarmament and non-proliferation of nuclear weapons;

(*b*) Elements of a draft declaration of the 2010s as the fourth disarmament decade;

(*c*) Practical confidence-building measures in the field of conventional weapons. This item will be taken up upon the conclusion of the preparation of the elements of a draft declaration of the 2010s as the fourth disarmament decade, preferably by 2010 and in any case no later than 2011;

8. *Requests* the Disarmament Commission to meet for a period not exceeding three weeks during 2010, namely from 29 March to 16 April, and to submit a substantive report to the General Assembly at its sixty-fifth session;

9. *Requests* the Secretary-General to transmit to the Disarmament Commission the annual report of the Conference on Disarmament,[4] together with all the official records of the sixty-fourth session of the General Assembly relating to disarmament matters, and to render all assistance that the Commission may require for implementing the present resolution;

10. *Also requests* the Secretary-General to ensure full provision to the Disarmament Commission and its subsidiary bodies of interpretation and translation facilities in the official languages and to assign, as a matter of priority, all the necessary resources and services, including verbatim records, to that end;

11. *Decides* to include in the provisional agenda of its sixty-fifth session the item entitled "Report of the Disarmament Commission".

Action by the General Assembly

Date: 2 December 2009 Meeting: 55th plenary meeting
Vote: Adopted without a vote Report: A/64/393

Sponsors

Poland, on behalf of the members of the extended Bureau of the Disarmament Commission, namely Azerbaijan, Benin, Bolivia

---

[3] A/CN.10/137.
[4] *Official Records of the General Assembly, Sixty-fourth Session, Supplement No. 27* (A/64/27).

(Plurinational State of), Italy, Netherlands, Poland, South Africa, Switzerland, Venezuela (Bolivarian Republic of)

Co-sponsors

Brazil, Colombia, the Comoros, Kazakhstan, Philippines

Action by the First Committee

Date: 28 October 2009　　　Meeting:　　20th meeting
Vote: Adopted without a vote　　Draft resolution: A/C.1/64/L.52

Agenda item 99

64/66 The risk of nuclear proliferation in the Middle East

Text

The General Assembly,

Bearing in mind its relevant resolutions,

Taking note of the relevant resolutions adopted by the General Conference of the International Atomic Energy Agency, the latest of which are resolutions GC(53)/RES/16, adopted on 17 September 2009 and GC(53)/RES/17, adopted on 18 September 2009,[1]

Cognizant that the proliferation of nuclear weapons in the region of the Middle East would pose a serious threat to international peace and security,

Mindful of the immediate need for placing all nuclear facilities in the region of the Middle East under full-scope safeguards of the Agency,

Recalling the decision on principles and objectives for nuclear non-proliferation and disarmament adopted by the 1995 Review and Extension Conference of the Parties to the Treaty on the Non-Proliferation of Nuclear Weapons on 11 May 1995,[2] in which the Conference urged universal adherence to the Treaty[3] as an urgent priority and called upon all States not yet parties to the Treaty to accede to it at the earliest date, particularly those States that operate unsafeguarded nuclear facilities,

Recognizing with satisfaction that, in the Final Document of the 2000 Review Conference of the Parties to the Treaty on the Non-Proliferation of Nuclear Weapons, the Conference undertook to make determined efforts towards the achievement of the goal of universality of the Treaty, called upon those remaining States not parties to the Treaty to accede to it, thereby accepting an international legally binding commitment not to acquire nuclear weapons or nuclear explosive devices and to accept Agency safeguards on all their nuclear activities, and underlined the necessity of universal adherence to the Treaty and of strict compliance by all parties with their obligations under the Treaty,[4]

---

[1] See International Atomic Energy Agency, *Resolutions and Other Decisions of the General Conference, Fifty-third Regular Session, 14–18 September 2009* (GC(53)/RES/DEC(2009)).

[2] See *1995 Review and Extension Conference of the Parties to the Treaty on the Non-Proliferation of Nuclear Weapons, Final Document, Part I* (NPT/CONF.1995/32 (Part I) and Corr.2), annex.

[3] United Nations, *Treaty Series*, vol. 729, No. 10485.

[4] See *2000 Review Conference of the Parties to the Treaty on the Non-Proliferation of Nuclear Weapons, Final Document*, vol. I (NPT/CONF.2000/28 (Parts I and II)), part I, section entitled "Article IX".

Recalling the resolution on the Middle East adopted by the 1995 Review and Extension Conference on 11 May 1995,[2] in which the Conference noted with concern the continued existence in the Middle East of unsafeguarded nuclear facilities, reaffirmed the importance of the early realization of universal adherence to the Treaty and called upon all States in the Middle East that had not yet done so, without exception, to accede to the Treaty as soon as possible and to place all their nuclear facilities under full-scope Agency safeguards,

Noting that Israel remains the only State in the Middle East that has not yet become party to the Treaty,

Concerned about the threats posed by the proliferation of nuclear weapons to the security and stability of the Middle East region,

Stressing the importance of taking confidence-building measures, in particular the establishment of a nuclear-weapon-free zone in the Middle East, in order to enhance peace and security in the region and to consolidate the global non-proliferation regime,

Emphasizing the need for all parties directly concerned to seriously consider taking the practical and urgent steps required for the implementation of the proposal to establish a nuclear-weapon-free zone in the region of the Middle East in accordance with the relevant resolutions of the General Assembly and, as a means of promoting this objective, inviting the countries concerned to adhere to the Treaty and, pending the establishment of the zone, to agree to place all their nuclear activities under Agency safeguards,

Noting that one hundred and eighty-one States have signed the Comprehensive Nuclear-Test-Ban Treaty,[5] including a number of States in the region,

1. *Welcomes* the conclusions on the Middle East of the 2000 Review Conference of the Parties to the Treaty on the Non-Proliferation of Nuclear Weapons;[6]

2. *Reaffirms* the importance of Israel's accession to the Treaty on the Non-Proliferation of Nuclear Weapons[3] and placement of all its nuclear facilities under comprehensive International Atomic Energy Agency safeguards, in realizing the goal of universal adherence to the Treaty in the Middle East;

3. *Calls upon* that State to accede to the Treaty without further delay and not to develop, produce, test or otherwise acquire nuclear weapons, and to renounce possession of nuclear weapons, and to place all its unsafeguarded

---

[5] See resolution 50/245.
[6] See *2000 Review Conference of the Parties to the Treaty on the Non-Proliferation of Nuclear Weapons, Final Document*, vol. I (NPT/CONF.2000/28 (Parts I and II)), part I, section entitled "Article VII and the security of non-nuclear-weapon States", para. 16.

nuclear facilities under full-scope Agency safeguards as an important confidence-building measure among all States of the region and as a step towards enhancing peace and security;

4. *Requests* the Secretary-General to report to the General Assembly at its sixty-fifth session on the implementation of the present resolution;

5. *Decides* to include in the provisional agenda of its sixty-fifth session the item entitled "The risk of nuclear proliferation in the Middle East".

Action by the General Assembly

Date: 2 December 2009
Vote: 167-6-6, as a whole
164-5-5, p.p. 6

Meeting: 55th plenary meeting
Report: A/64/394

Sponsors

Algeria, Bahrain, Comoros, Djibouti, **Egypt**, Iraq, Jordan, Kuwait, Lebanon, Libyan Arab Jamahiriya, Mauritania, Morocco, Oman, Qatar, Saudi Arabia, Sudan, Syrian Arab Republic, Tunisia, United Arab Emirates, Yemen, Palestine

Co-sponsors

Bolivia, Gabon, Somalia

Recorded vote

As a whole*

In favour:

Afghanistan, Albania, Algeria, Andorra, Angola, Antigua and Barbuda, Argentina, Armenia, Austria, Azerbaijan, Bahamas, Bahrain, Bangladesh, Barbados, Belarus, Belgium, Belize, Benin, Bhutan, Bolivia (Plurinational State of), Bosnia and Herzegovina, Botswana, Brazil, Brunei Darussalam, Bulgaria, Burkina Faso, Burundi, Cambodia, Cape Verde, Chile, China, Colombia, Comoros, Congo, Costa Rica, Croatia, Cuba, Cyprus, Czech Republic, Democratic People's Republic of Korea, Democratic Republic of the Congo, Denmark, Djibouti, Dominica, Dominican Republic, Ecuador, Egypt, El Salvador, Equatorial Guinea, Eritrea, Estonia, Fiji, Finland, France, Gambia, Georgia, Germany, Ghana, Greece, Grenada, Guatemala, Guinea, Guinea-Bissau, Guyana, Haiti, Honduras, Hungary, Iceland, Indonesia, Iran (Islamic Republic of), Iraq, Ireland, Italy, Jamaica, Japan, Jordan, Kazakhstan, Kenya, Kuwait, Kyrgyzstan, Lao People's Democratic Republic, Latvia, Lebanon, Lesotho, Liberia, Libyan Arab Jamahiriya, Liechtenstein,

---

* Subsequently, the delegation of Ethiopia advised the Secretariat that it had intended to abstain.

Lithuania, Luxembourg, Madagascar, Malawi, Malaysia, Maldives, Mali, Malta, Mauritania, Mauritius, Mexico, Monaco, Mongolia, Montenegro, Morocco, Mozambique, Myanmar, Namibia, Nepal, Netherlands, New Zealand, Nicaragua, Niger, Nigeria, Norway, Oman, Pakistan, Papua New Guinea, Paraguay, Peru, Philippines, Poland, Portugal, Qatar, Republic of Korea, Republic of Moldova, Romania, Russian Federation, Saint Kitts and Nevis, Saint Lucia, Saint Vincent and the Grenadines, Samoa, San Marino, Saudi Arabia, Senegal, Serbia, Sierra Leone, Singapore, Slovakia, Slovenia, Solomon Islands, South Africa, Spain, Sri Lanka, Sudan, Suriname, Swaziland, Sweden, Switzerland, Syrian Arab Republic, Tajikistan, Thailand, the former Yugoslav Republic of Macedonia, Togo, Trinidad and Tobago, Tunisia, Turkey, Turkmenistan, Uganda, Ukraine, United Arab Emirates, United Kingdom, United Republic of Tanzania, Uruguay, Uzbekistan, Venezuela (Bolivarian Republic of), Viet Nam, Yemen, Zambia, Zimbabwe

Against:
Israel, Marshall Islands, Micronesia (Federated States of), Nauru, Palau, United States

Abstaining:
Australia, Cameroon, Canada, Côte d'Ivoire, India, Panama

Sixth preambular paragraph*

In favour:
Afghanistan, Albania, Algeria, Andorra, Angola, Antigua and Barbuda, Argentina, Armenia, Australia, Austria, Azerbaijan, Bahamas, Bahrain, Bangladesh, Barbados, Belarus, Belgium, Belize, Benin, Bolivia (Plurinational State of), Bosnia and Herzegovina, Botswana, Brazil, Brunei Darussalam, Bulgaria, Burkina Faso, Burundi, Cambodia, Cameroon, Canada, Cape Verde, Chile, China, Colombia, Congo, Costa Rica, Croatia, Cuba, Cyprus, Czech Republic, Democratic Republic of the Congo, Denmark, Djibouti, Dominica, Dominican Republic, Ecuador, Egypt, El Salvador, Equatorial Guinea, Eritrea, Estonia, Fiji, Finland, France, Gambia, Georgia, Germany, Ghana, Greece, Grenada, Guatemala, Guinea, Guinea-Bissau, Guyana, Haiti, Honduras, Hungary, Iceland, Indonesia, Iran (Islamic Republic of), Iraq, Ireland, Italy, Jamaica, Japan, Jordan, Kazakhstan, Kenya, Kuwait, Kyrgyzstan, Lao People's Democratic Republic, Latvia, Lebanon, Lesotho, Liberia, Libyan Arab Jamahiriya, Liechtenstein, Lithuania, Luxembourg, Madagascar, Malawi, Malaysia, Maldives, Mali, Malta, Mauritania, Mexico, Monaco, Mongolia, Montenegro, Morocco, Mozambique, Myanmar, Namibia, Nepal, Netherlands, New Zealand, Nicaragua, Niger, Nigeria, Norway,

---

* Subsequently, the delegation of Ethiopia advised the Secretariat that it had intended to abstain. The voting tally above does not reflect this information.

Oman, Papua New Guinea, Paraguay, Peru, Philippines, Poland, Portugal, Qatar, Republic of Korea, Republic of Moldova, Romania, Russian Federation, Saint Kitts and Nevis, Saint Lucia, Saint Vincent and the Grenadines, Samoa, San Marino, Saudi Arabia, Senegal, Serbia, Singapore, Slovakia, Slovenia, Solomon Islands, South Africa, Spain, Sri Lanka, Sudan, Suriname, Swaziland, Sweden, Switzerland, Syrian Arab Republic, Tajikistan, Thailand, the former Yugoslav Republic of Macedonia, Togo, Trinidad and Tobago, Tunisia, Turkey, Turkmenistan, Uganda, Ukraine, United Arab Emirates, United Kingdom, United Republic of Tanzania, Uruguay, Uzbekistan, Venezuela (Bolivarian Republic of), Viet Nam, Yemen, Zambia, Zimbabwe

Against:
India, Israel, Marshall Islands, Palau, United States

Abstaining:
Bhutan, Côte d'Ivoire, Democratic People's Republic of Korea, Mauritius, Pakistan

Action by the First Committee

Date: 27 October 2009   Meeting: 19th meeting
Vote: 164-5-6   Draft resolution: A/C.1/64/L.4
      163-4-6, p.p. 6

Agenda item 100

64/67 Convention on Prohibitions or Restrictions on the Use of Certain Conventional Weapons Which May Be Deemed to Be Excessively Injurious or to Have Indiscriminate Effects

Text

The General Assembly,

Recalling its resolution 63/85 of 2 December 2008,

Recalling with satisfaction the adoption and the entry into force of the Convention on Prohibitions or Restrictions on the Use of Certain Conventional Weapons Which May Be Deemed to Be Excessively Injurious or to Have Indiscriminate Effects,[1] and its amended article 1,[2] and the Protocol on Non-Detectable Fragments (Protocol I),[1] the Protocol on Prohibitions or Restrictions on the Use of Mines, Booby Traps and Other Devices (Protocol II)[1] and its amended version,[3] the Protocol on Prohibitions or Restrictions on the Use of Incendiary Weapons (Protocol III),[1] the Protocol on Blinding Laser Weapons (Protocol IV)[4] and the Protocol on Explosive Remnants of War (Protocol V),[5]

Welcoming the results of the Third Review Conference of the High Contracting Parties to the Convention on Prohibitions or Restrictions on the Use of Certain Conventional Weapons Which May Be Deemed to Be Excessively Injurious or to Have Indiscriminate Effects, held from 7 to 17 November 2006 in Geneva,

Welcoming also the results of the 2008 Meeting of the High Contracting Parties to the Convention, held on 13 and 14 November 2008 in Geneva,

Welcoming further the results of the Tenth Annual Conference of the High Contracting Parties to Amended Protocol II, held on 12 November 2008 in Geneva,

Welcoming the results of the Second Conference of the High Contracting Parties to Protocol V, held on 10 and 11 November 2008 in Geneva,

Recalling the role played by the International Committee of the Red Cross in the elaboration of the Convention and the Protocols thereto, and welcoming the particular efforts of various international, non-governmental

---

[1] United Nations, *Treaty Series*, vol. 1342, No. 22495.
[2] Ibid., vol. 2260, No. 22495.
[3] Ibid., vol. 2048, No. 22495.
[4] Ibid., vol. 2024, No. 22495.
[5] Ibid., vol. 2399, No. 22495.

and other organizations in raising awareness of the humanitarian consequences of explosive remnants of war,

1. *Calls upon* all States that have not yet done so to take all measures to become parties, as soon as possible, to the Convention on Prohibitions or Restrictions on the Use of Certain Conventional Weapons Which May Be Deemed to Be Excessively Injurious or to Have Indiscriminate Effects[1] and the Protocols thereto, as amended, with a view to achieving the widest possible adherence to these instruments at an early date, and so as to ultimately achieve their universality;

2. *Calls upon* all States parties to the Convention that have not yet done so to express their consent to be bound by the Protocols to the Convention and the amendment extending the scope of the Convention and the Protocols thereto to include armed conflicts of a non-international character;

3. *Emphasizes* the importance of the universalization of the Protocol on Explosive Remnants of War (Protocol V);[5]

4. *Welcomes* the additional ratifications and acceptances of or accessions to the Convention, as well as the consents to be bound by the Protocols thereto;

5. *Also welcomes* the adoption by the Third Review Conference of the High Contracting Parties to the Convention of a Plan of Action to promote universality of the Convention and its annexed Protocols,[6] and expresses appreciation for the continued efforts of the Secretary-General, as depositary of the Convention and its annexed Protocols, the Chairperson of the Meeting of the High Contracting Parties to the Convention, the President of the Second Conference of the High Contracting Parties to Protocol V and the President of the Tenth Annual Conference of the High Contracting Parties to Amended Protocol II, on behalf of the High Contracting Parties, to achieve the goal of universality;

6. *Recalls* the decision by the Third Review Conference to establish a Sponsorship Programme within the framework of the Convention,[7] and, with recognition of the value and importance of the programme, encourages States to contribute to the Sponsorship Programme;

7. *Welcomes* the commitment by States parties to continue to address the humanitarian problems caused by certain specific types of munitions in all their aspects, including cluster munitions, with a view to minimizing the humanitarian impact of these munitions;

8. *Expresses support* for the work conducted in 2009 by the Group of Governmental Experts of the High Contracting Parties to the Convention to continue its negotiations to address urgently the humanitarian impact of

---

[6] See CCW/CONF.III/11 (Part II), annex III.
[7] Ibid., annex IV.

cluster munitions, while striking a balance between military and humanitarian considerations, in accordance with the mandate given to it by the Meeting of the High Contracting Parties, in November 2008;[8]

9. *Welcomes* the commitment of States parties to the Protocol on Explosive Remnants of War (Protocol V) to the effective and efficient implementation of the Protocol and the implementation of the decisions of the First and Second Conferences of the High Contracting Parties to the Protocol establishing a comprehensive framework for the exchange of information and cooperation,[9] and also welcomes the holding of the second Meeting of Experts of the High Contracting Parties to the Protocol, from 22 to 24 April 2009 in Geneva, as a mechanism for consultation and cooperation among the States parties;

10. *Notes* the decision of the Tenth Annual Conference of the High Contracting Parties to Amended Protocol II to establish an informal open-ended Group of Experts,[10] and welcomes the holding of the first session of the Group of Experts of the High Contracting Parties to Amended Protocol II, on 20 and 21 April 2009 in Geneva, to exchange national practices and experiences and to assess the implementation of the Protocol;

11. *Also notes* that, in conformity with article 8 of the Convention, conferences may be convened to examine amendments to the Convention or to any of the Protocols thereto, to examine additional protocols concerning other categories of conventional weapons not covered by existing Protocols or to review the scope and application of the Convention and the Protocols thereto and to examine any proposed amendments or additional protocols;

12. *Requests* the Secretary-General to render the necessary assistance and to provide such services, including summary records, as may be required for the Third Conference of the High Contracting Parties to Protocol V, to be held on 9 and 10 November 2009, for the Eleventh Annual Conference of the High Contracting Parties to Amended Protocol II, to be held on 11 November 2009, and for the Meeting of the High Contracting Parties to the Convention, to be held on 12 and 13 November 2009, as well as for any continuation of work after the meetings;

13. *Also requests* the Secretary-General, in his capacity as depositary of the Convention and the Protocols thereto, to continue to inform the General Assembly periodically, by electronic means, of ratifications and acceptances of and accessions to the Convention, its amended article 1[2] and the Protocols thereto;

14. *Decides* to include in the provisional agenda of its sixty-fifth session the item entitled "Convention on Prohibitions or Restrictions on the Use of

---

[8] See CCW/MSP/2008/4, para. 34.
[9] See CCW/P.V/CONF/2007/1 and Corr.1 and 2, and CCW/P.V/CONF/2008/12.
[10] See CCW/AP.II/CONF.10/2, para. 23.

Certain Conventional Weapons Which May Be Deemed to Be Excessively Injurious or to Have Indiscriminate Effects".

Action by the General Assembly

    Date: 2 December 2009   Meeting: 55th plenary meeting
    Vote: Adopted without a vote   Report: A/64/395

Sponsors

    Lithuania, Pakistan, **Sweden**, Switzerland

Action by the First Committee

    Date: 29 October 2009   Meeting: 21st meeting
    Vote: Adopted without a vote   Draft resolution: A/C.1/64/L.37

Agenda item 101

64/68 Strengthening of security and cooperation in the Mediterranean region

Text

The General Assembly,

Recalling its previous resolutions on the subject, including resolution 63/86 of 2 December 2008,

Reaffirming the primary role of the Mediterranean countries in strengthening and promoting peace, security and cooperation in the Mediterranean region,

Welcoming the efforts deployed by the Euro-Mediterranean countries to strengthen their cooperation in combating terrorism, in particular by the adoption of the Euro-Mediterranean Code of Conduct on Countering Terrorism by the Euro-Mediterranean Summit, held in Barcelona, Spain, on 27 and 28 November 2005,

Bearing in mind all the previous declarations and commitments, as well as all the initiatives taken by the riparian countries at the recent summits, ministerial meetings and various forums concerning the question of the Mediterranean region,

Welcoming, in this regard, the adoption on 13 July 2008 of the joint Declaration of the Paris Summit, which launched a reinforced partnership, "the Barcelona Process: Union for the Mediterranean", and the common political will to revive efforts to transform the Mediterranean into an area of peace, democracy, cooperation and prosperity,

Welcoming also the entry into force of the African Nuclear-Weapon-Free Zone Treaty (Treaty of Pelindaba)[1] as a contribution to the strengthening of peace and security both regionally and internationally,

Recognizing the indivisible character of security in the Mediterranean and that the enhancement of cooperation among Mediterranean countries with a view to promoting the economic and social development of all peoples of the region will contribute significantly to stability, peace and security in the region,

Recognizing also the efforts made so far and the determination of the Mediterranean countries to intensify the process of dialogue and consultations with a view to resolving the problems existing in the Mediterranean region and to eliminating the causes of tension and the consequent threat to peace and security, and their growing awareness of the need for further joint efforts

---

[1] A/50/426, annex.

to strengthen economic, social, cultural and environmental cooperation in the region,

Recognizing further that prospects for closer Euro-Mediterranean cooperation in all spheres can be enhanced by positive developments worldwide, in particular in Europe, in the Maghreb and in the Middle East,

Reaffirming the responsibility of all States to contribute to the stability and prosperity of the Mediterranean region and their commitment to respecting the purposes and principles of the Charter of the United Nations as well as the provisions of the Declaration on Principles of International Law concerning Friendly Relations and Cooperation among States in accordance with the Charter of the United Nations,[2]

Noting the peace negotiations in the Middle East, which should be of a comprehensive nature and represent an appropriate framework for the peaceful settlement of contentious issues in the region,

Expressing its concern at the persistent tension and continuing military activities in parts of the Mediterranean that hinder efforts to strengthen security and cooperation in the region,

Taking note of the report of the Secretary-General,[3]

1. *Reaffirms* that security in the Mediterranean is closely linked to European security as well as to international peace and security;

2. *Expresses its satisfaction* at the continuing efforts by Mediterranean countries to contribute actively to the elimination of all causes of tension in the region and to the promotion of just and lasting solutions to the persistent problems of the region through peaceful means, thus ensuring the withdrawal of foreign forces of occupation and respecting the sovereignty, independence and territorial integrity of all countries of the Mediterranean and the right of peoples to self-determination, and therefore calls for full adherence to the principles of non-interference, non-intervention, non-use of force or threat of use of force and the inadmissibility of the acquisition of territory by force, in accordance with the Charter and the relevant resolutions of the United Nations;

3. *Commends* the Mediterranean countries for their efforts in meeting common challenges through coordinated overall responses, based on a spirit of multilateral partnership, towards the general objective of turning the Mediterranean basin into an area of dialogue, exchanges and cooperation, guaranteeing peace, stability and prosperity, encourages them to strengthen such efforts through, inter alia, a lasting multilateral and action-oriented cooperative dialogue among States of the region, and recognizes the role of the United Nations in promoting regional and international peace and security;

---

[2] Resolution 2625 (XXV), annex.
[3] A/64/119 and Add.1.

4. *Recognizes* that the elimination of the economic and social disparities in levels of development and other obstacles as well as respect and greater understanding among cultures in the Mediterranean area will contribute to enhancing peace, security and cooperation among Mediterranean countries through the existing forums;

5. *Calls upon* all States of the Mediterranean region that have not yet done so to adhere to all the multilaterally negotiated legal instruments related to the field of disarmament and non-proliferation, thus creating the conditions necessary for strengthening peace and cooperation in the region;

6. *Encourages* all States of the region to favour the conditions necessary for strengthening the confidence-building measures among them by promoting genuine openness and transparency on all military matters, by participating, inter alia, in the United Nations system for the standardized reporting of military expenditures and by providing accurate data and information to the United Nations Register of Conventional Arms;[4]

7. *Encourages* the Mediterranean countries to strengthen further their cooperation in combating terrorism in all its forms and manifestations, including the possible resort by terrorists to weapons of mass destruction, taking into account the relevant resolutions of the United Nations, and in combating international crime and illicit arms transfers and illicit drug production, consumption and trafficking, which pose a serious threat to peace, security and stability in the region and therefore to the improvement of the current political, economic and social situation and which jeopardize friendly relations among States, hinder the development of international cooperation and result in the destruction of human rights, fundamental freedoms and the democratic basis of pluralistic society;

8. *Requests* the Secretary-General to submit a report on means to strengthen security and cooperation in the Mediterranean region;

9. *Decides* to include in the provisional agenda of its sixty-fifth session the item entitled "Strengthening of security and cooperation in the Mediterranean region".

Action by the General Assembly

Date: 2 December 2009 Meeting: 55th plenary meeting
Vote: Adopted without a vote Report: A/64/396

Sponsors

Albania, **Algeria**, Andorra, Australia, Austria, Belgium, Bulgaria, Croatia, Cyprus, Czech Republic, Denmark, Egypt, Finland, France, Germany, Greece, Hungary, Iceland, Ireland, Italy, Jordan, Latvia,

---

[4] See resolution 46/36 L.

Lithuania, Luxembourg, Malta, Monaco, Montenegro, Morocco, Poland, Portugal, Republic of Moldova, Romania, San Marino, Serbia, Slovakia, Slovenia, Spain, Sudan, Sweden, Tunisia, Turkey

Co-sponsors

Bosnia and Herzegovina, Estonia, Fiji, the Netherlands, Norway, the former Yugoslav Republic of Macedonia, Timor-Leste

Action by the First Committee

Date: 28 October 2009   Meeting: 20th meeting
Vote: Adopted without a vote   Draft resolution: A/C.1/64/L.49

Agenda item 102

64/69   Comprehensive Nuclear-Test-Ban Treaty

Text

The General Assembly,

Reiterating that the cessation of nuclear-weapon test explosions or any other nuclear explosions constitutes an effective nuclear disarmament and non-proliferation measure, and convinced that this is a meaningful step in the realization of a systematic process to achieve nuclear disarmament,

Recalling that the Comprehensive Nuclear-Test-Ban Treaty, adopted by its resolution 50/245 of 10 September 1996, was opened for signature on 24 September 1996,

Stressing that a universal and effectively verifiable Treaty constitutes a fundamental instrument in the field of nuclear disarmament and non-proliferation and that, after more than twelve years, its entry into force is more urgent than ever before,

Encouraged by the signing of the Treaty by one hundred and eighty-two States, including forty-one of the forty-four needed for its entry into force, and welcoming the ratification of one hundred and fifty States, including thirty-five of the forty-four needed for its entry into force, among which there are three nuclear-weapon States,

Recalling its resolution 63/87 of 2 December 2008,

Welcoming the Joint Ministerial Statement on the Comprehensive Nuclear-Test-Ban Treaty, adopted at the Ministerial Meeting held in New York on 24 September 2008,[1]

Welcoming also the Final Declaration of the Sixth Conference on Facilitating the Entry into Force of the Comprehensive Nuclear-Test-Ban Treaty, held in New York on 24 and 25 September 2009, pursuant to article XIV of the Treaty,[2] and noting the improved prospects for ratification in several Annex 2 countries,

1.   *Stresses* the vital importance and urgency of signature and ratification, without delay and without conditions, to achieve the earliest entry into force of the Comprehensive Nuclear-Test-Ban Treaty;[3]

2.   *Welcomes* the contributions by the States signatories to the work of the Preparatory Commission for the Comprehensive Nuclear-Test-Ban Treaty Organization, in particular its efforts to ensure that the Treaty's verification

---
[1]   A/63/634, annex.
[2]   See CTBT-Art.XIV/2009/6, annex.
[3]   See resolution 50/245.

regime will be capable of meeting the verification requirements of the Treaty upon its entry into force, in accordance with article IV of the Treaty;

3. *Underlines* the need to maintain momentum towards completion of all elements of the verification regime;

4. *Urges* all States not to carry out nuclear-weapon test explosions or any other nuclear explosions, to maintain their moratoriums in this regard and to refrain from acts that would defeat the object and purpose of the Treaty, while stressing that these measures do not have the same permanent and legally binding effect as the entry into force of the Treaty;

5. *Recalls* Security Council resolutions 1718 (2006) of 14 October 2006 and 1874 (2009) of 12 June 2009, calls for their early implementation, and calls for early resumption of the Six-Party Talks;

6. *Urges* all States that have not yet signed the Treaty to sign and ratify it as soon as possible;

7. *Urges* all States that have signed but not yet ratified the Treaty, in particular those whose ratification is needed for its entry into force, to accelerate their ratification processes with a view to ensuring their earliest successful conclusion;

8. *Welcomes*, since the last session of the General Assembly, the ratification of the Treaty by Lebanon, Liberia, Malawi, Mozambique and Saint Vincent and the Grenadines, as well as the signature by Trinidad and Tobago, as significant steps towards the early entry into force of the Treaty;

9. *Urges* all States to remain seized of the issue at the highest political level and, where in a position to do so, to promote adherence to the Treaty through bilateral and joint outreach, seminars and other means;

10. *Requests* the Secretary-General, in consultation with the Preparatory Commission for the Comprehensive Nuclear-Test-Ban Treaty Organization, to prepare a report on the efforts of States that have ratified the Treaty towards its universalization and possibilities for providing assistance on ratification procedures to States that so request it, and to submit such a report to the General Assembly at its sixty-fifth session;

11. *Decides* to include in the provisional agenda of its sixty-fifth session the item entitled "Comprehensive Nuclear-Test-Ban Treaty".

Action by the General Assembly

Date: 2 December 2009
Vote: 175-1-3, as a whole
169-1-6, o.p. 5
Meeting: 55th plenary meeting
Report: A/64/397

Sponsors

Afghanistan, Andorra, Antigua and Barbuda, Argentina, Armenia, **Australia**, Austria, Belgium, Bosnia and Herzegovina, Brazil, Bulgaria, Cambodia, Canada, China, Colombia, Comoros, Costa Rica, Croatia, Cyprus, Czech Republic, Denmark, Eritrea, Estonia, Fiji, Finland, France, Germany, Greece, Grenada, Guyana, Hungary, Iceland, Ireland, Italy, Japan, Kazakhstan, Latvia, Liechtenstein, Lithuania, Luxembourg, Malaysia, Malta, Mexico, Micronesia (Federated States of), Monaco, Mongolia, Morocco, Netherlands, New Zealand, Norway, Peru, Philippines, Poland, Portugal, Republic of Korea, Republic of Moldova, Romania, Russian Federation, Saint Lucia, Saint Vincent and the Grenadines, Samoa, San Marino, Serbia, Slovakia, Slovenia, Spain, Suriname, Sweden, Switzerland, Tajikistan, the former Yugoslav Republic of Macedonia, Trinidad and Tobago, Turkey, Ukraine, United Kingdom, United States, Uruguay

Co-sponsors

Chile, Jamaica, Montenegro

Recorded vote

As a whole*

In favour:
Afghanistan, Albania, Algeria, Andorra, Angola, Antigua and Barbuda, Argentina, Armenia, Australia, Austria, Azerbaijan, Bahamas, Bahrain, Bangladesh, Barbados, Belarus, Belgium, Belize, Benin, Bhutan, Bolivia (Plurinational State of), Bosnia and Herzegovina, Botswana, Brazil, Brunei Darussalam, Bulgaria, Burkina Faso, Burundi, Cambodia, Cameroon, Canada, Cape Verde, Chile, China, Colombia, Comoros, Congo, Costa Rica, Côte d'Ivoire, Croatia, Cuba, Cyprus, Czech Republic, Democratic Republic of the Congo, Denmark, Djibouti, Dominica, Dominican Republic, Ecuador, Egypt, El Salvador, Equatorial Guinea, Eritrea, Estonia, Fiji, Finland, France, Gambia, Georgia, Germany, Ghana, Greece, Grenada, Guatemala, Guinea, Guinea-Bissau, Guyana, Haiti, Honduras, Hungary, Iceland, Indonesia, Iran (Islamic Republic of), Iraq, Ireland, Israel, Italy, Jamaica, Japan, Jordan, Kazakhstan, Kenya, Kuwait, Kyrgyzstan, Lao People's Democratic Republic, Latvia, Lebanon, Lesotho, Liberia, Libyan Arab Jamahiriya, Liechtenstein, Lithuania, Luxembourg, Madagascar, Malawi, Malaysia, Maldives, Mali, Malta, Marshall Islands, Mauritania, Mexico, Micronesia (Federated States of), Monaco, Mongolia, Montenegro, Morocco, Mozambique, Myanmar, Namibia, Nepal, Netherlands, New Zealand, Nicaragua,

---

* Subsequently, the delegation of Ethiopia advised the Secretariat that it had intended to vote in favour. The voting tally above does not reflect this information.

Niger, Nigeria, Norway, Oman, Pakistan, Palau, Panama, Papua New Guinea, Paraguay, Peru, Philippines, Poland, Portugal, Qatar, Republic of Korea, Republic of Moldova, Romania, Russian Federation, Saint Kitts and Nevis, Saint Lucia, Saint Vincent and the Grenadines, Samoa, San Marino, Saudi Arabia, Senegal, Serbia, Sierra Leone, Singapore, Slovakia, Slovenia, Solomon Islands, Somalia, South Africa, Spain, Sri Lanka, Suriname, Swaziland, Sweden, Switzerland, Tajikistan, Thailand, the former Yugoslav Republic of Macedonia, Togo, Tonga, Trinidad and Tobago, Tunisia, Turkey, Turkmenistan, Uganda, Ukraine, United Arab Emirates, United Kingdom, United Republic of Tanzania, United States, Uruguay, Uzbekistan, Venezuela (Bolivarian Republic of), Viet Nam, Yemen, Zambia, Zimbabwe

Against:
Democratic People's Republic of Korea

Abstaining:
India, Mauritius, Syrian Arab Republic

Operative paragraph 5*

In favour:
Afghanistan, Albania, Algeria, Andorra, Angola, Antigua and Barbuda, Argentina, Armenia, Australia, Austria, Azerbaijan, Bahamas, Bahrain, Bangladesh, Barbados, Belarus, Belgium, Belize, Benin, Bhutan, Bolivia (Plurinational State of), Bosnia and Herzegovina, Botswana, Brazil, Brunei Darussalam, Bulgaria, Burkina Faso, Burundi, Cambodia, Cameroon, Canada, Cape Verde, Chile, China, Colombia, Comoros, Congo, Costa Rica, Côte d'Ivoire, Croatia, Cyprus, Czech Republic, Democratic Republic of the Congo, Denmark, Djibouti, Dominica, Dominican Republic, Ecuador, Egypt, El Salvador, Equatorial Guinea, Eritrea, Estonia, Fiji, Finland, France, Gambia, Georgia, Germany, Ghana, Greece, Grenada, Guatemala, Guinea, Guinea-Bissau, Guyana, Haiti, Honduras, Hungary, Iceland, India, Indonesia, Iraq, Ireland, Israel, Italy, Jamaica, Japan, Jordan, Kazakhstan, Kenya, Kuwait, Kyrgyzstan, Latvia, Lebanon, Lesotho, Liberia, Libyan Arab Jamahiriya, Liechtenstein, Lithuania, Luxembourg, Madagascar, Malawi, Malaysia, Maldives, Mali, Malta, Marshall Islands, Mauritania, Mauritius, Mexico, Micronesia (Federated States of), Monaco, Mongolia, Montenegro, Morocco, Mozambique, Myanmar, Nepal, Netherlands, New Zealand, Niger, Nigeria, Norway, Oman, Pakistan, Panama, Papua New Guinea, Paraguay, Peru, Philippines, Poland, Portugal, Qatar, Republic of Korea, Republic of Moldova, Romania, Russian Federation, Saint Kitts and Nevis, Saint Lucia, Saint Vincent and the Grenadines, Samoa, San

---

* Subsequently, the delegations of Chile and Ethiopia advised the Secretariat that they had intended to vote in favour. The voting tally above does not reflect this information.

Marino, Saudi Arabia, Senegal, Serbia, Singapore, Slovakia, Slovenia, Solomon Islands, Somalia, South Africa, Spain, Sri Lanka, Sudan, Suriname, Swaziland, Sweden, Switzerland, Tajikistan, Thailand, the former Yugoslav Republic of Macedonia, Togo, Tonga, Trinidad and Tobago, Tunisia, Turkey, Turkmenistan, Ukraine, United Arab Emirates, United Kingdom, United Republic of Tanzania, United States, Uruguay, Uzbekistan, Viet Nam, Yemen, Zambia, Zimbabwe

Against:
Democratic People's Republic of Korea

Abstaining:
Cuba, Iran (Islamic Republic of), Namibia, Nicaragua, Syrian Arab Republic, Venezuela (Bolivarian Republic of)

Action by the First Committee

Date: 30 October 2009 Meeting: 22nd meeting
Vote: 175-1-3, as a whole Draft resolution: A/C.1/64/L.47/Rev.1
166-1-5, o.p. 5

Agenda item 103

64/70   Convention on the Prohibition of the Development, Production and Stockpiling of Bacteriological (Biological) and Toxin Weapons and on Their Destruction

Text

The General Assembly,

Recalling its previous resolutions relating to the complete and effective prohibition of bacteriological (biological) and toxin weapons and to their destruction,

Noting with satisfaction that there are one hundred and sixty-three States parties to the Convention on the Prohibition of the Development, Production and Stockpiling of Bacteriological (Biological) and Toxin Weapons and on Their Destruction,[1] including all of the permanent members of the Security Council,

Bearing in mind its call upon all States parties to the Convention to participate in the implementation of the recommendations of the Review Conferences, including the exchange of information and data agreed to in the Final Declaration of the Third Review Conference of the Parties to the Convention,[2] and to provide such information and data in conformity with standardized procedure to the Secretary-General on an annual basis and no later than 15 April,

Welcoming the reaffirmation made in the Final Declaration of the Fourth Review Conference[3] that under all circumstances the use of bacteriological (biological) and toxin weapons and their development, production and stockpiling are effectively prohibited under article I of the Convention,

Recalling the decision reached at the Sixth Review Conference to hold four annual meetings of the States parties of one week's duration each year commencing in 2007, prior to the Seventh Review Conference, which is to be held no later than the end of 2011, and to hold a one-week meeting of experts to prepare for each meeting of the States parties,[4]

1.   *Notes* the increase in the number of States parties to the Convention on the Prohibition of the Development, Production and Stockpiling of Bacteriological (Biological) and Toxin Weapons and on Their Destruction,[1] reaffirms the call upon all signatory States that have not yet ratified the

---

[1] United Nations, *Treaty Series*, vol. 1015, No. 14860.
[2] BWC/CONF.III/23, part II.
[3] BWC/CONF.IV/9, part II.
[4] BWC/CONF.VI/6, part III, para. 7.

Convention to do so without delay, and calls upon those States that have not signed the Convention to become parties thereto at an early date, thus contributing to the achievement of universal adherence to the Convention;

2. *Welcomes* the information and data provided to date, and reiterates its call upon all States parties to the Convention to participate in the exchange of information and data agreed to in the Final Declaration of the Third Review Conference of the Parties to the Convention;[2]

3. *Also welcomes* the successful holding of meetings as part of the 2007–2010 intersessional process, and in this context also welcomes the discussion aimed at the promotion of common understanding and effective action on topics agreed at the Sixth Review Conference,[5] and urges States parties to continue to participate actively in the remaining intersessional process;

4. *Notes with satisfaction* that the Sixth Review Conference agreed on several measures to update the mechanism for the transmission of information within the framework of the confidence-building measures;

5. *Recalls* the decisions reached at the Sixth Review Conference,[6] and calls upon States parties to the Convention to participate in their implementation;

6. *Urges* States parties to continue to work closely with the Implementation Support Unit of the Office for Disarmament Affairs of the Secretariat in fulfilling its mandate, in accordance with the decision of the Sixth Review Conference;

7. *Requests* the Secretary-General to continue to render the necessary assistance to the depositary Governments and to provide such services as may be required for the implementation of the decisions and recommendations of the Review Conferences, including all assistance to the annual meetings of the States parties and the meetings of experts;

8. *Decides* to include in the provisional agenda of its sixty-fifth session the item entitled "Convention on the Prohibition of the Development, Production and Stockpiling of Bacteriological (Biological) and Toxin Weapons and on Their Destruction".

Action by the General Assembly

Date: 2 December 2009　　Meeting: 55th plenary meeting
Vote: Adopted without a vote　　Report: A/64/398

---

[5] BWC/CONF.VI/6.
[6] Ibid., part III, paras. 1 and 7.

Sponsors

Hungary

Action by the First Committee

Date: 28 October 2009   Meeting: 20th meeting
Vote: Adopted without a vote   Draft resolution: A/C.1/64/L.15

Decisions

Agenda item 89

64/512 Verification in all its aspects, including the role of the United Nations in the field of verification

Text

The General Assembly, recalling its resolution 62/21 unanimously adopted on 5 December 2007, decides to include in the provisional agenda of its sixty-sixth session the item entitled "Verification in all its aspects, including the role of the United Nations in the field of verification".

Action by the General Assembly

Date: 2 December 2009 Meeting: 55th plenary meeting
Vote: Adopted without a vote Report: A/64/384

Sponsors

Canada*

Action by the First Committee

Date: 28 October 2009 Meeting: 20th meeting
Vote: Adopted without a vote Draft resolution: A/C.1/64/L.2

---

* The draft decision was submitted by Canada.

Agenda item 90

64/513 Review of the implementation of the Declaration on the Strengthening of International Security

Text

The General Assembly decides to include in the provisional agenda of its sixty-sixth session the item entitled "Review of the implementation of the Declaration on the Strengthening of International Security".

Action by the General Assembly

> Date: 2 December 2009 Meeting: 55th plenary meeting
> Vote: Adopted without a vote Report: A/64/385

Sponsors

> **Indonesia**, on behalf of the States Members of the United Nations that are members of the Movement of Non-Aligned Countries

Action by the First Committee

> Date: 28 October 2009 Meeting: 20th meeting
> Vote: Adopted without a vote Draft resolution: A/C.1/64/L.7

Agenda item 95

64/514   Role of science and technology in the context of international security and disarmament

Text

The General Assembly decides to include in the provisional agenda of its sixty-fifth session the item entitled "Role of science and technology in the context of international security and disarmament".

Action by the General Assembly

    Date: 2 December 2009   Meeting: 55th plenary meeting
    Vote: Adopted without a vote Report: A/64/390

Sponsors

    India

Action by the First Committee

    Date: 28 October 2009   Meeting: 20th meeting
    Vote: Adopted without a vote Draft resolution: A/C.1/64/L.21

Agenda item 96 (aa)

64/515 Convening of the fourth special session of the General Assembly devoted to disarmament

Text

The General Assembly,

Recalling its resolution 62/29 of 5 December 2007 and its decisions 62/552 of 11 September 2008 and 63/519 of 2 December 2008, decides to include in the provisional agenda of its sixty-fifth session the item entitled "Convening of the fourth special session of the General Assembly devoted to disarmament".

Action by the General Assembly

Date: 2 December 2009　　Meeting: 55th plenary meeting
Vote: Adopted without a vote　　Report: A/64/391

Sponsors

Indonesia, on behalf of the States Members of the United Nations that are members of the Movement of Non-Aligned Countries

Action by the First Committee

Date: 28 October 2009　　Meeting: 20th meeting
Vote: Adopted without a vote　　Draft resolution: A/C.1/64/L.9

Agenda item 96 (e)

64/516 Preventing the acquisition by terrorists of radioactive materials and sources

Text

The General Assembly,

Recalling its resolution 62/46 unanimously adopted on 5 December 2007,

Decides to include in the provisional agenda of its sixty-fifth session the item entitled "Preventing the acquisition by terrorists of radioactive materials and sources".

Action by the General Assembly

    Date: 2 December 2009   Meeting: 55th plenary meeting
    Vote: Adopted without a vote   Report: A/64/391

Sponsors

    France*

Action by the First Committee

    Date: 27 October 2009   Meeting: 19th meeting
    Vote: Adopted without a vote   Draft resolution: A/C.1/64/L.17

---

* The draft decision was submitted by France.

Annex

List of reports and notes of the Secretary-General

Agenda item 86	**Reduction of military budgets**
(a)	*Reduction of military budgets*
(b)	*Objective information on military matters, including transparency of military expenditures*
A/64/113 and Add.1	Objective information on military matters, including transparency of military expenditures
Agenda item 87	**Implementation of the Declaration of the Indian Ocean as a Zone of Peace**
Agenda item 88	**African Nuclear-Weapon-Free Zone Treaty**
Agenda item 89	**Verification in all its aspects, including the role of the United Nations in the field of verification**
Agenda item 90	**Review of the implementation of the Declaration on the Strengthening of International Security**
Agenda item 91	**Developments in the field of information and telecommunications in the context of international security**
A/64/129 and Add.1	Developments in the field of information and telecommunications in the context of international security
Agenda item 92	**Establishment of a nuclear-weapon-free zone in the region of the Middle East**
A/64/124 (Part I) and Add.1	Establishment of a nuclear-weapon-free zone in the region of the Middle East
Agenda item 93	**Conclusion of effective international arrangements to assure non-nuclear-weapon States against the use or threat of use of nuclear weapons**
Agenda item 94	**Prevention of an arms race in outer space**
Agenda item 95	**Role of science and technology in the context of international security and disarmament**
Agenda item 96	**General and complete disarmament**

A/64/81	Letter dated 12 May 2009 from the Permanent Representative of Namibia to the United Nations addressed to the Secretary-General
(a)	Notification of nuclear tests
(b)	Follow-up to nuclear disarmament obligations agreed to at the 1995 and 2000 Review Conferences of the Parties to the Treaty on the Non-Proliferation of Nuclear Weapons
(c)	Treaty on the South-East Asia Nuclear-Weapon-Free Zone (Bangkok Treaty)
(d)	Prohibition of the dumping of radioactive wastes
(e)	Preventing the acquisition by terrorists of radioactive materials and sources
(f)	Regional disarmament
(g)	Conventional arms control at the regional and subregional levels
A/64/126	Conventional arms control at the regional and subregional levels
(h)	Confidence-building measures in the regional and subregional context
A/64/114 and Add.1	Confidence-building measures in the regional and subregional context
(i)	Nuclear disarmament
A/64/139	Follow-up to the advisory opinion of the International Court of Justice on the *Legality of the Threat or Use of Nuclear Weapons*
(j)	Reducing nuclear danger
A/64/139	Follow-up to the advisory opinion of the International Court of Justice on the *Legality of the Threat or Use of Nuclear Weapons*
(k)	Implementation of the Convention on the Prohibition of the Development, Production, Stockpiling and Use of Chemical Weapons and on Their Destruction
A/64/156	Implementation of the Convention on the Prohibition of the Development, Production, Stockpiling and Use of Chemical Weapons and on Their Destruction
(l)	Follow-up to the advisory opinion of the International Court of Justice on the *Legality of the Threat or Use of Nuclear Weapons*

A/64/139	Follow-up to the advisory opinion of the International Court of Justice on the *Legality of the Threat or Use of Nuclear Weapons*
(m)	*Promotion of multilateralism in the area of disarmament and non-proliferation*
A/64/117 and Add.1	Promotion of multilateralism in the area of disarmament and non-proliferation
(n)	*Observance of environmental norms in the drafting and implementation of agreements on disarmament and arms control (resolution 63/51);*
A/64/118 and Add.1	Observance of environmental norms in the drafting and implementation of agreements on disarmament and arms control
(o)	*Relationship between disarmament and development*
A/64/153	Relationship between disarmament and development
(p)	*Towards a nuclear-weapon-free world: accelerating the implementation of nuclear disarmament commitments*
(q)	*Measures to prevent terrorists from acquiring weapons of mass destruction*
A/64/140 and Add.1	Measures to prevent terrorists from acquiring weapons of mass destruction
(r)	*Problems arising from the accumulation of conventional ammunition stockpiles in surplus*
(s)	*The Hague Code of Conduct against Ballistic Missile Proliferation*
(t)	*Nuclear-weapon-free southern hemisphere and adjacent areas*
(u)	*Assistance to States for curbing the illicit traffic in small arms and light weapons and collecting them*
A/64/173	The illicit trade in small arms and light weapons in all its aspects
(v)	*Transparency and confidence-building measures in outer space activities*
A/64/138 and Add.1	Transparency and confidence-building measures in outer space activities
(w)	*Transparency in armaments*
A/64/135 and Add.1	United Nations Register of Conventional Arms

A/64/296	Note by the Secretary-General transmitting the report of the Group of Governmental Experts on the continuing operation of the United Nations Register of Conventional Arms and its further development
(x)	*The illicit trade in small arms and light weapons in all its aspects*
A/64/173	The illicit trade in small arms and light weapons in all its aspects
(y)	*Renewed determination towards the total elimination of nuclear weapons*
(z)	*Towards an arms trade treaty: establishing common international standards for the import, export and transfer of conventional arms*
(aa)	*Convening of the fourth special session of the General Assembly devoted to disarmament*
(bb)	*United Nations conference to identify appropriate ways of eliminating nuclear dangers in the context of nuclear disarmament*
Agenda item 97	**Review and implementation of the Concluding Document of the Twelfth Special Session of the General Assembly**
(a)	*United Nations Regional Centre for Peace, Disarmament and Development in Latin America and the Caribbean*
A/64/116	United Nations Regional Centre for Peace, Disarmament and Development in Latin America and the Caribbean
(b)	*Convention on the Prohibition of the Use of Nuclear Weapons*
(c)	*United Nations regional centres for peace and disarmament*
(d)	*United Nations Regional Centre for Peace and Disarmament in Asia and the Pacific*
A/64/111	United Nations Regional Centre for Peace and Disarmament in Asia and the Pacific
(e)	*Regional confidence-building measures: activities of the United Nations Standing Advisory Committee on Security Questions in Central Africa*
A/64/163	Regional confidence-building measures: activities of the United Nations Standing Advisory Committee on Security Questions in Central Africa

A/64/85-S/2009/288	Letter dated 3 June 2009 from the Chargé d'affaires a.i. of Gabon to the United Nations addressed to the Secretary-General
(f)	*United Nations Regional Centre for Peace and Disarmament in Africa*
A/64/112	United Nations Regional Centre for Peace and Disarmament in Africa
Agenda item 98	**Review of the implementation of the recommendations and decisions adopted by the General Assembly at its tenth special session**
A/64/261	United Nations Institute for Disarmament Research
A/64/286	Work of the Advisory Board on Disarmament Matters
(a)	*Report of the Conference on Disarmament*
A/64/27	Report of the Conference on Disarmament
(b)	*Report of the Disarmament Commission*
A/64/42	Report of the Disarmament Commission for 2009
Agenda item 99	**The risk of nuclear proliferation in the Middle East**
A/64/124 (Part II)	The risk of nuclear proliferation in the Middle East
Agenda item 100	**Convention on Prohibitions or Restrictions on the Use of Certain Conventional Weapons Which May Be Deemed to Be Excessively Injurious or to Have Indiscriminate Effects**
Agenda item 101	**Strengthening of security and cooperation in the Mediterranean region**
A/64/119 and Add.1	Strengthening of security and cooperation in the Mediterranean region
Agenda item 102	**Comprehensive Nuclear-Test-Ban Treaty**
A/64/137 and Add.1	Comprehensive Nuclear-Test-Ban Treaty
A/64/155	Note by the Secretary-General transmitting the report of the Executive Secretary of the Preparatory Commission for the Comprehensive Nuclear-Test-Ban Treaty Organization covering the year 2008
Agenda item 103	**Convention on the Prohibition of the Development, Production and Stockpiling of Bacteriological (Biological) and Toxin Weapons and on Their Destruction**